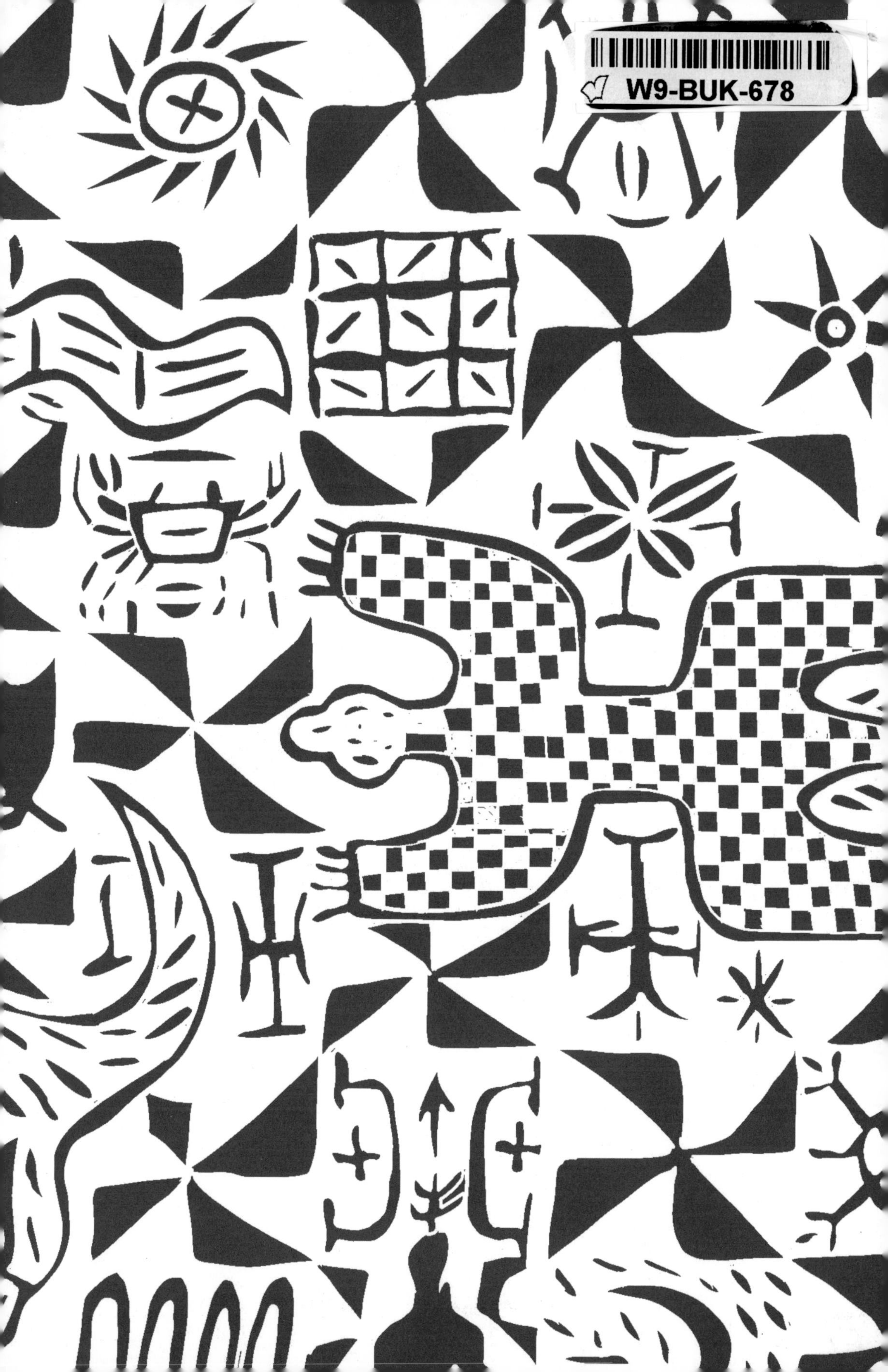

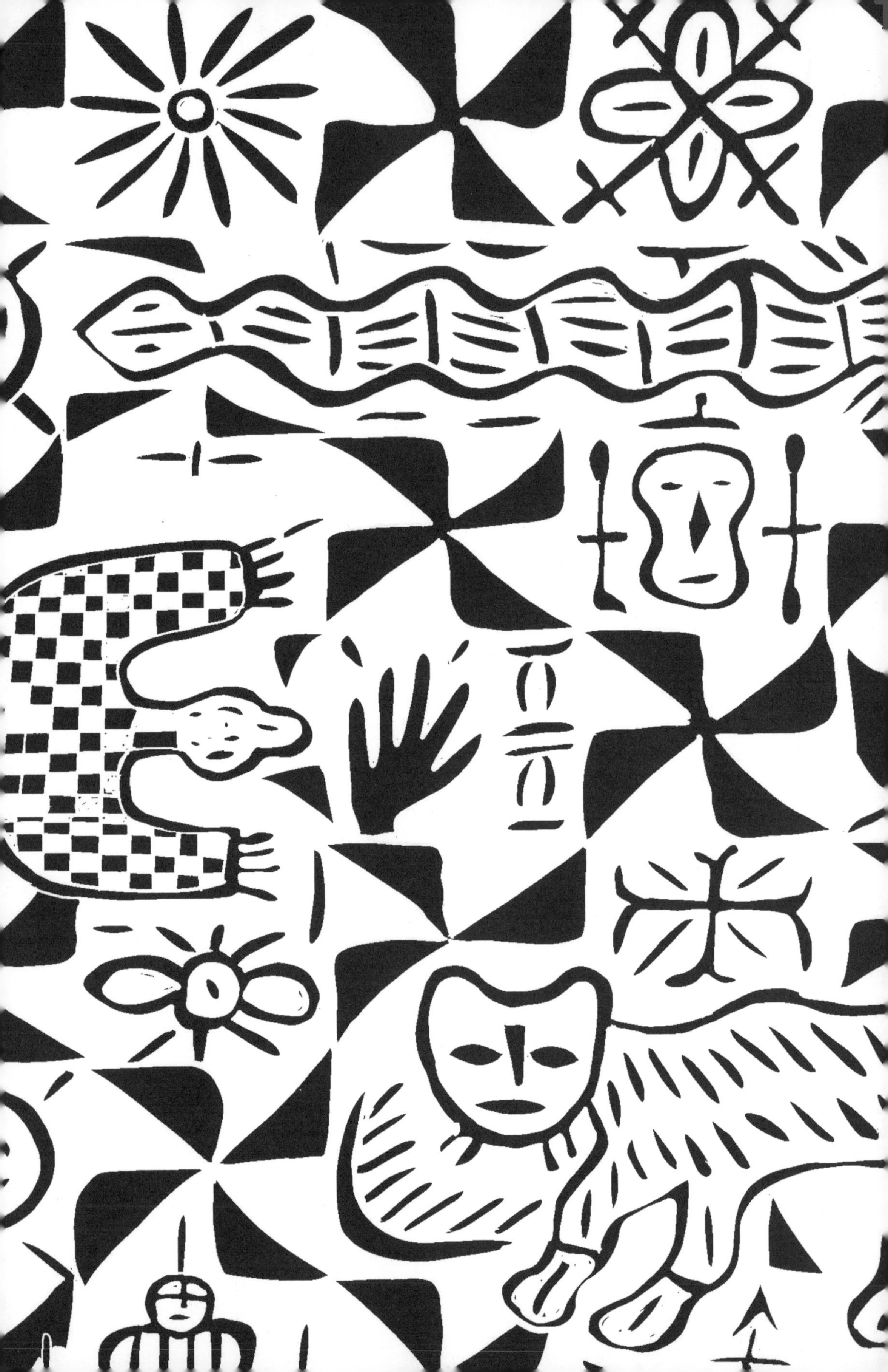

AFTER THE RAIN

Adapted from the short story "On the Road" by
NNEDI OKORAFOR

Written by JOHN JENNINGS · Illustrated by DAVID BRAME
Lettering by DAMIAN DUFFY

ABRAMS COMICARTS · NEW YORK

MEGASCOPE Curator: John Jennings
Editor: Charlotte Greenbaum
Editorial Assistant: Jazmine Joyner
Designer: Charice Silverman
Managing Editor: Annalea Manalili
Production Manager: Alison Gervais

Cataloging-in-Publication Data has been
applied for and may be obtained from the
Library of Congress.

ISBN 978-1-4197-4355-9
eISBN 978-1-68335-834-3

Adapted from the short story "On the Road"
by Nnedi Okorafor, originally published in the
anthology *Kabu Kabu* by Prime Books in 2013.

Printed and bound in China
10 9 8 7 6 5 4 3 2 1

Abrams ComicArts books are available at
special discounts when purchased in quantity
for premiums and promotions as well as
fundraising or educational use. Special editions
can also be created to specification. For details,
contact specialsales@abramsbooks.com or the
address below.

ABRAMS The Art of Books
195 Broadway, New York, NY 10007
abramsbooks.com

ABRAMS COMIC ARTS MEGASCOPE

MEGASCOPE is dedicated to show-
casing speculative works by and
about people of color, with a focus
on science fiction, fantasy, horror,
and stories of magical realism. The
megascope is a fictional device
imagined by W. E. B. Du Bois that
can peer through time and space into
other realities. This magical invention
represents the idea that so much of
our collective past has not seen the
light of day, and that there is so much
history that we have yet to discover.
MEGASCOPE will serve as a lens
through which we can broaden our
view of history, the present, and the
future, and as a method by which
previously unheard voices can find
their way to an ever-growing diverse
audience.

MEGASCOPE ADVISORY BOARD

To Octavia E. Butler, Amos Tutuola, and
W. E. B. Du Bois for introducing us to
and showing us how to embrace our
most beautiful of ghosts

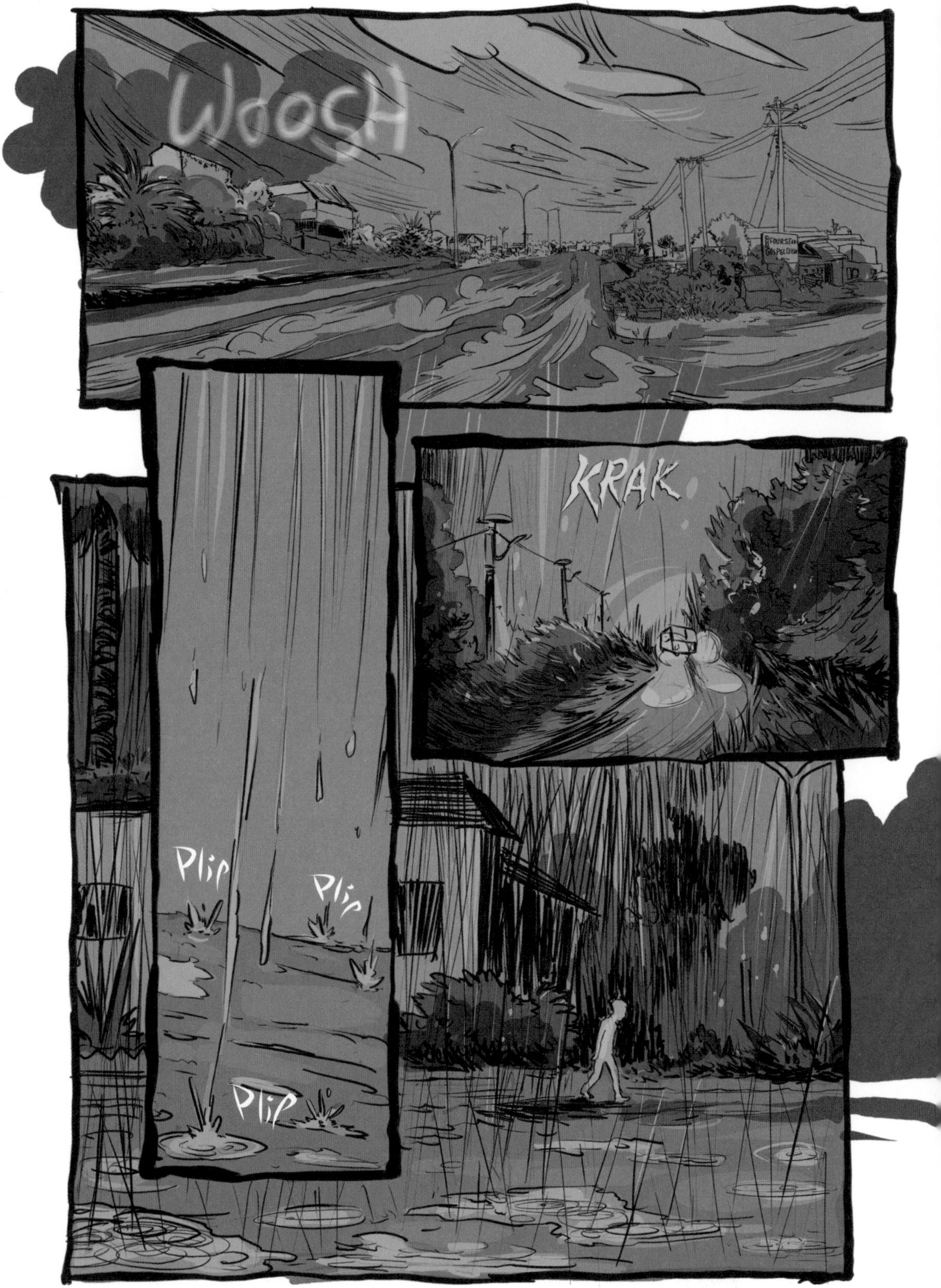
WOOSH
KRAK
Plip
Plip
Plip

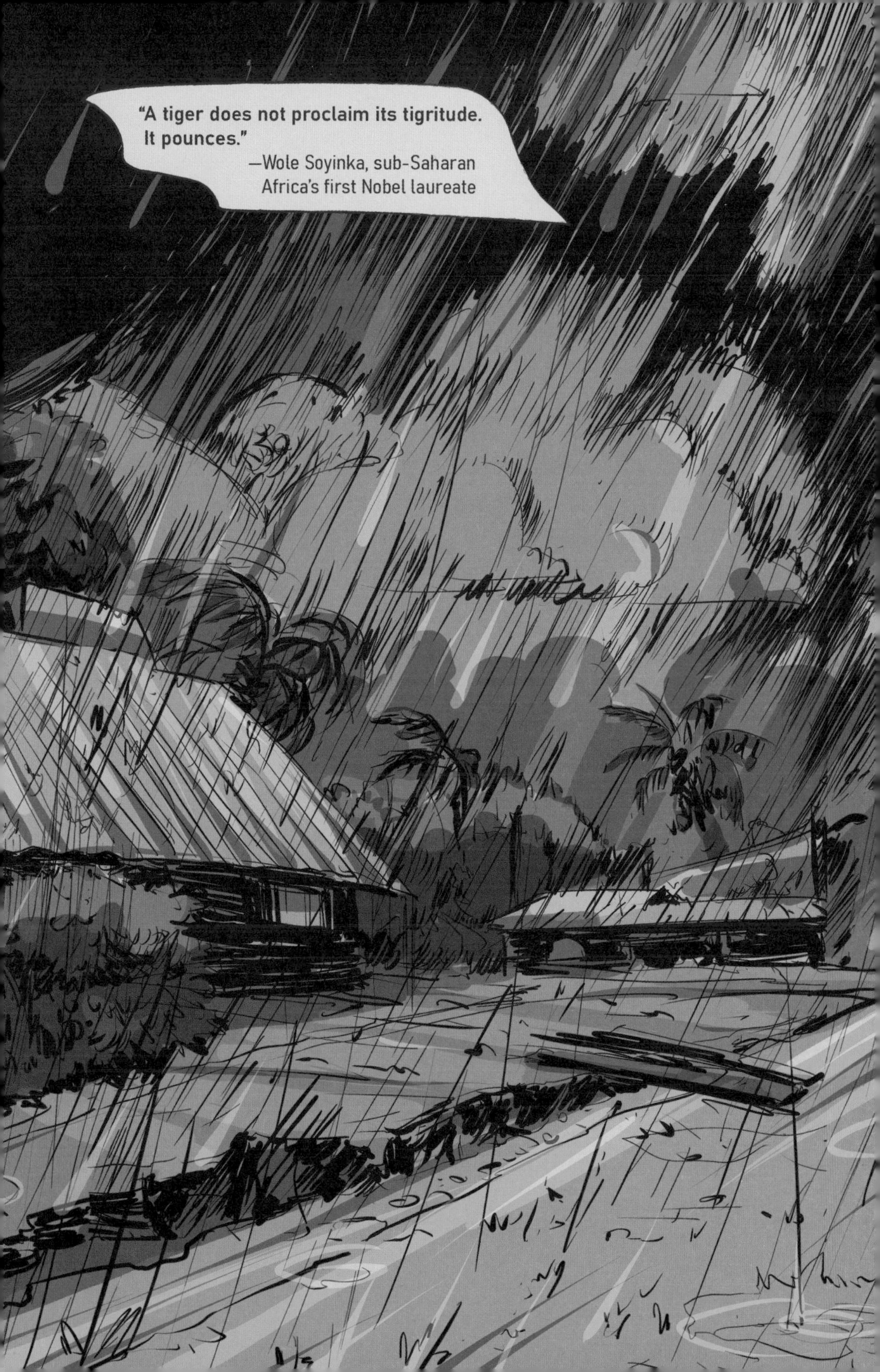
"A tiger does not proclaim its tigritude. It pounces."
—Wole Soyinka, sub-Saharan Africa's first Nobel laureate

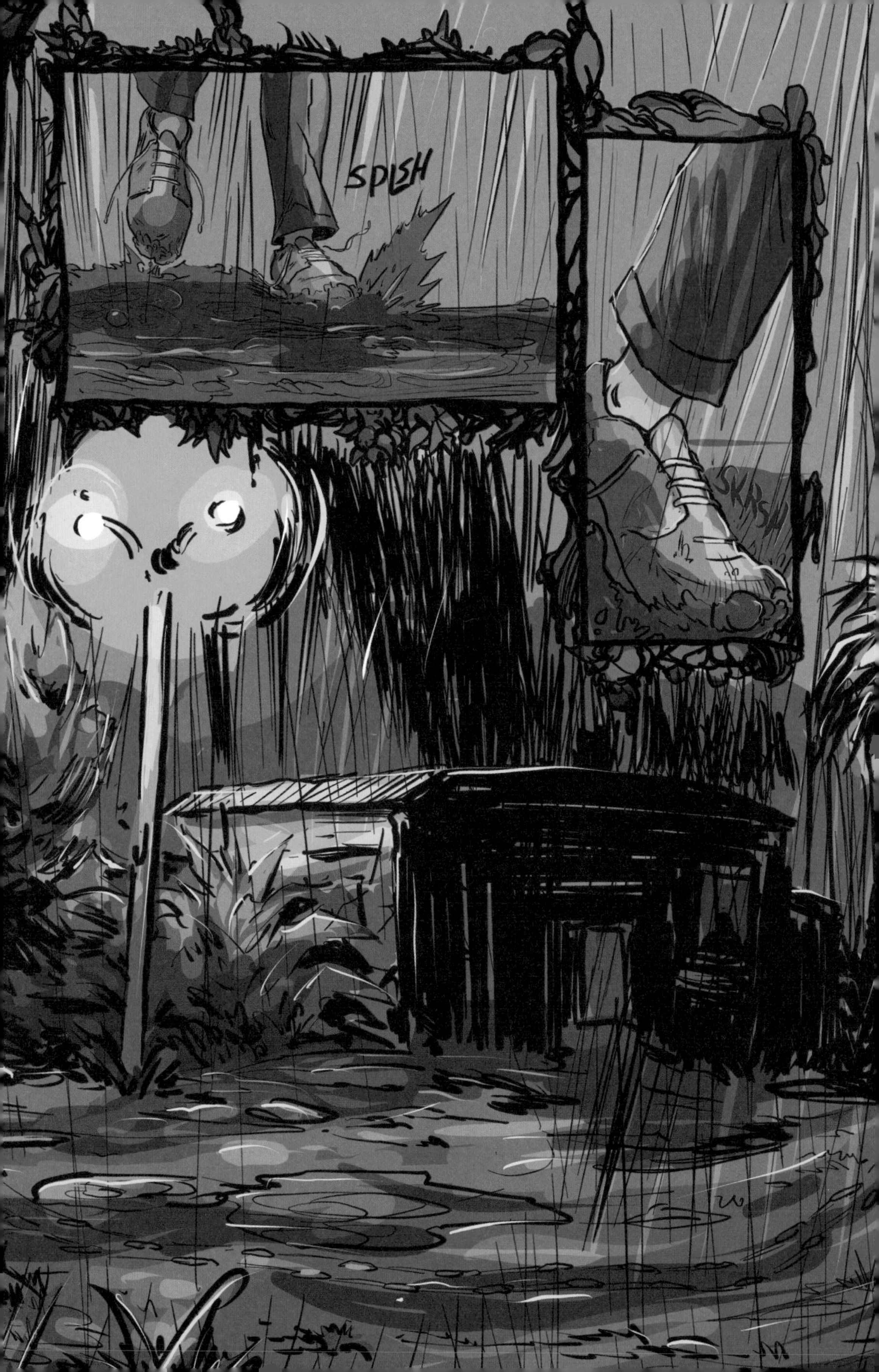
SPLSH
SKRSH

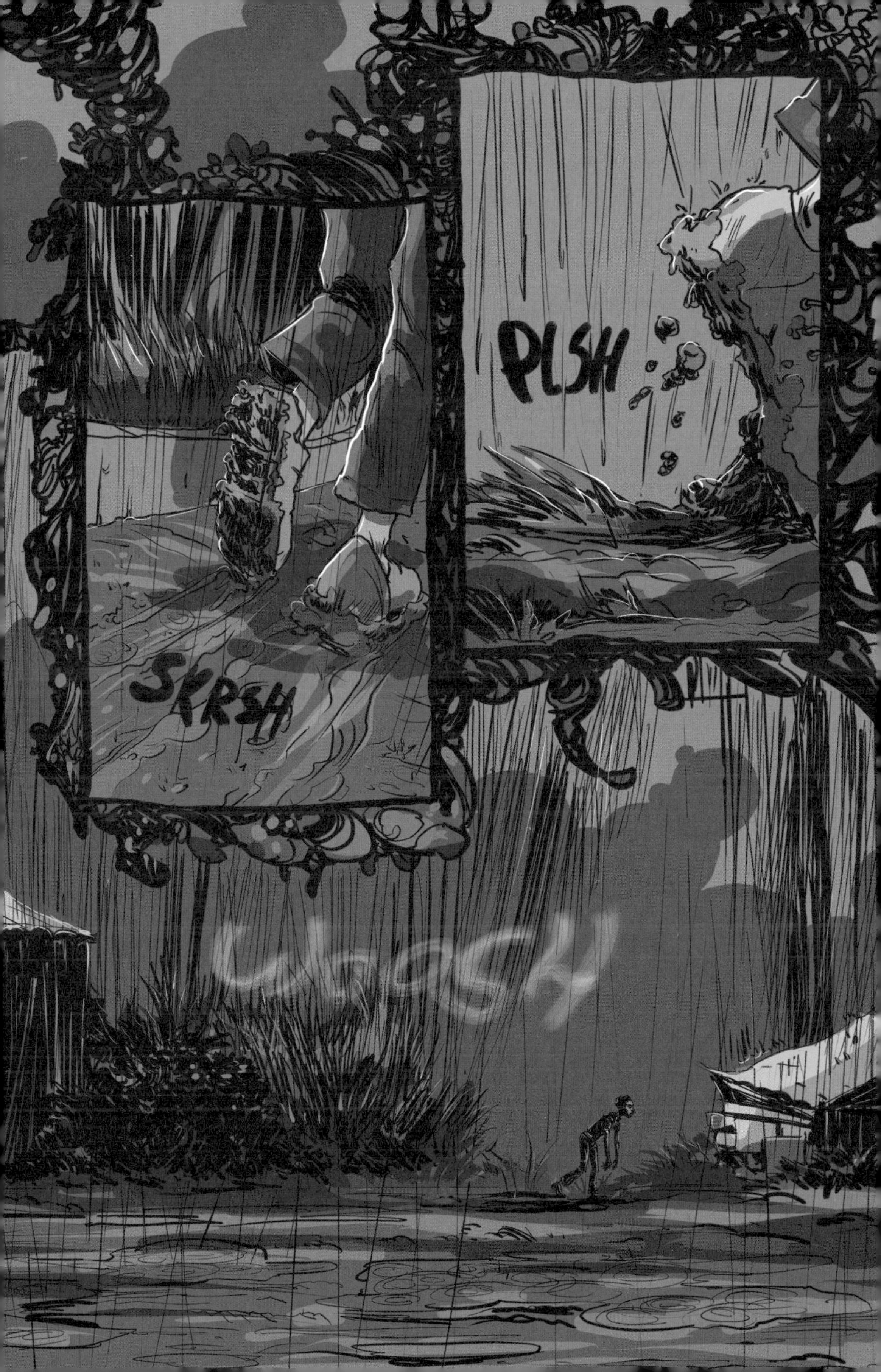
SKRSH
PLSH

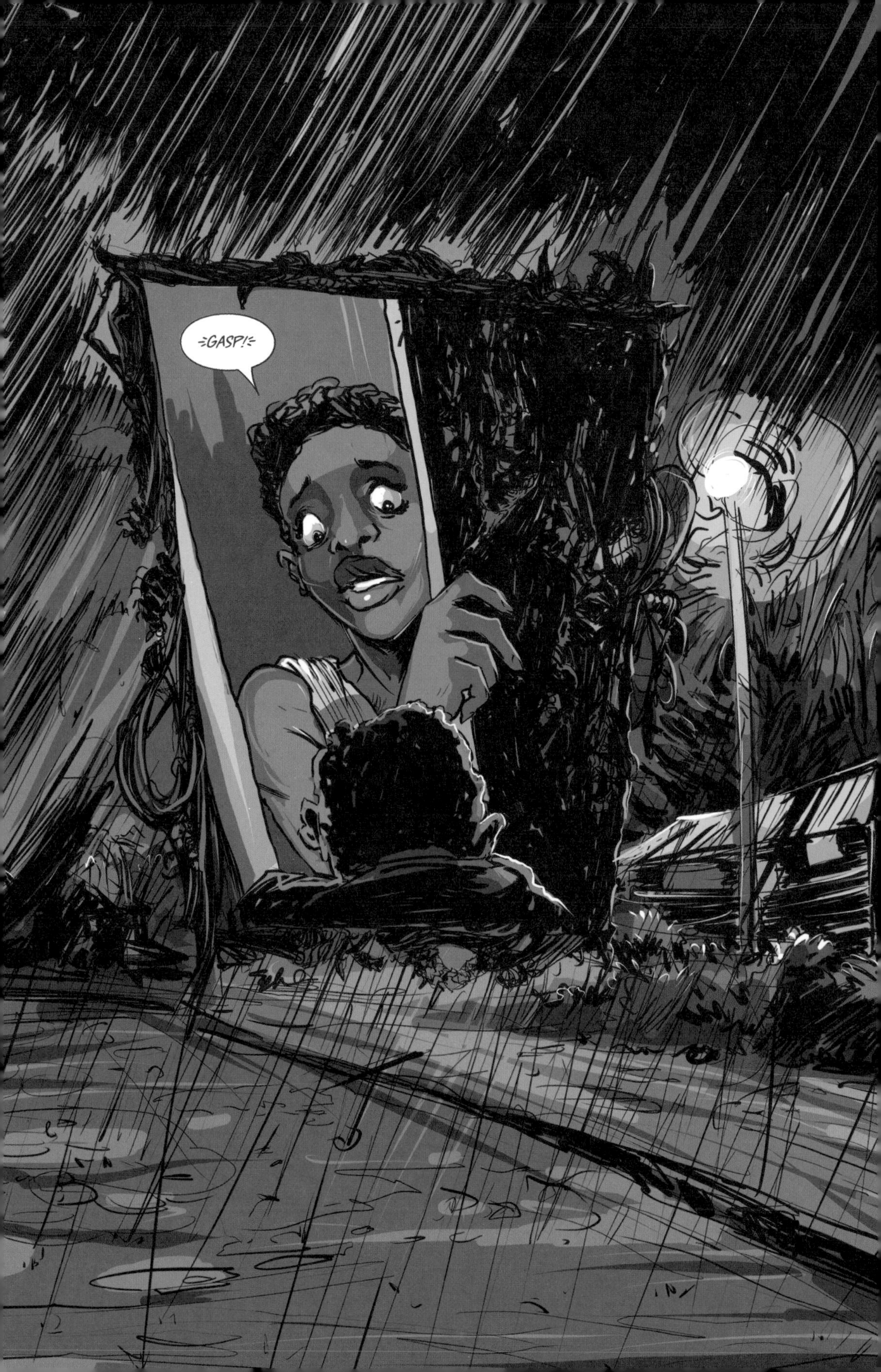
GASP!

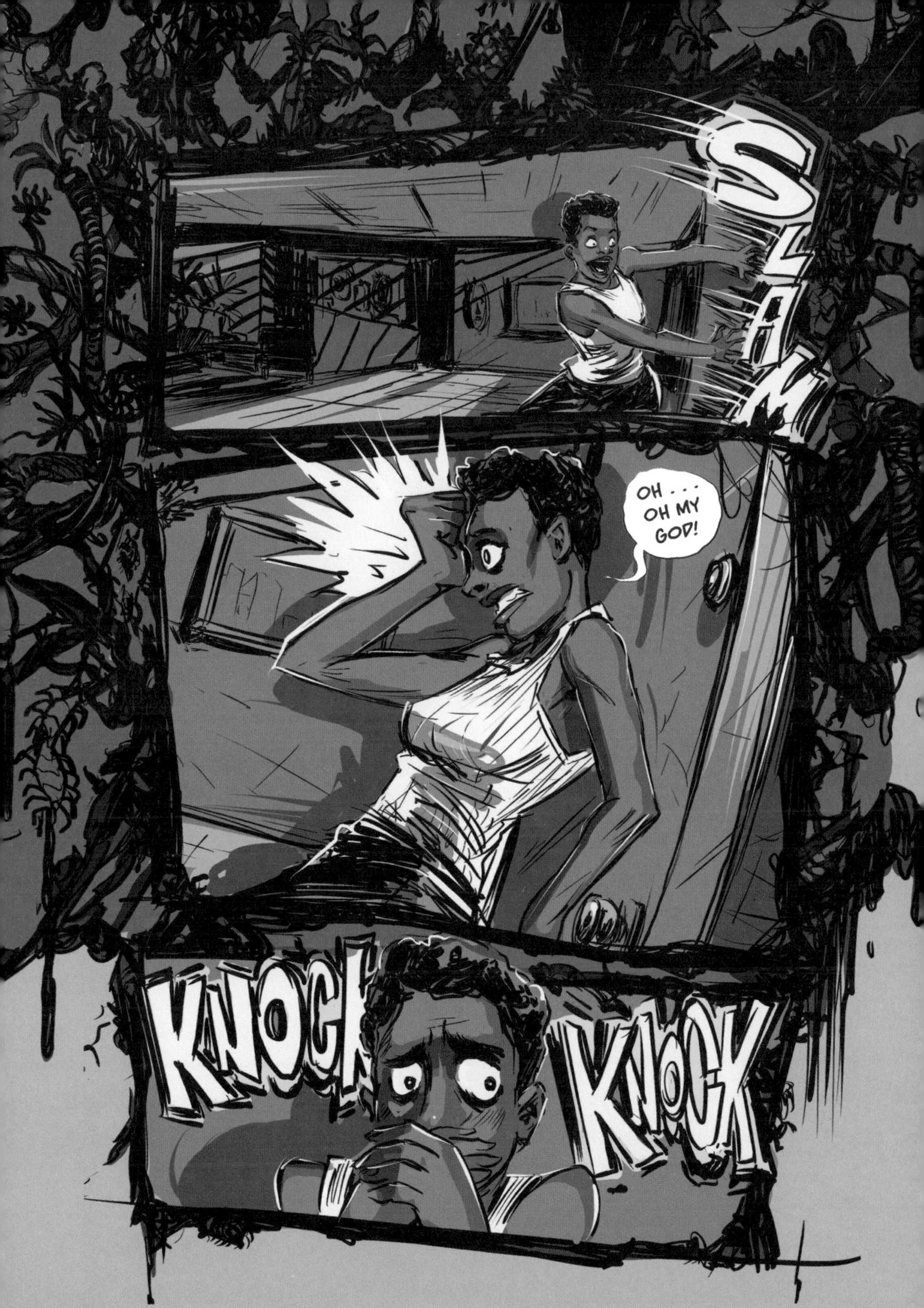
SLAM
OH . . .
OH MY
GOD!
KNOCK
KNOCK

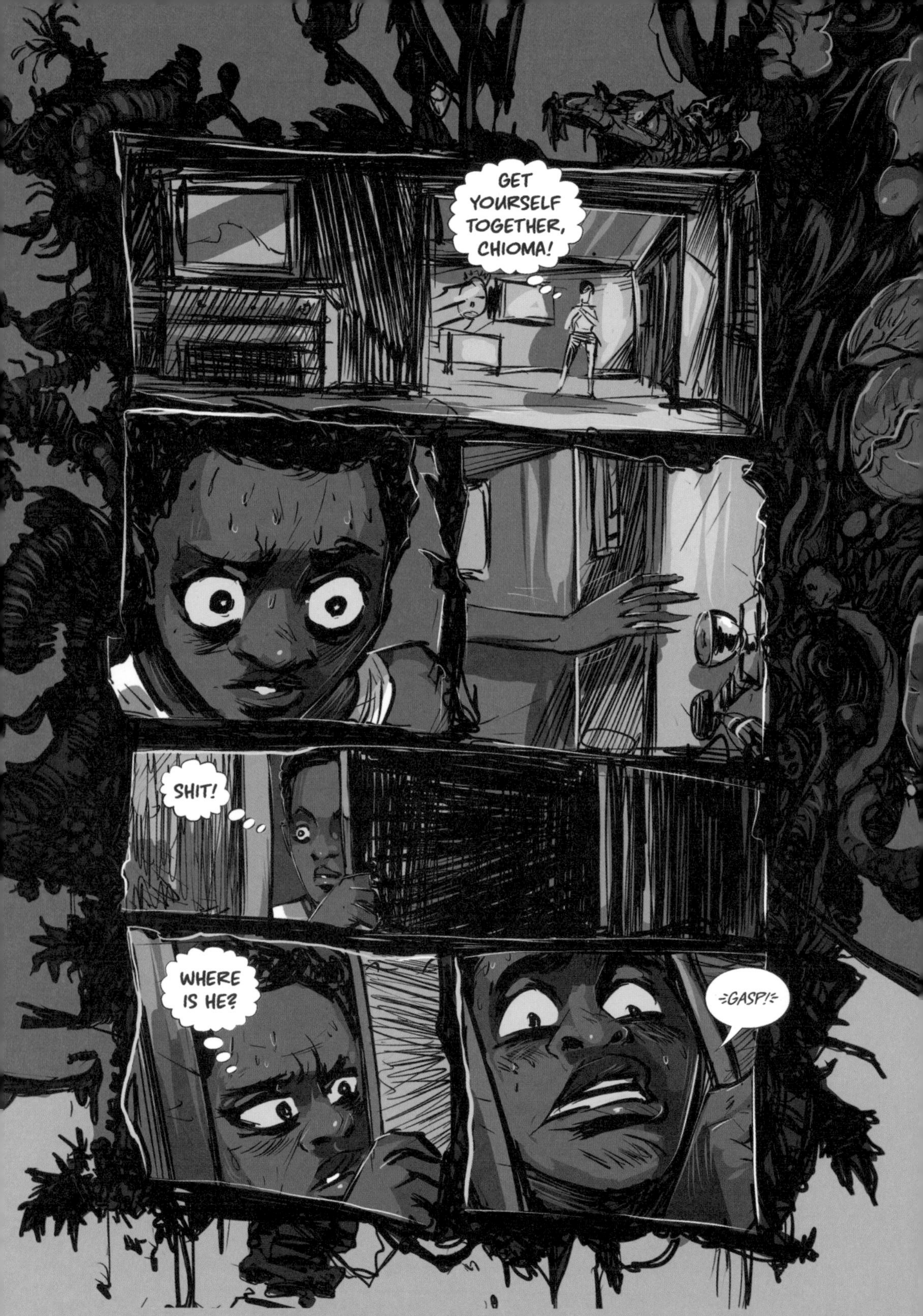
GET YOURSELF TOGETHER, CHIOMA!
SHIT!
WHERE IS HE?
GASP!

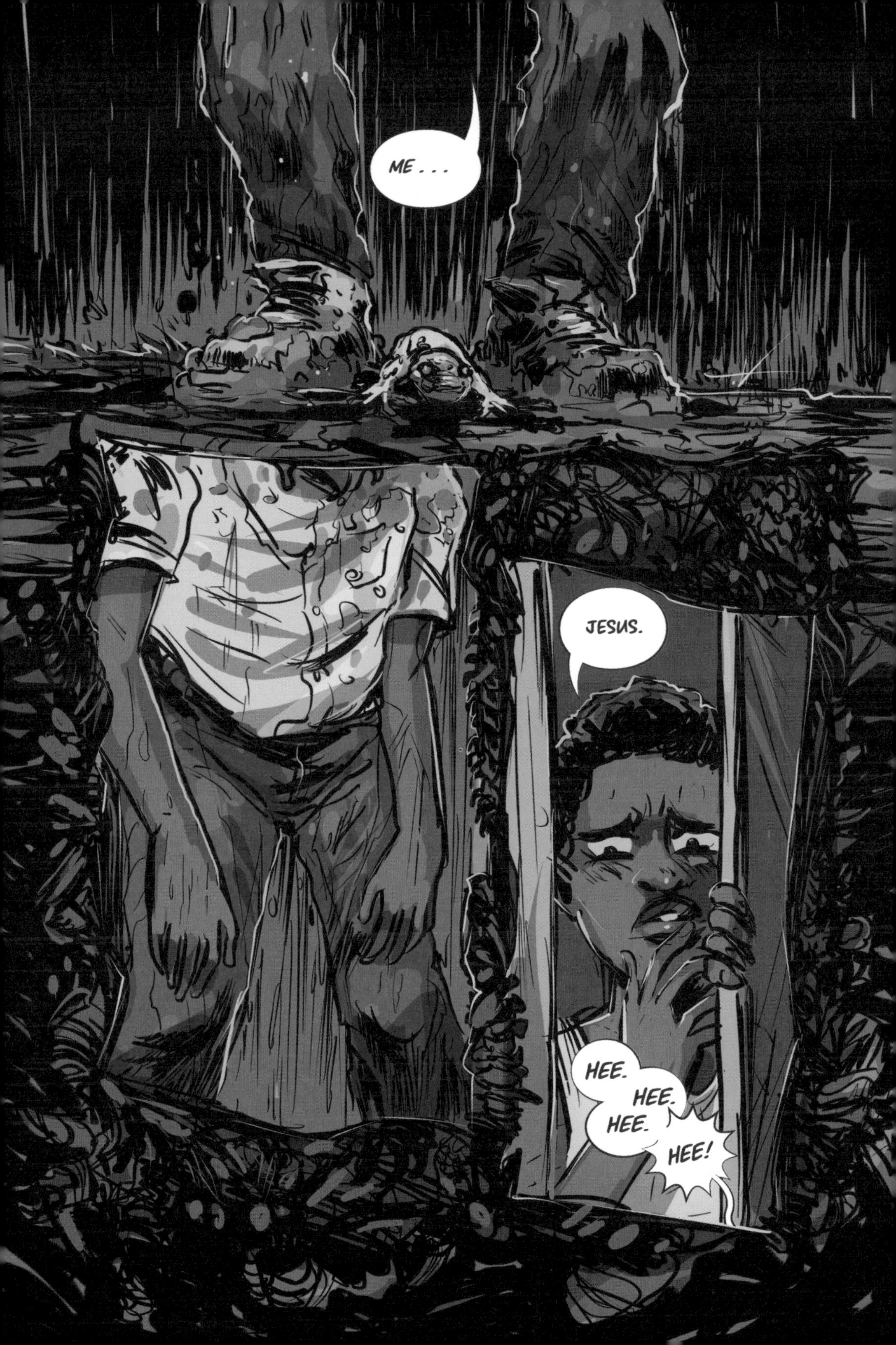
ME . . .
JESUS.
HEE.
HEE.
HEE.
HEE!

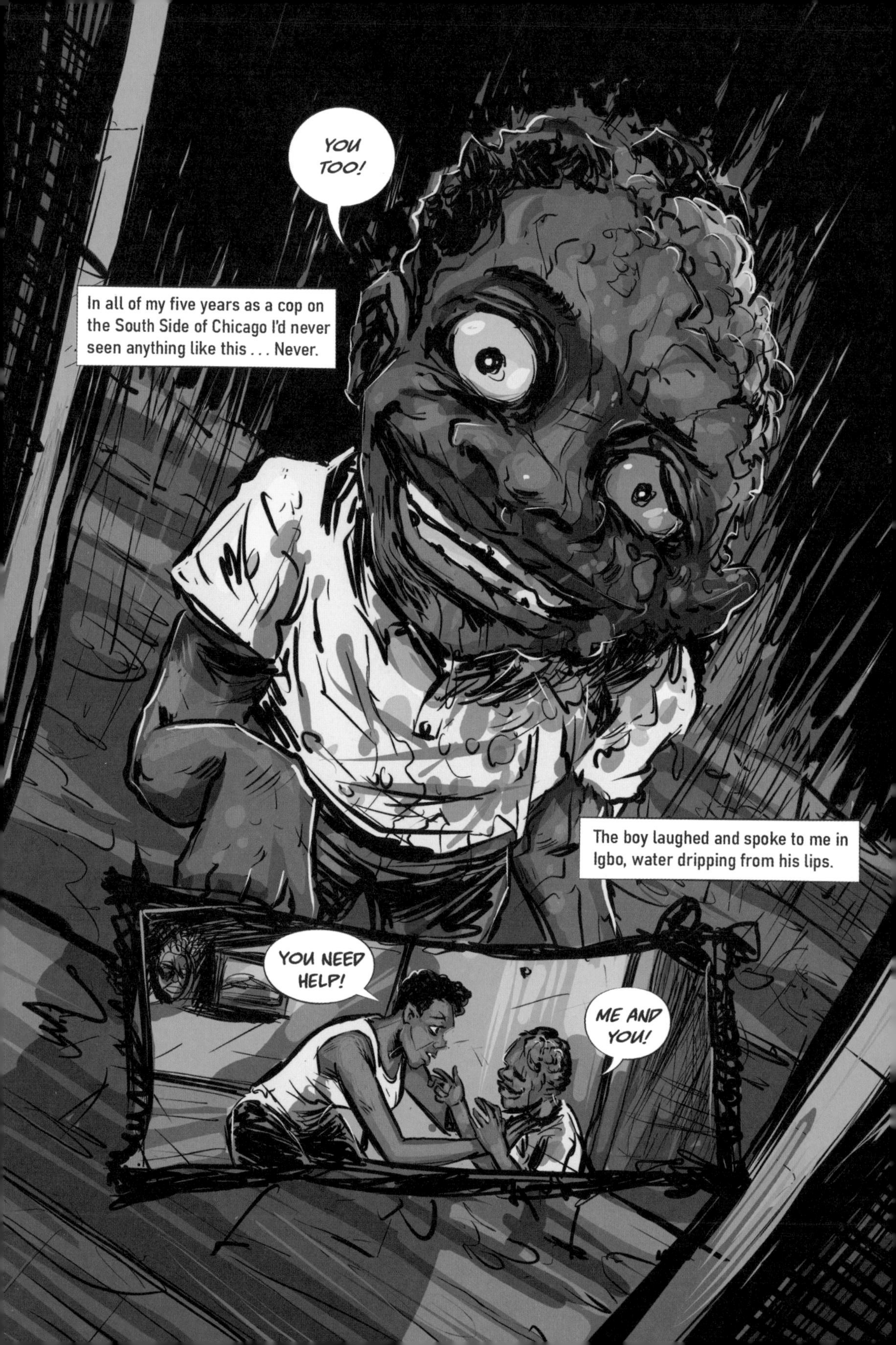
YOU TOO!
In all of my five years as a cop on the South Side of Chicago I'd never seen anything like this . . . Never.
The boy laughed and spoke to me in Igbo, water dripping from his lips.
YOU NEED HELP!
ME AND YOU!

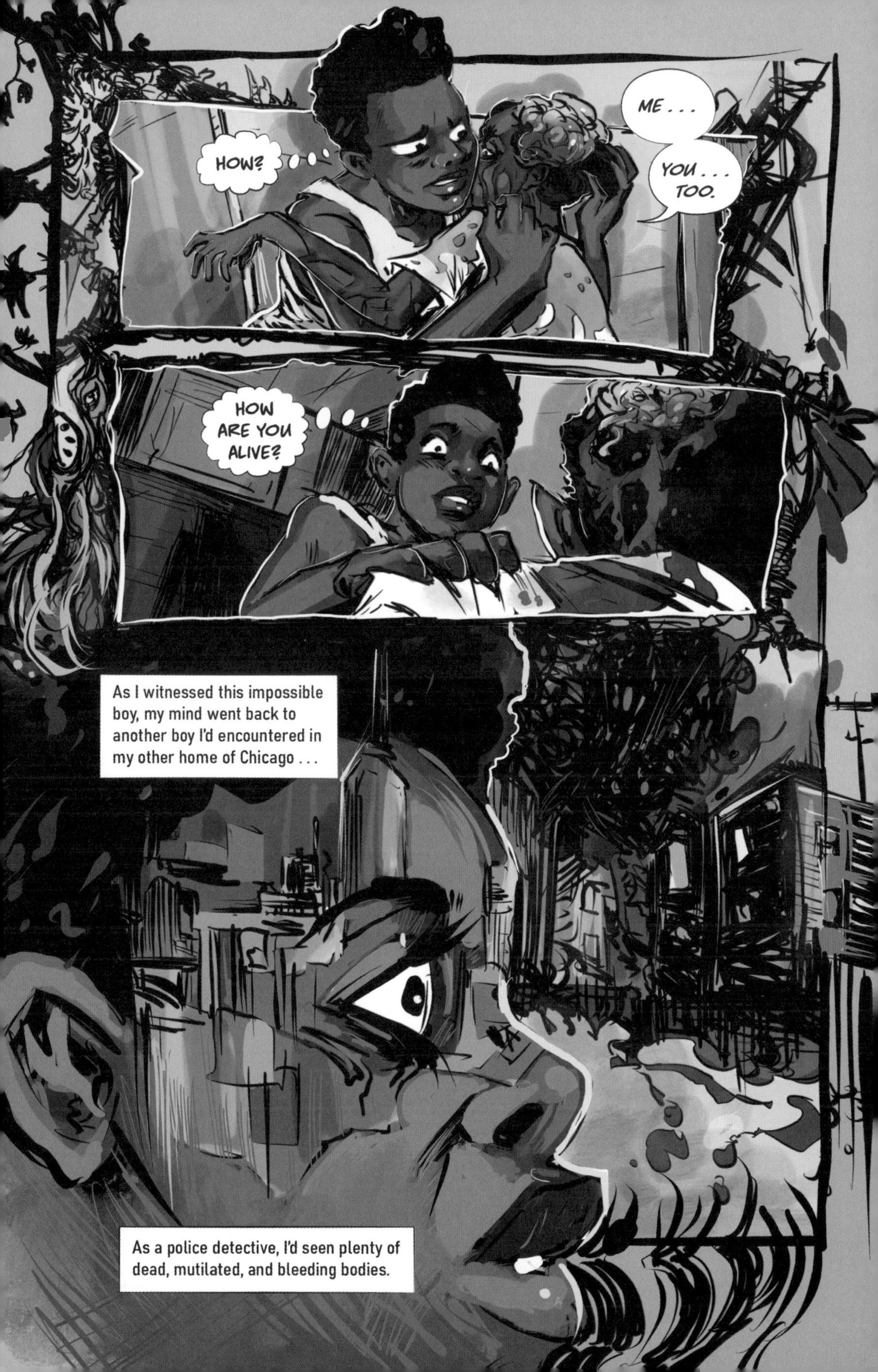
HOW?
ME . . .
YOU . . . TOO.
HOW ARE YOU ALIVE?
As I witnessed this impossible boy, my mind went back to another boy I'd encountered in my other home of Chicago . . .
As a police detective, I'd seen plenty of dead, mutilated, and bleeding bodies.

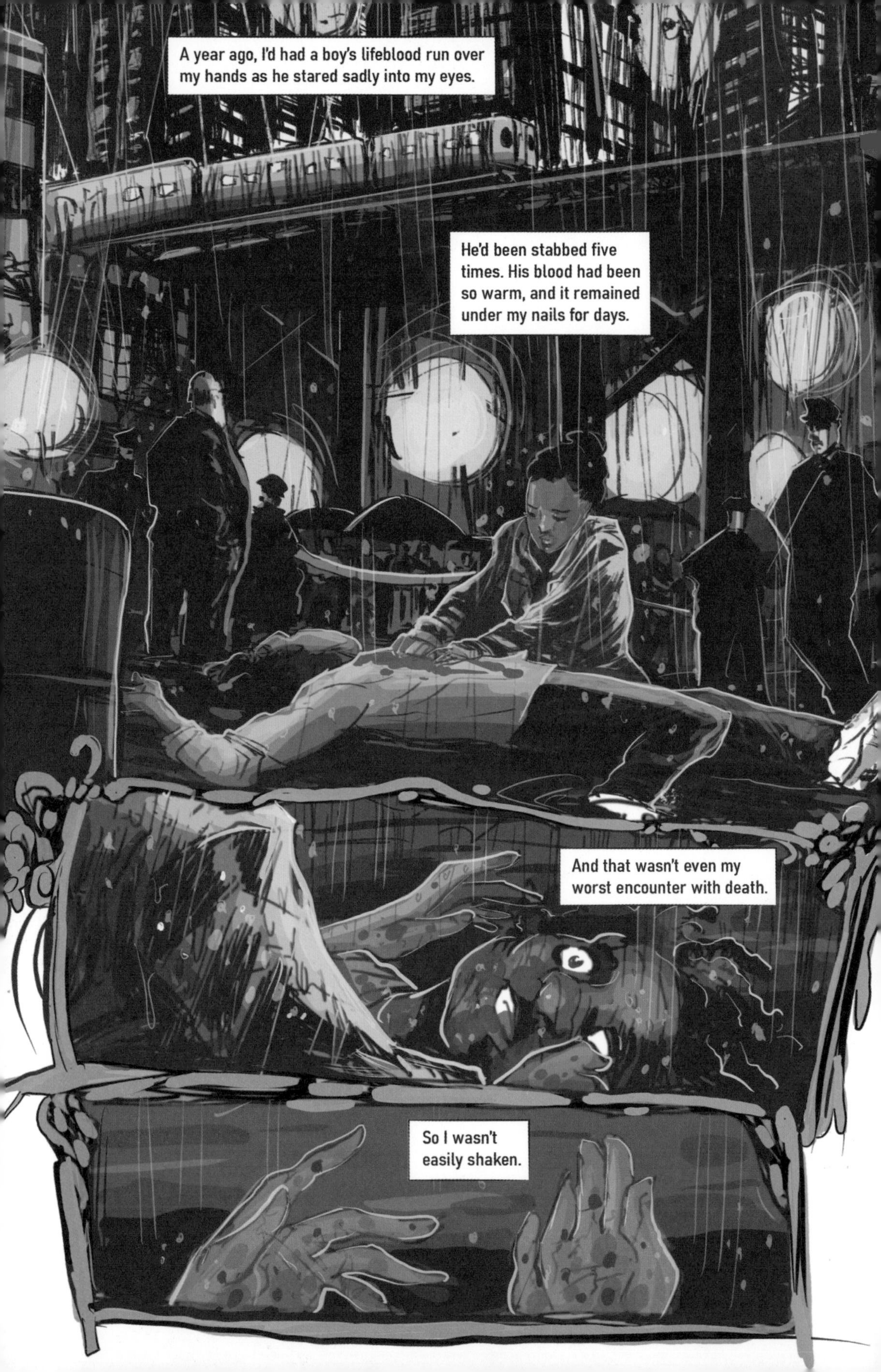
A year ago, I'd had a boy's lifeblood run over my hands as he stared sadly into my eyes.
He'd been stabbed five times. His blood had been so warm, and it remained under my nails for days.
And that wasn't even my worst encounter with death.
So I wasn't easily shaken.

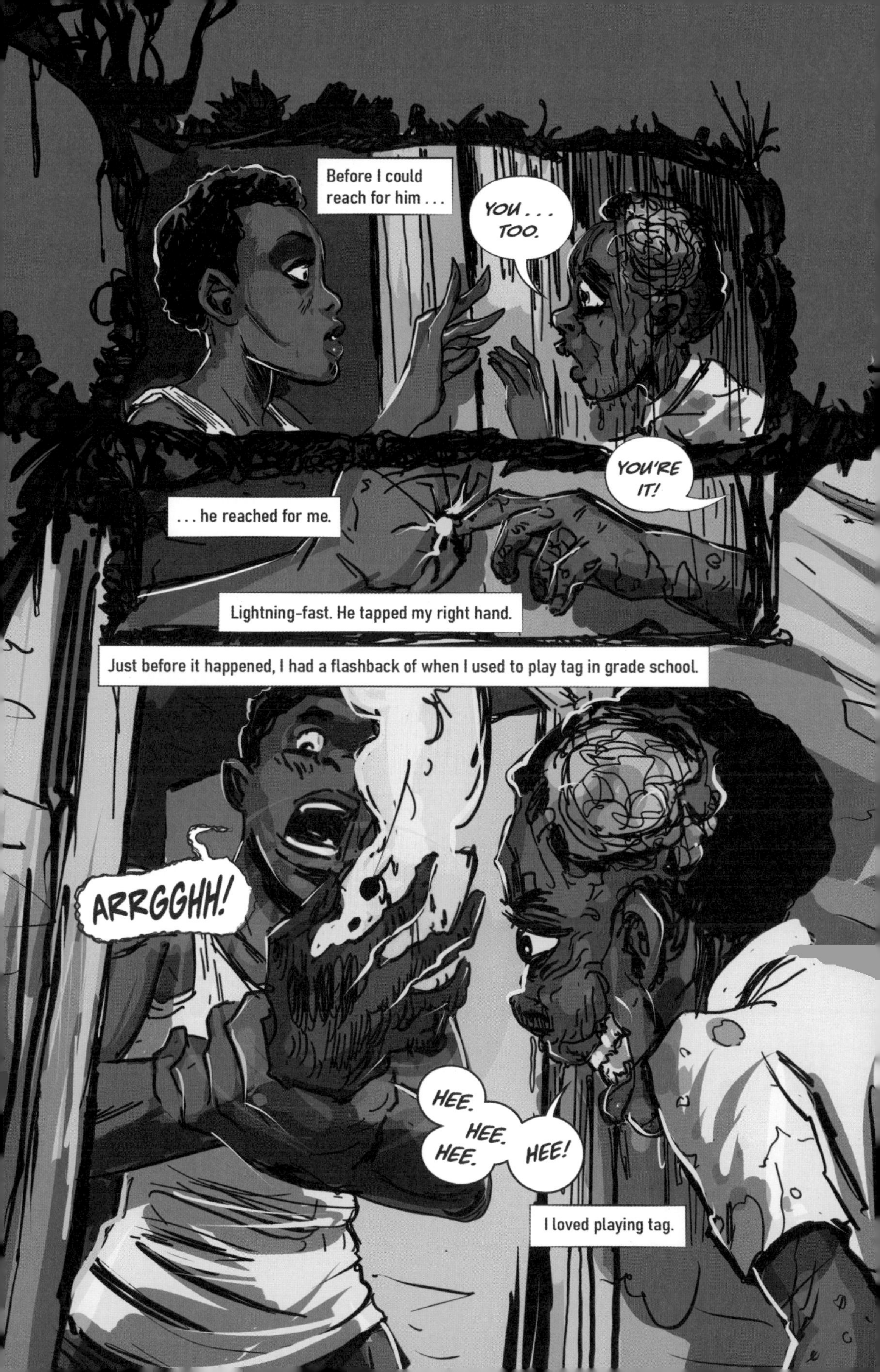

Before I could reach for him . . .
YOU . . . TOO.
. . . he reached for me.
YOU'RE IT!
Lightning-fast. He tapped my right hand.
Just before it happened, I had a flashback of when I used to play tag in grade school.
ARRGGHH!
HEE. HEE. HEE. HEE!
I loved playing tag.

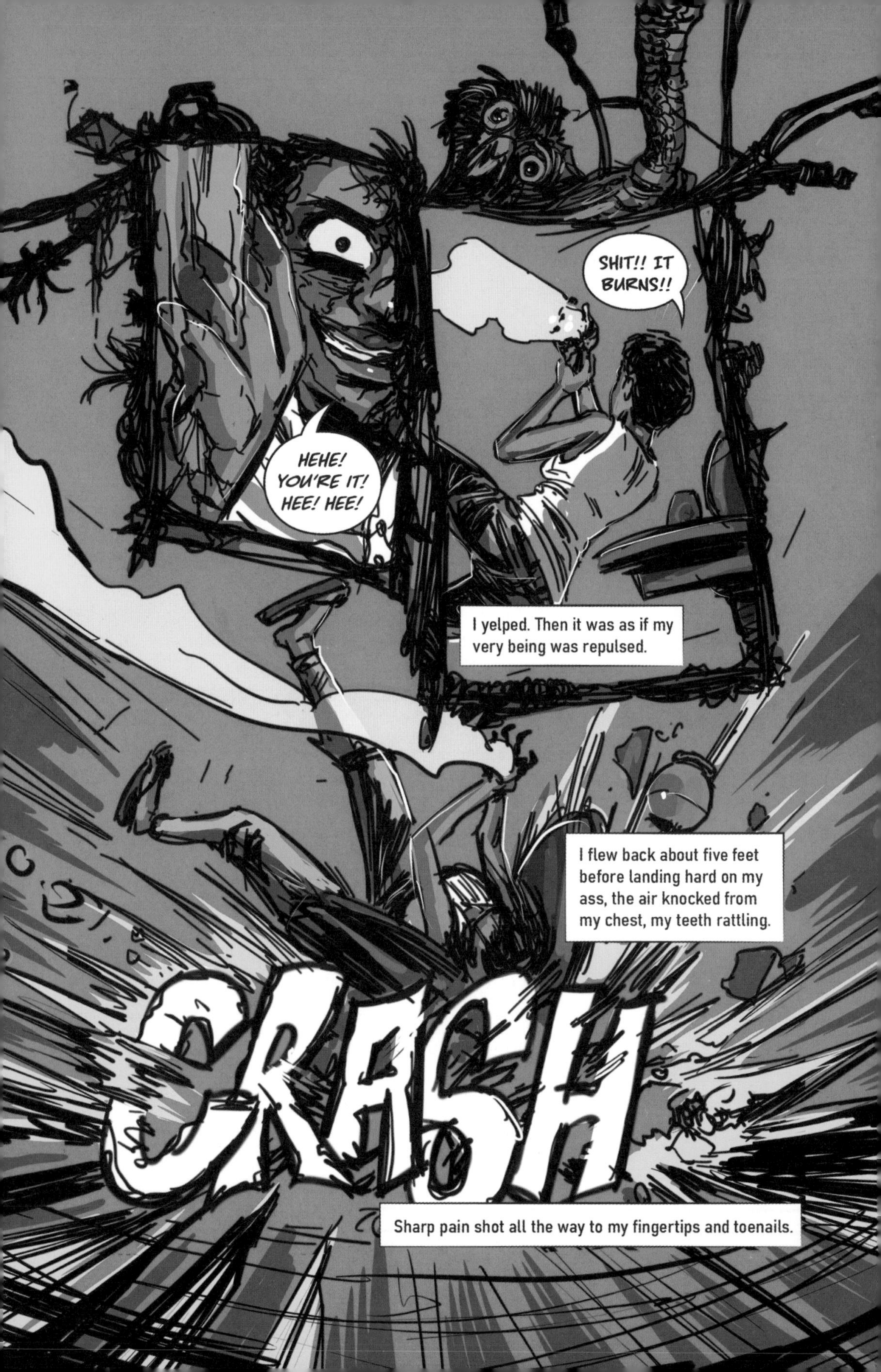

HEHE! YOU'RE IT! HEE! HEE!
SHIT!! IT BURNS!!
I yelped. Then it was as if my very being was repulsed.
I flew back about five feet before landing hard on my ass, the air knocked from my chest, my teeth rattling.
CRASH
Sharp pain shot all the way to my fingertips and toenails.

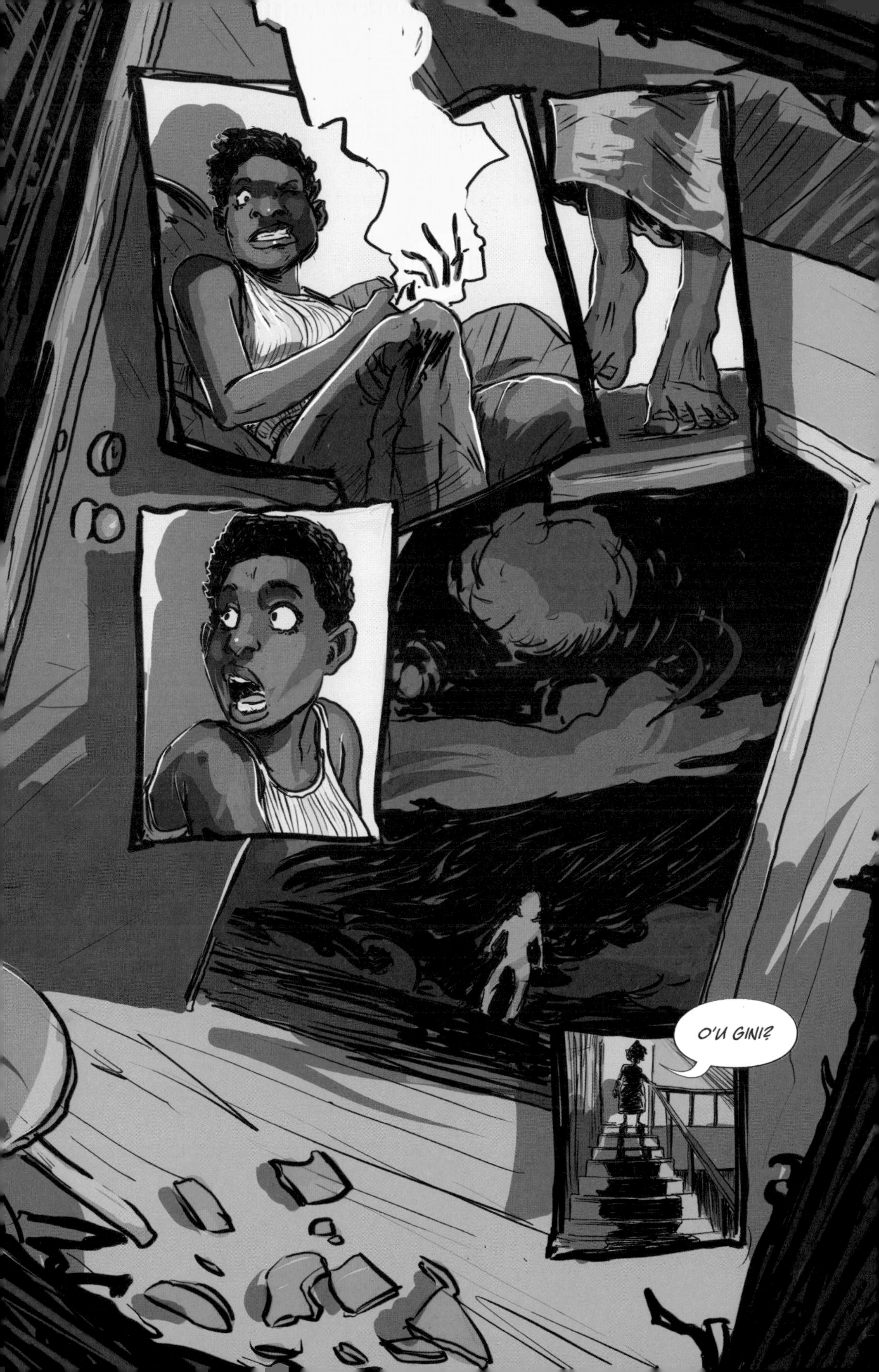
O'U GINI?

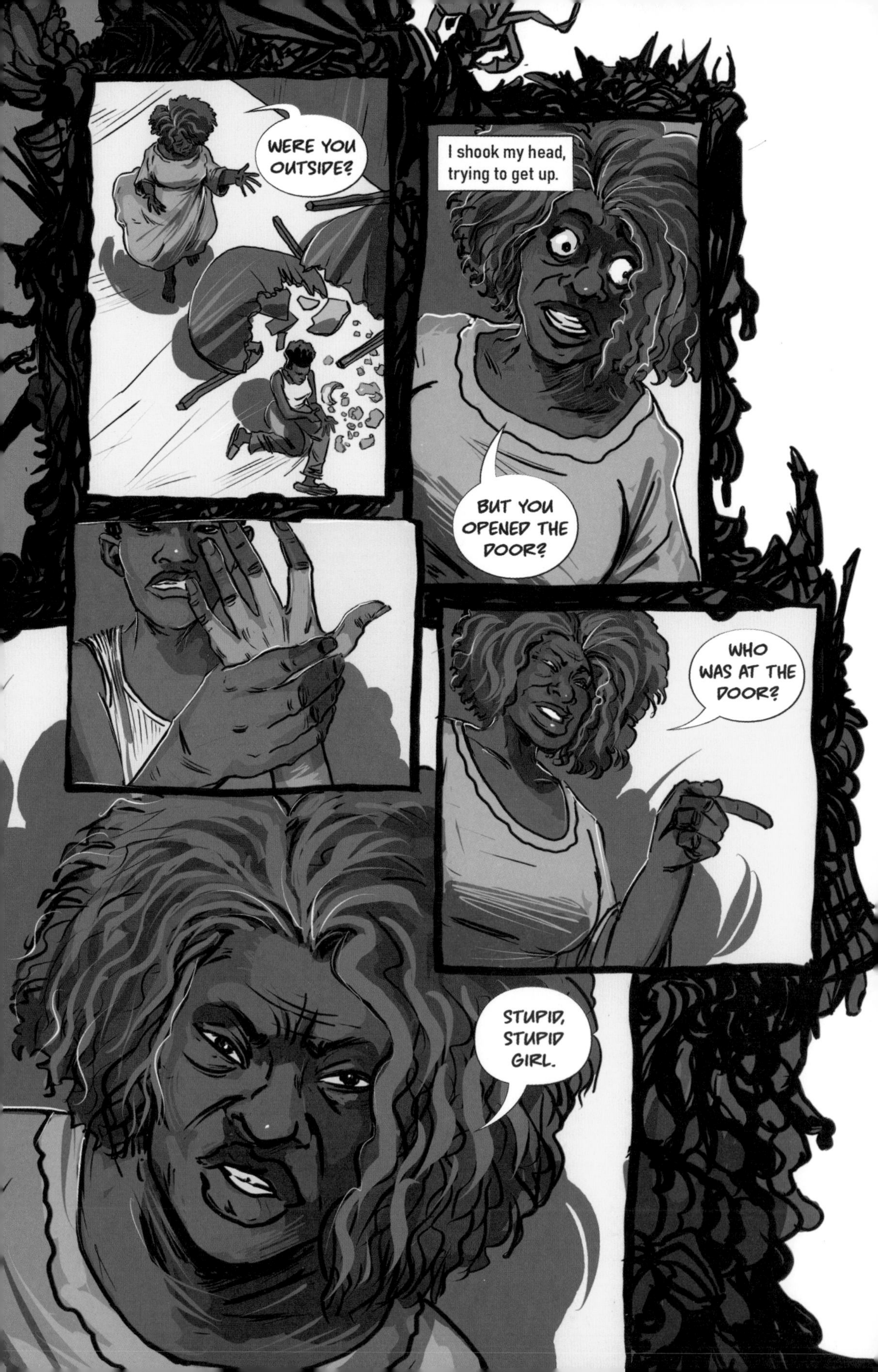
WERE YOU OUTSIDE?
I shook my head, trying to get up.
BUT YOU OPENED THE DOOR?
WHO WAS AT THE DOOR?
STUPID, STUPID GIRL.

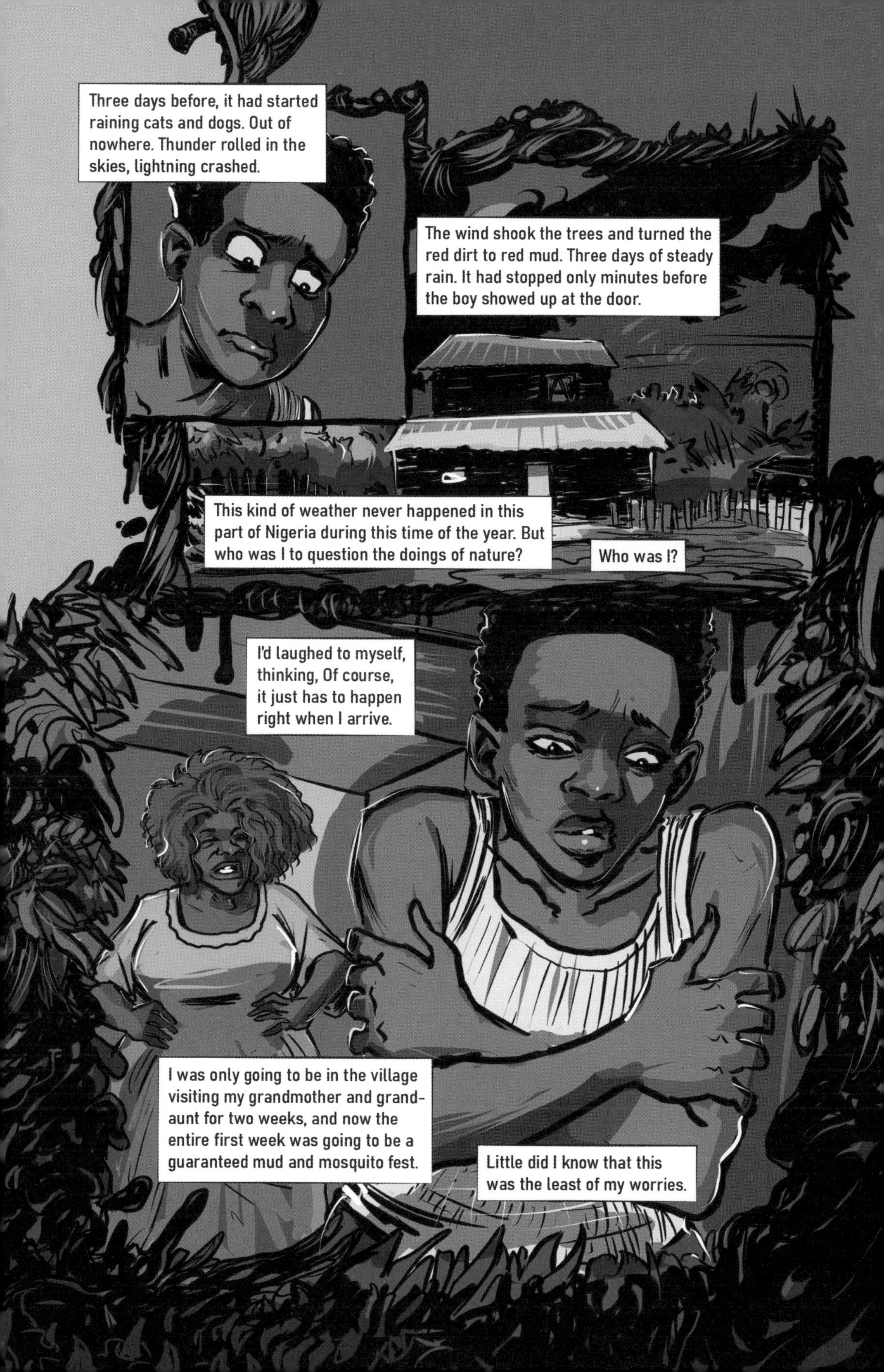
Three days before, it had started raining cats and dogs. Out of nowhere. Thunder rolled in the skies, lightning crashed.
The wind shook the trees and turned the red dirt to red mud. Three days of steady rain. It had stopped only minutes before the boy showed up at the door.
This kind of weather never happened in this part of Nigeria during this time of the year. But who was I to question the doings of nature?
Who was I?
I'd laughed to myself, thinking, Of course, it just has to happen right when I arrive.
I was only going to be in the village visiting my grandmother and grand-aunt for two weeks, and now the entire first week was going to be a guaranteed mud and mosquito fest.
Little did I know that this was the least of my worries.

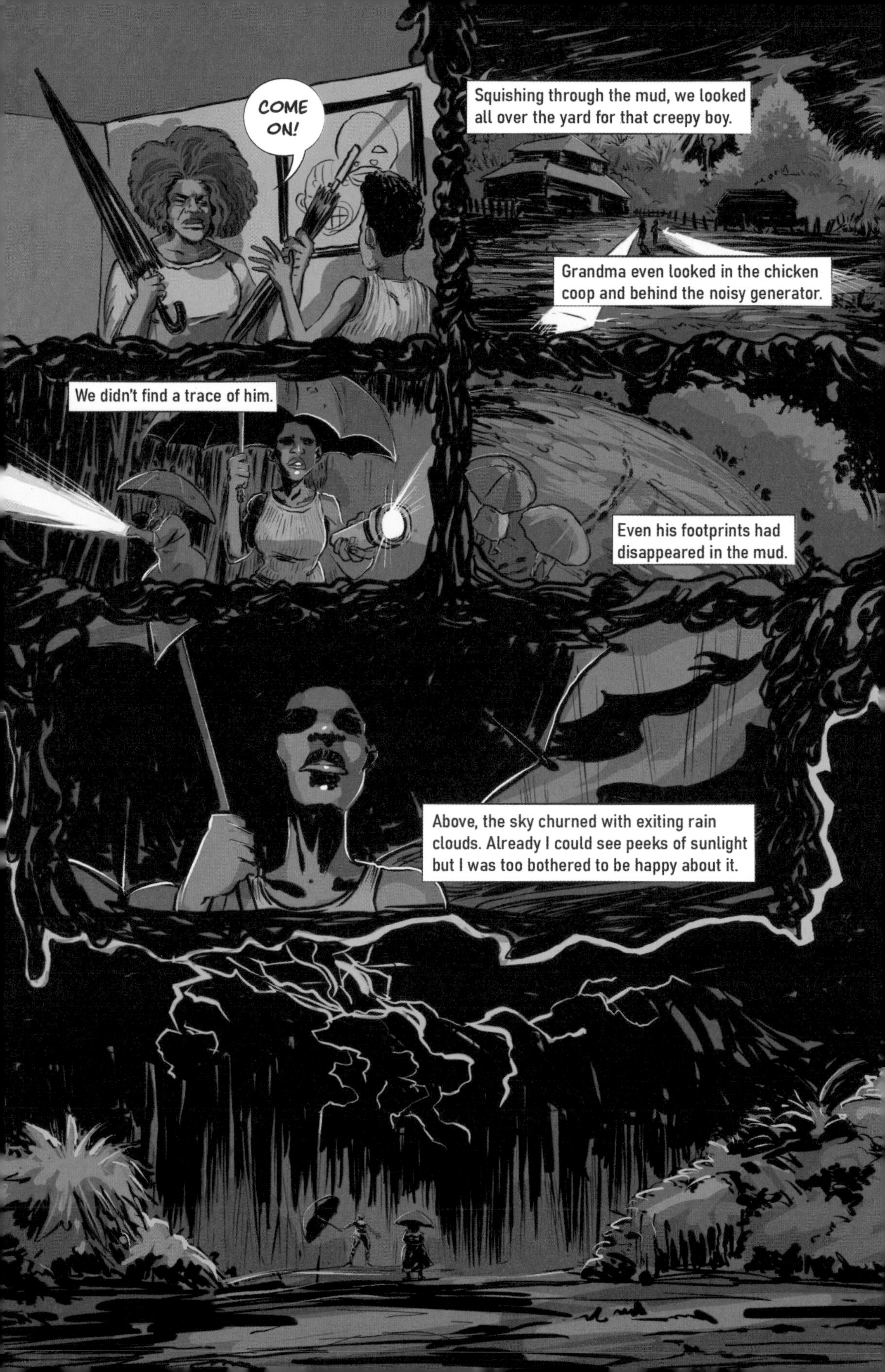
COME ON!
Squishing through the mud, we looked all over the yard for that creepy boy.
Grandma even looked in the chicken coop and behind the noisy generator.
We didn't find a trace of him.
Even his footprints had disappeared in the mud.
Above, the sky churned with exiting rain clouds. Already I could see peeks of sunlight but I was too bothered to be happy about it.

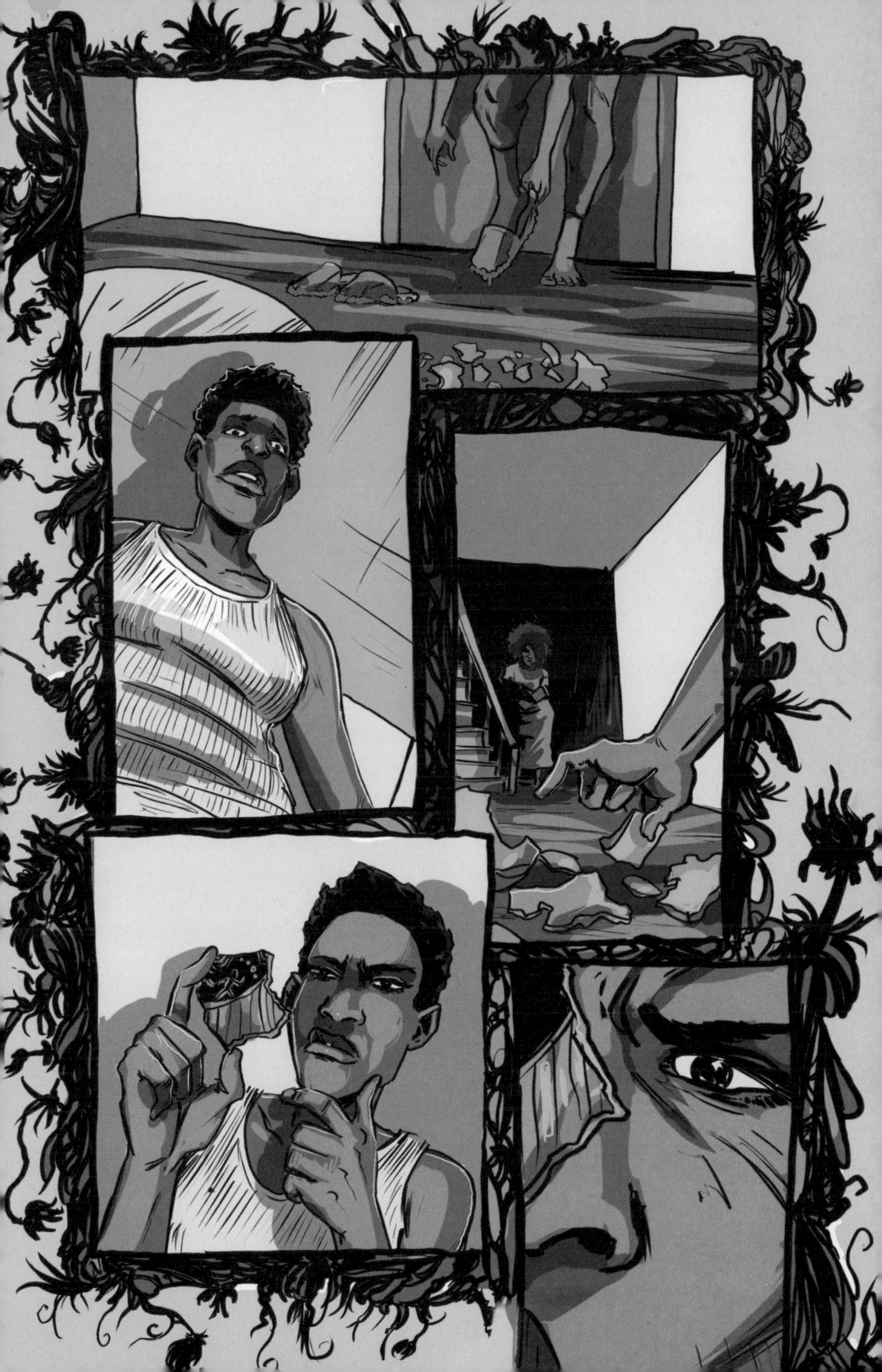

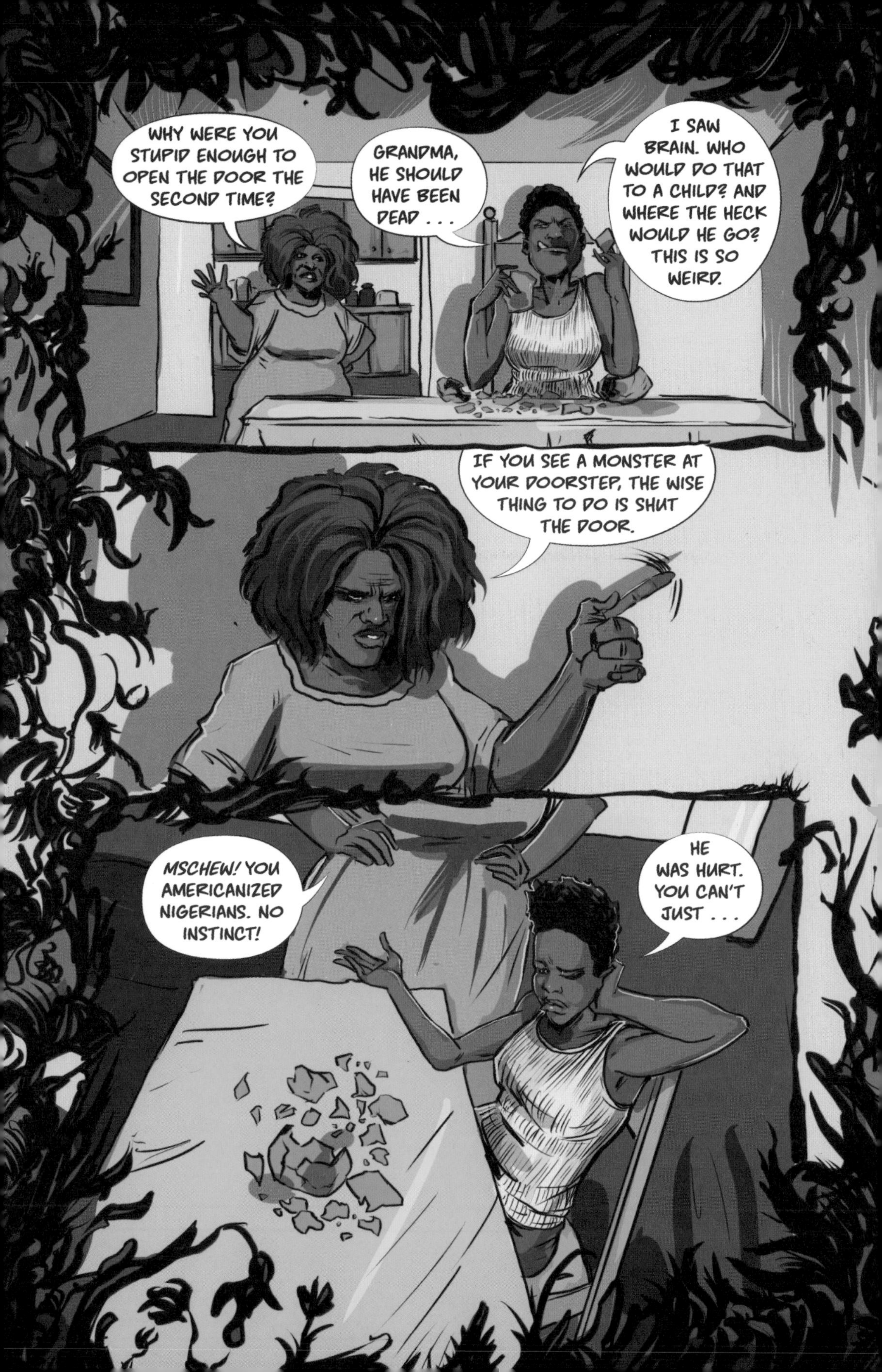
WHY WERE YOU STUPID ENOUGH TO OPEN THE DOOR THE SECOND TIME?
GRANDMA, HE SHOULD HAVE BEEN DEAD . . .
I SAW BRAIN. WHO WOULD DO THAT TO A CHILD? AND WHERE THE HECK WOULD HE GO? THIS IS SO WEIRD.
IF YOU SEE A MONSTER AT YOUR DOORSTEP, THE WISE THING TO DO IS SHUT THE DOOR.
MSCHEW! YOU AMERICANIZED NIGERIANS. NO INSTINCT!
HE WAS HURT. YOU CAN'T JUST . . .

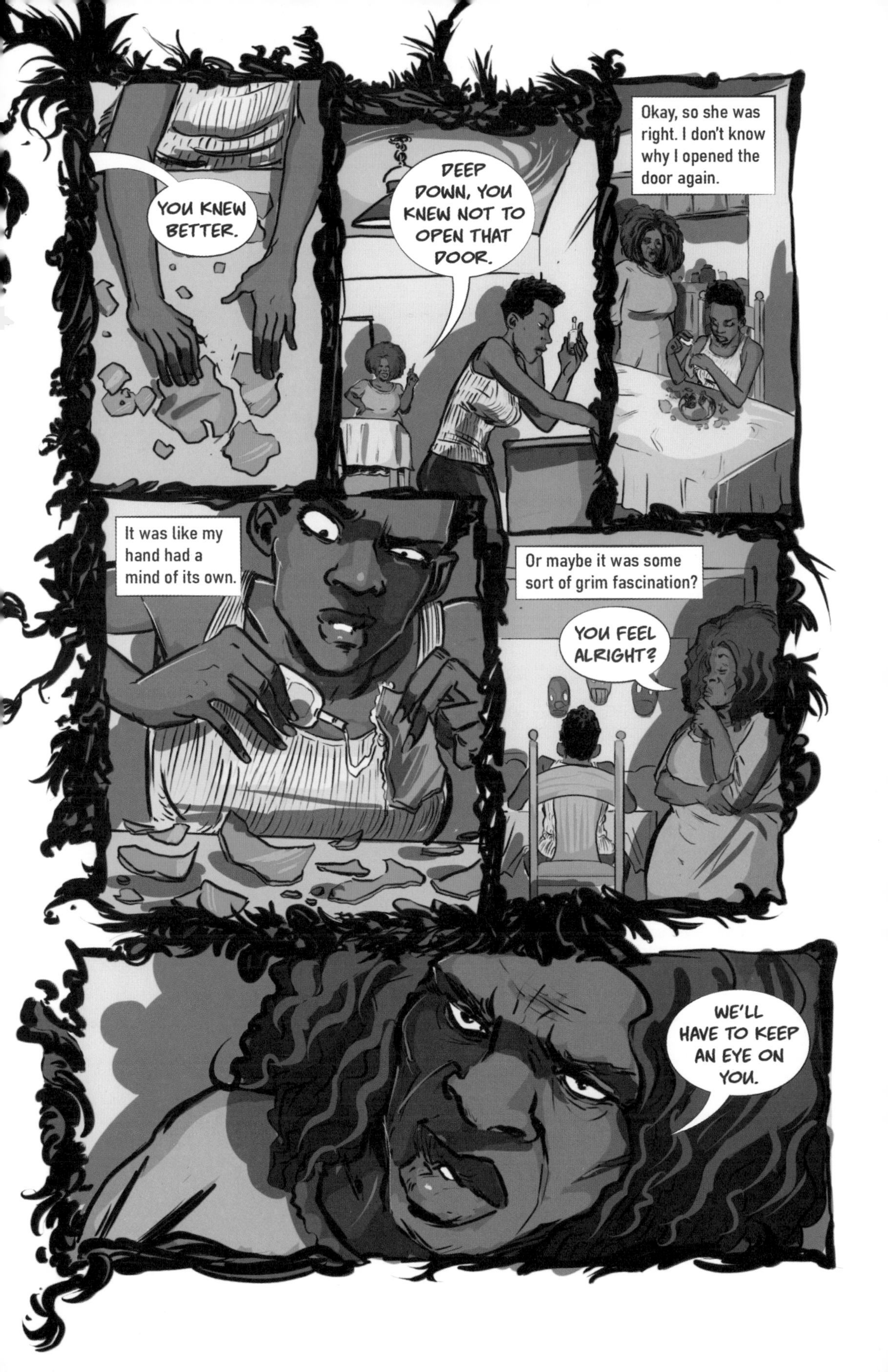
YOU KNEW BETTER.
DEEP DOWN, YOU KNEW NOT TO OPEN THAT DOOR.
Okay, so she was right. I don't know why I opened the door again.
It was like my hand had a mind of its own.
Or maybe it was some sort of grim fascination?
YOU FEEL ALRIGHT?
WE'LL HAVE TO KEEP AN EYE ON YOU.

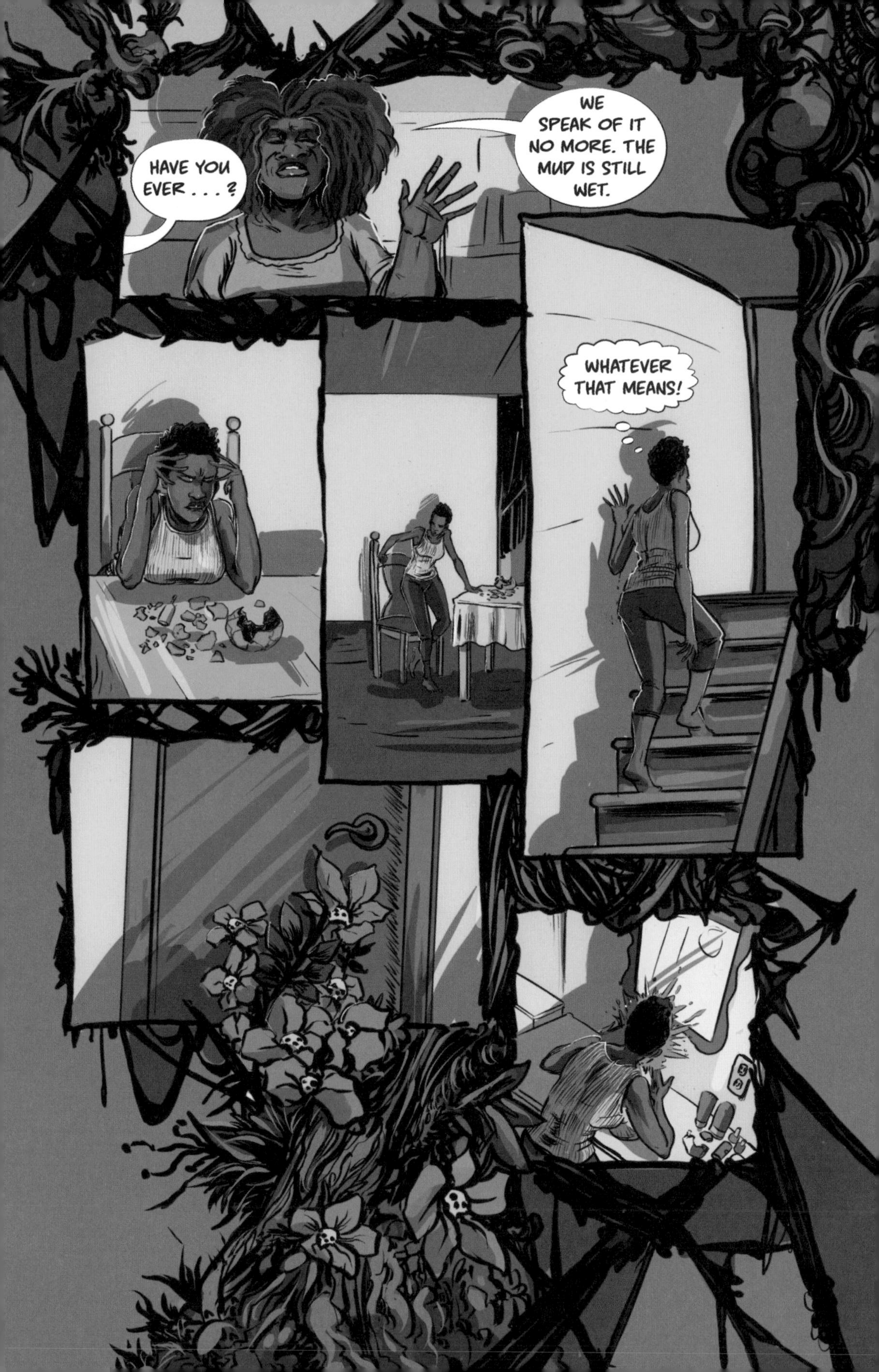
HAVE YOU EVER . . . ?
WE SPEAK OF IT NO MORE. THE MUD IS STILL WET.
WHATEVER THAT MEANS!

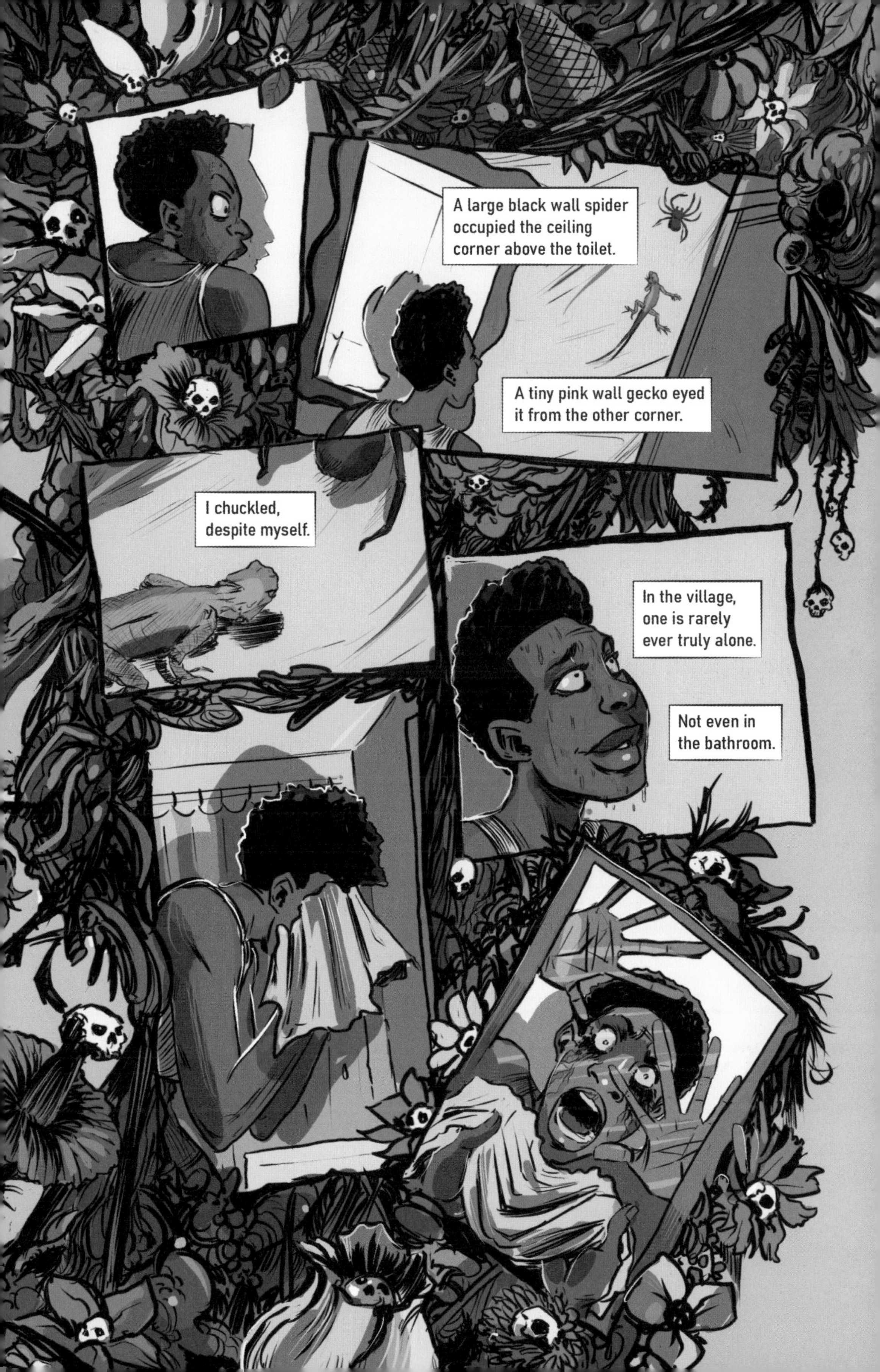
A large black wall spider occupied the ceiling corner above the toilet.
A tiny pink wall gecko eyed it from the other corner.
I chuckled, despite myself.
In the village, one is rarely ever truly alone.
Not even in the bathroom.

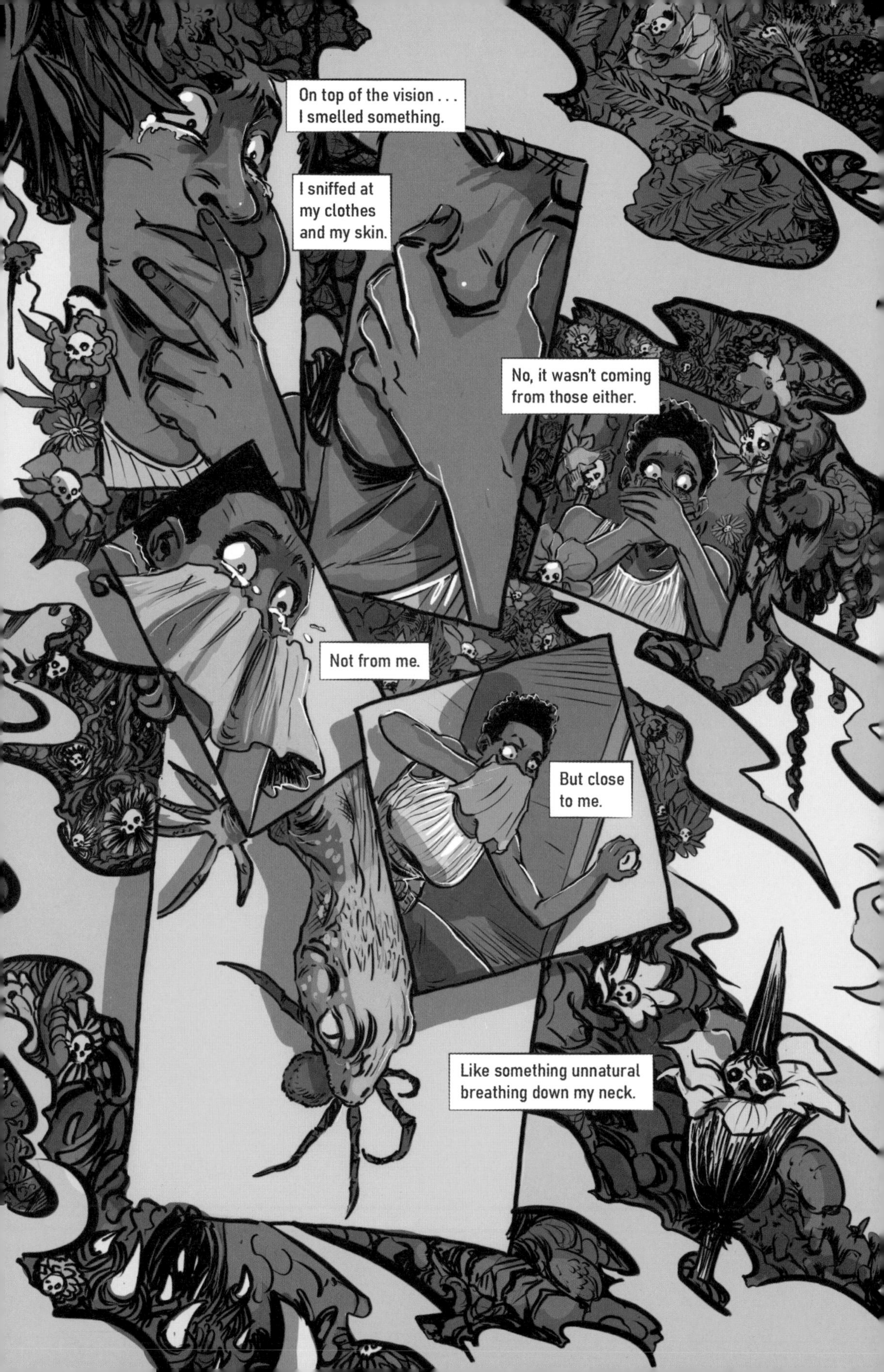
On top of the vision . . .
I smelled something.
I sniffed at
my clothes
and my skin.
No, it wasn't coming
from those either.
Not from me.
But close
to me.
Like something unnatural
breathing down my neck.

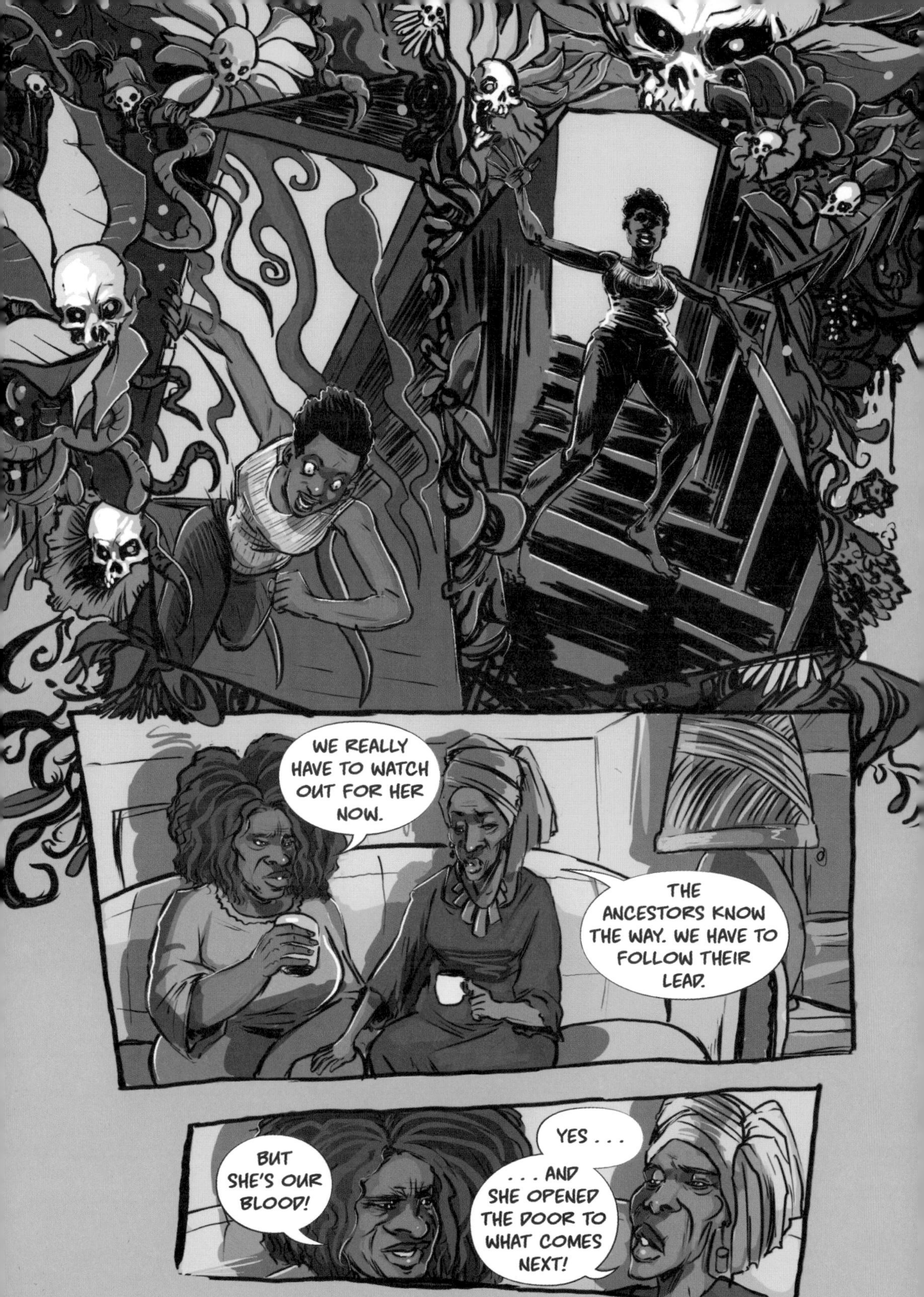
WE REALLY HAVE TO WATCH OUT FOR HER NOW.
THE ANCESTORS KNOW THE WAY. WE HAVE TO FOLLOW THEIR LEAD.
BUT SHE'S OUR BLOOD!
YES . . .
. . . AND SHE OPENED THE DOOR TO WHAT COMES NEXT!

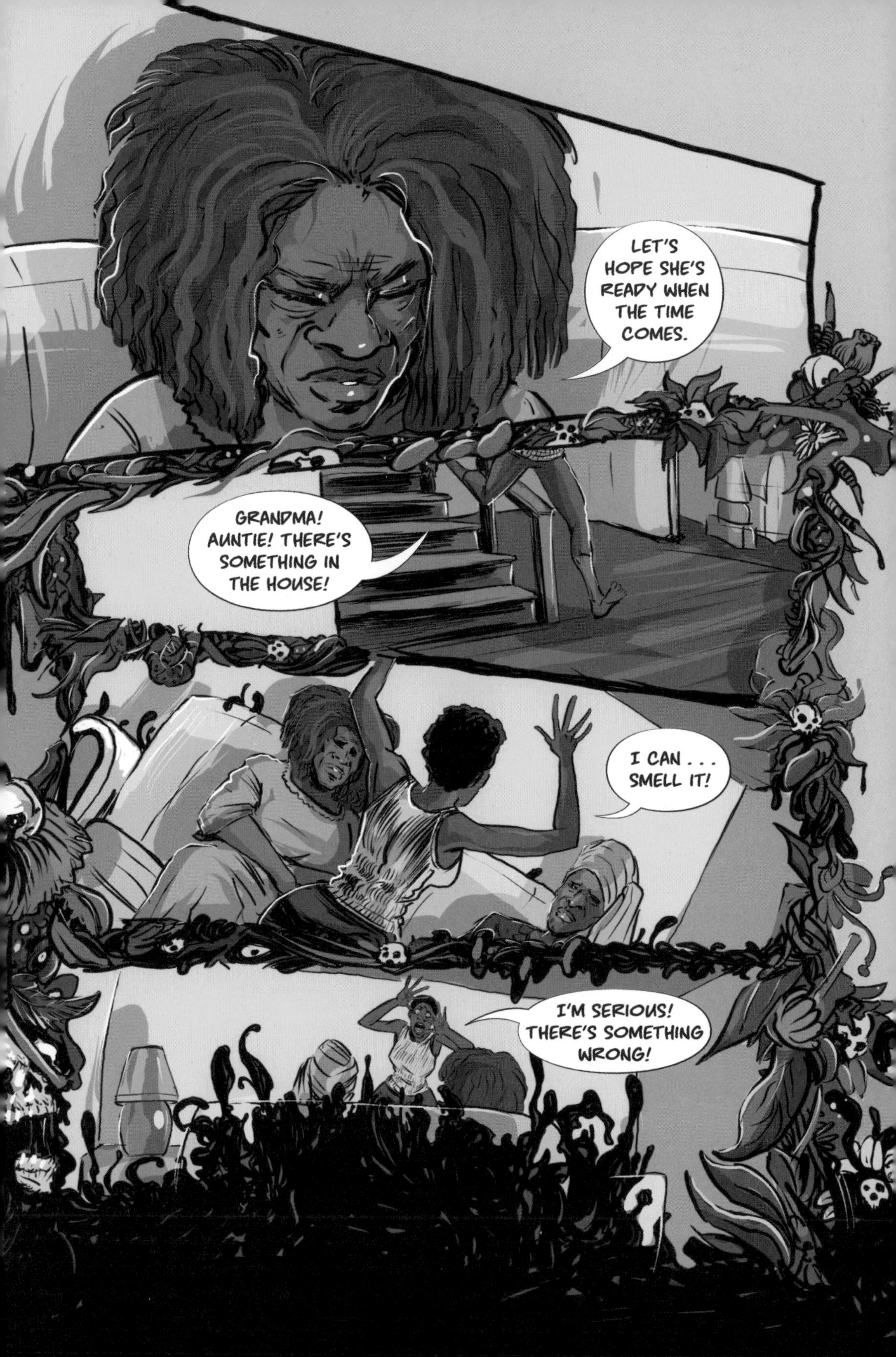
LET'S HOPE SHE'S READY WHEN THE TIME COMES.
GRANDMA! AUNTIE! THERE'S SOMETHING IN THE HOUSE!
I CAN . . . SMELL IT!
I'M SERIOUS! THERE'S SOMETHING WRONG!

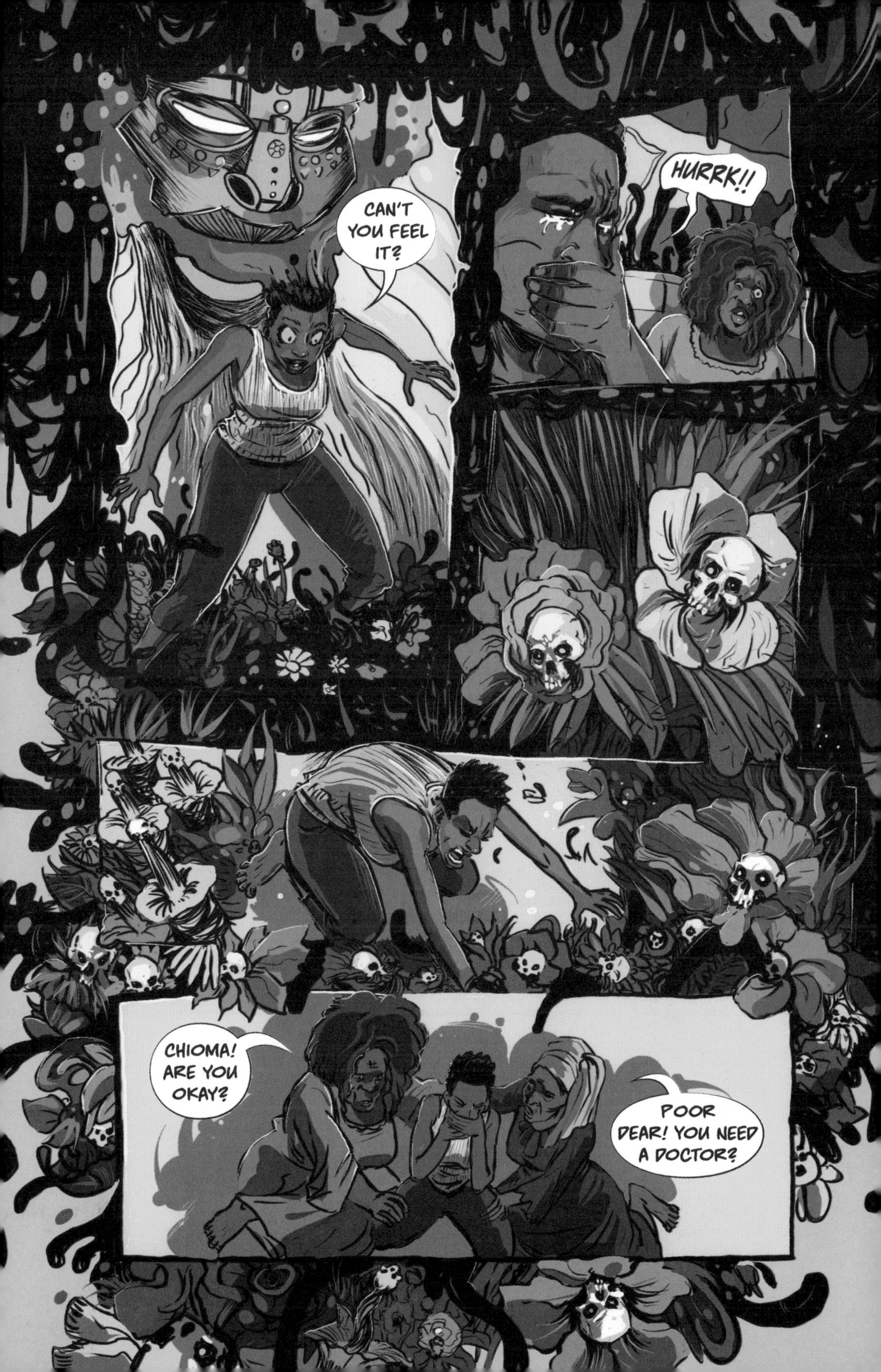
CAN'T YOU FEEL IT?
HURRK!!
CHIOMA! ARE YOU OKAY?
POOR DEAR! YOU NEED A DOCTOR?

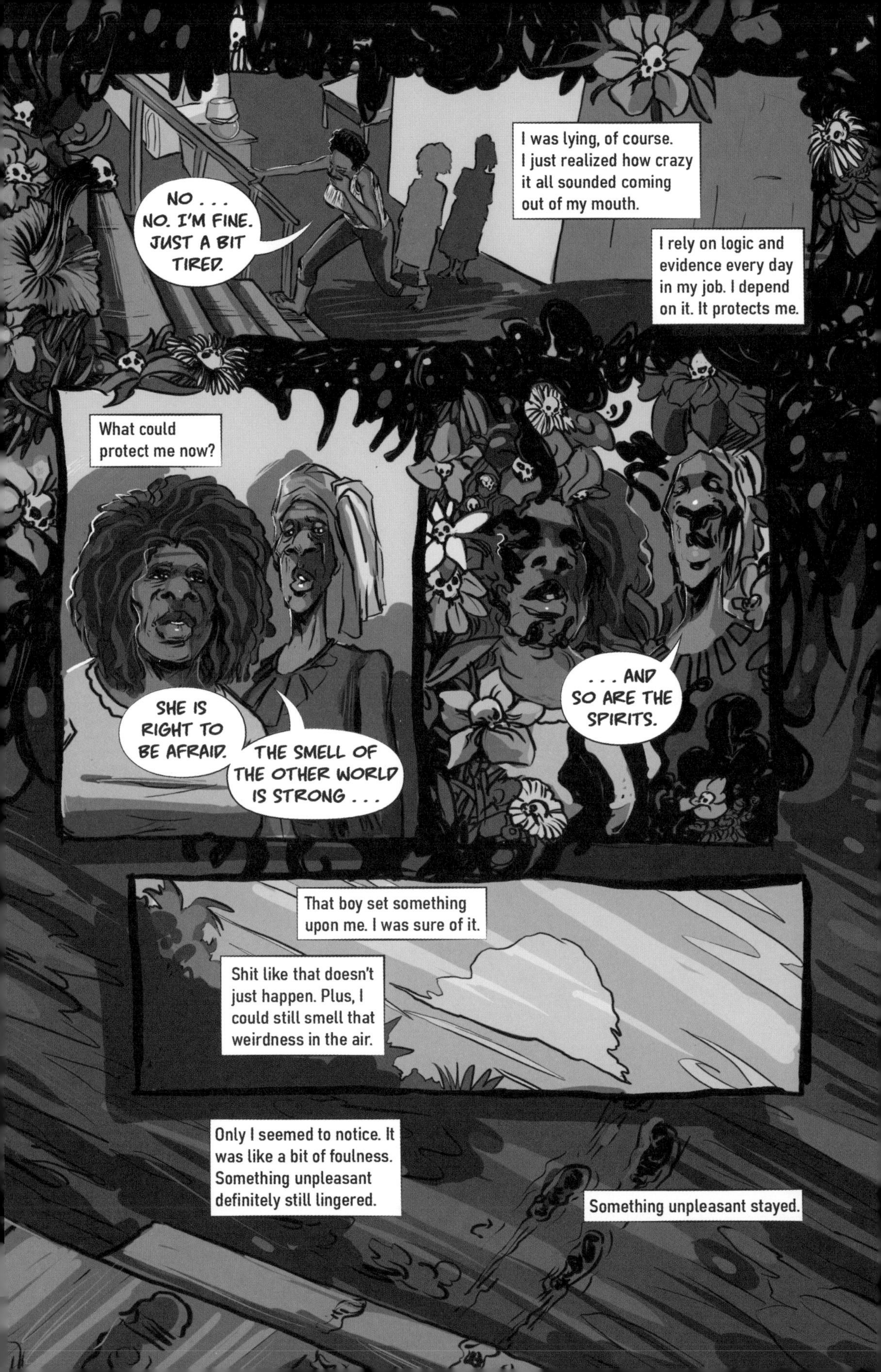
NO . . . NO. I'M FINE. JUST A BIT TIRED.
I was lying, of course. I just realized how crazy it all sounded coming out of my mouth.
I rely on logic and evidence every day in my job. I depend on it. It protects me.
What could protect me now?
SHE IS RIGHT TO BE AFRAID.
THE SMELL OF THE OTHER WORLD IS STRONG . . .
. . . AND SO ARE THE SPIRITS.
That boy set something upon me. I was sure of it.
Shit like that doesn't just happen. Plus, I could still smell that weirdness in the air.
Only I seemed to notice. It was like a bit of foulness. Something unpleasant definitely still lingered.
Something unpleasant stayed.

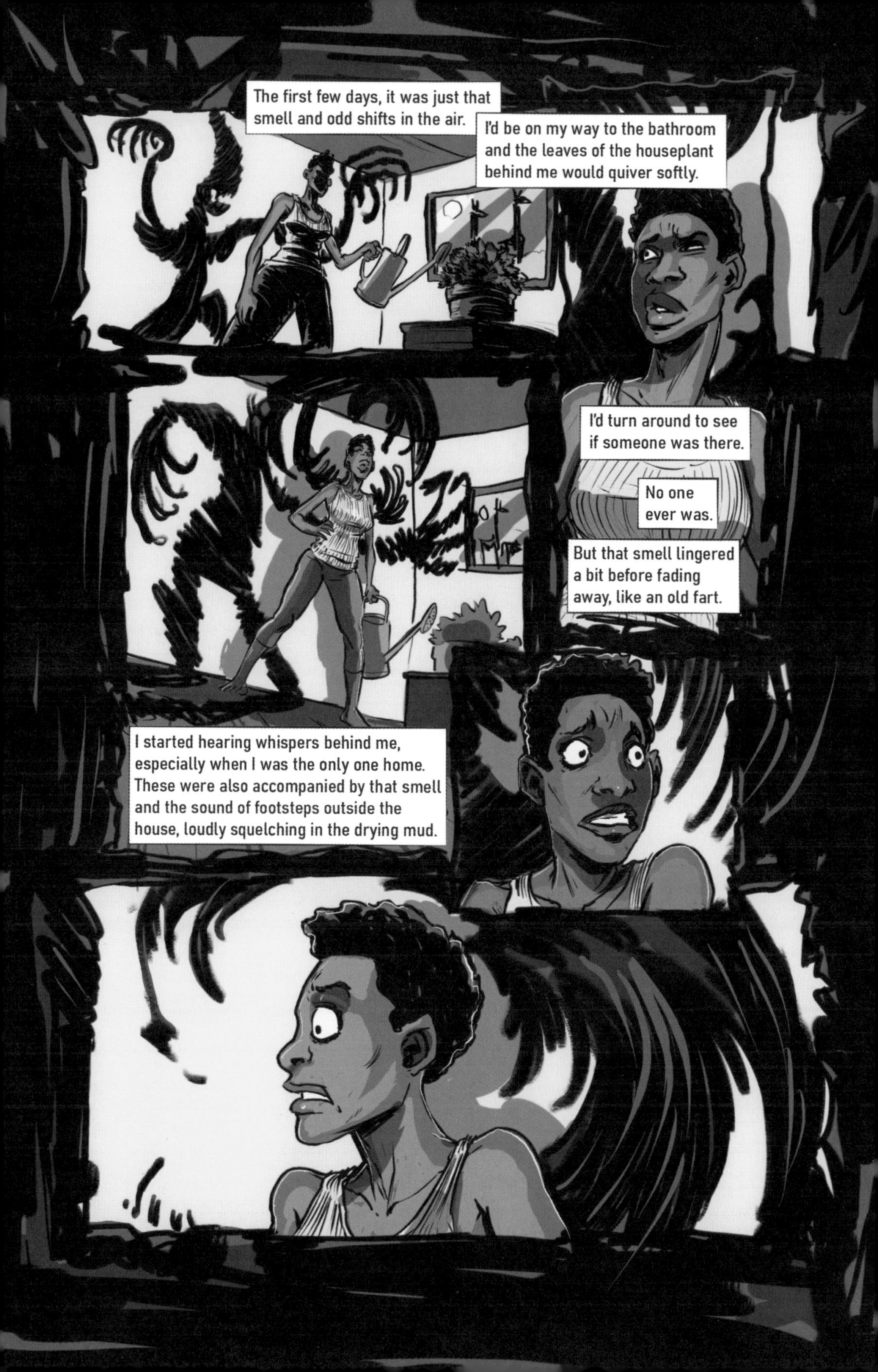
The first few days, it was just that smell and odd shifts in the air.
I'd be on my way to the bathroom and the leaves of the houseplant behind me would quiver softly.
I'd turn around to see if someone was there.
No one ever was.
But that smell lingered a bit before fading away, like an old fart.
I started hearing whispers behind me, especially when I was the only one home. These were also accompanied by that smell and the sound of footsteps outside the house, loudly squelching in the drying mud.

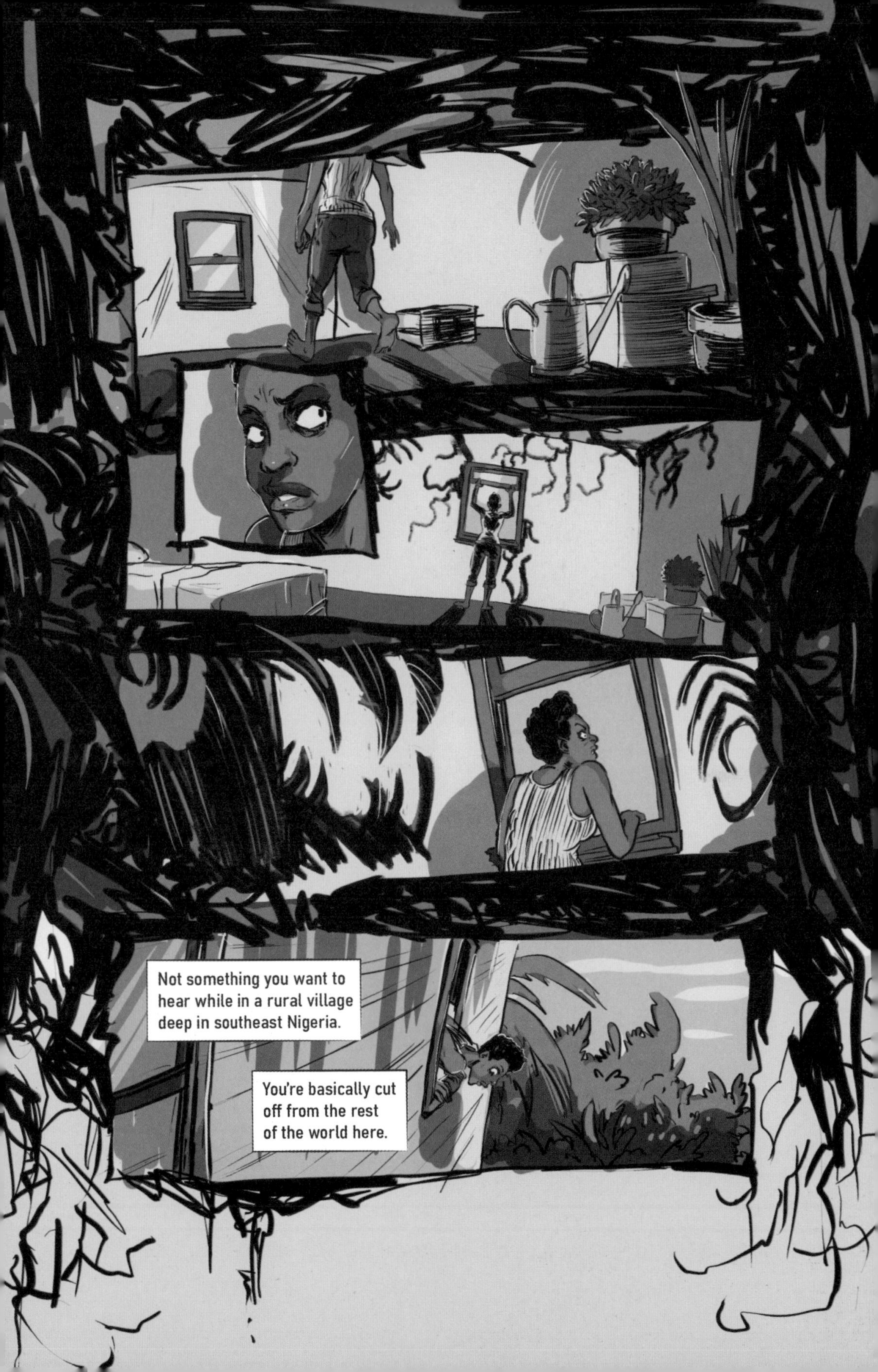
Not something you want to hear while in a rural village deep in southeast Nigeria.
You're basically cut off from the rest of the world here.

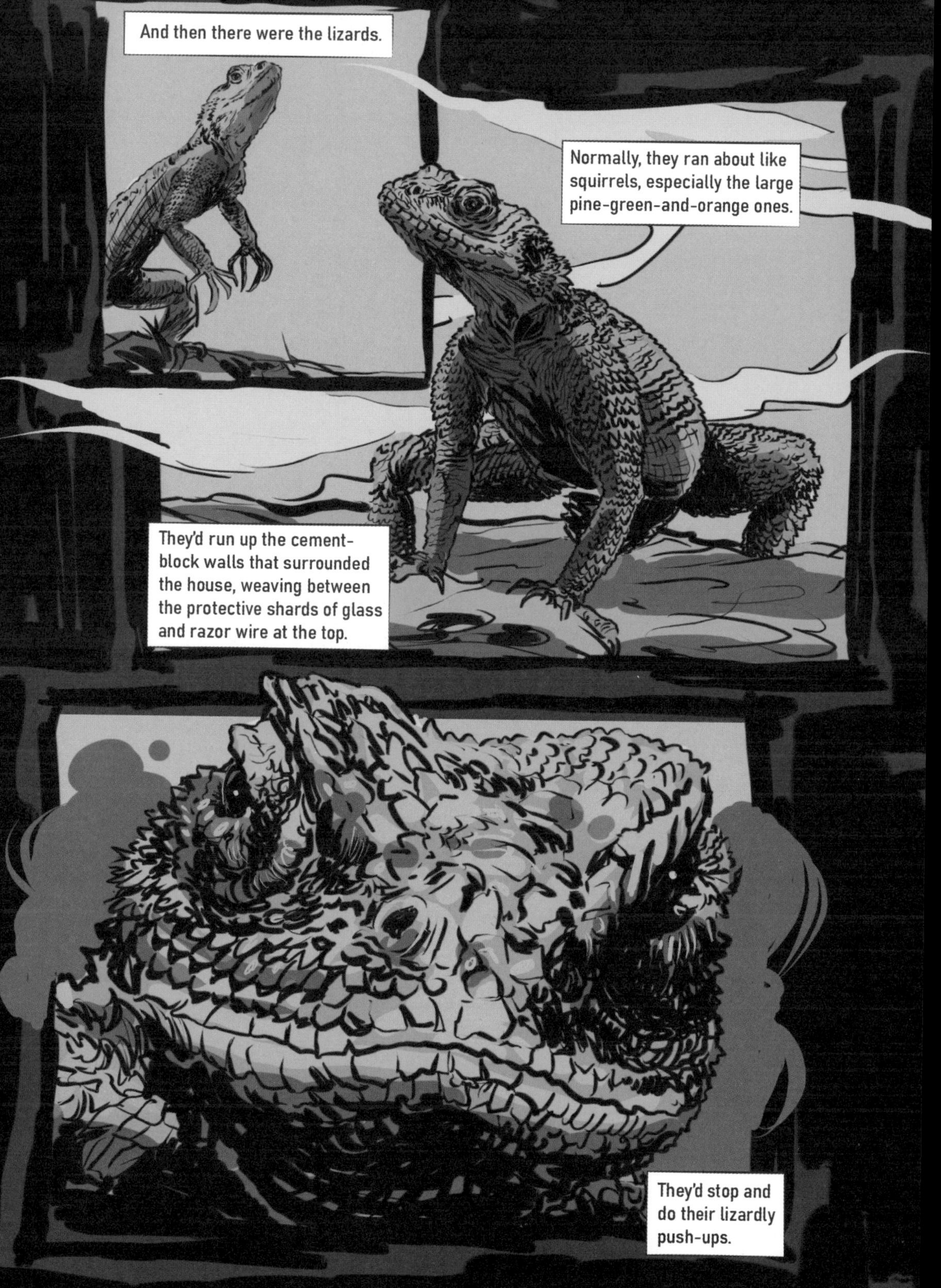
And then there were the lizards.
Normally, they ran about like squirrels, especially the large pine-green-and-orange ones.
They'd run up the cement-block walls that surrounded the house, weaving between the protective shards of glass and razor wire at the top.
They'd stop and do their lizardly push-ups.

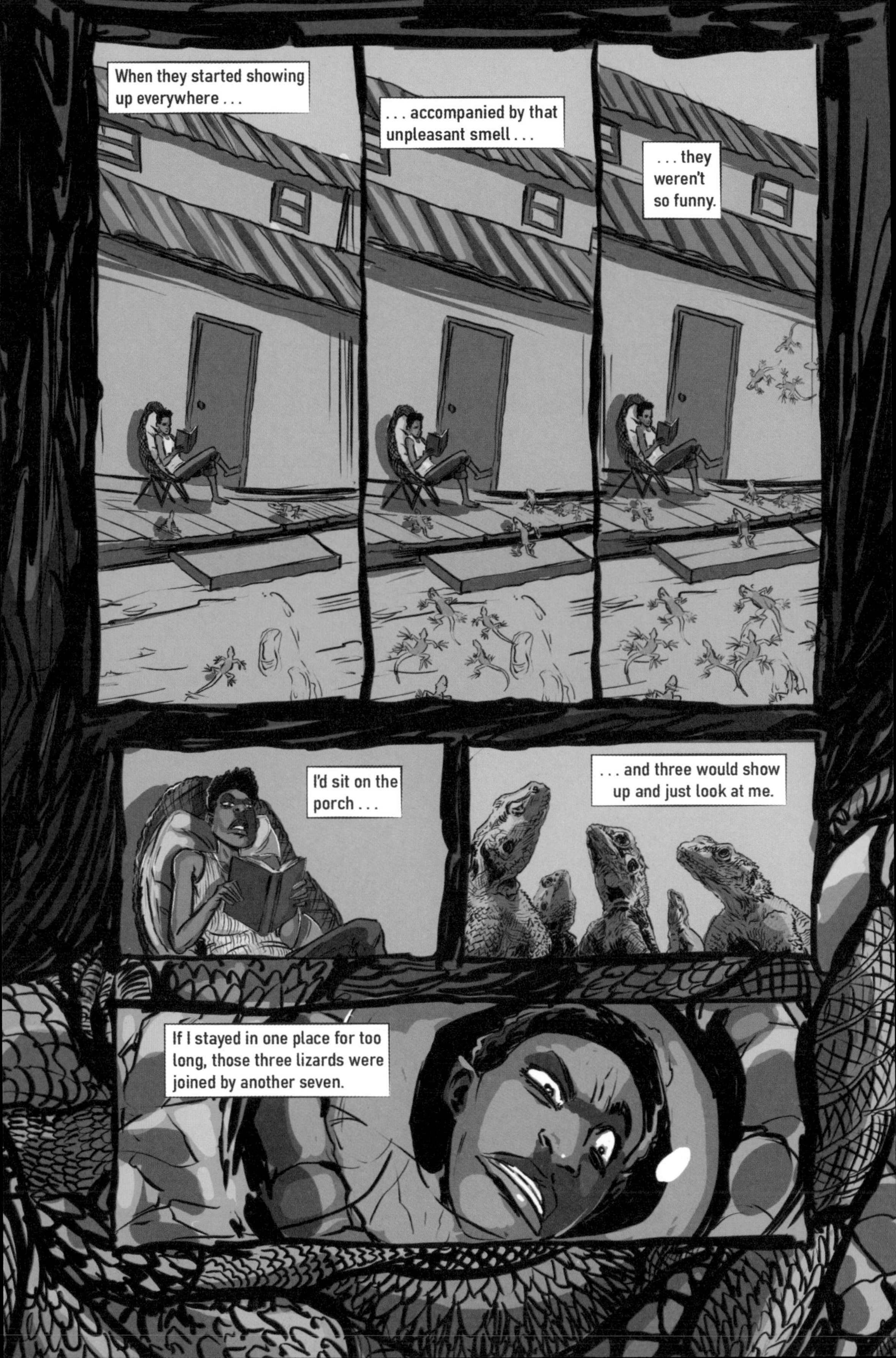
When they started showing up everywhere . . .
. . . accompanied by that unpleasant smell . . .
. . . they weren't so funny.
I'd sit on the porch . . .
. . . and three would show up and just look at me.
If I stayed in one place for too long, those three lizards were joined by another seven.

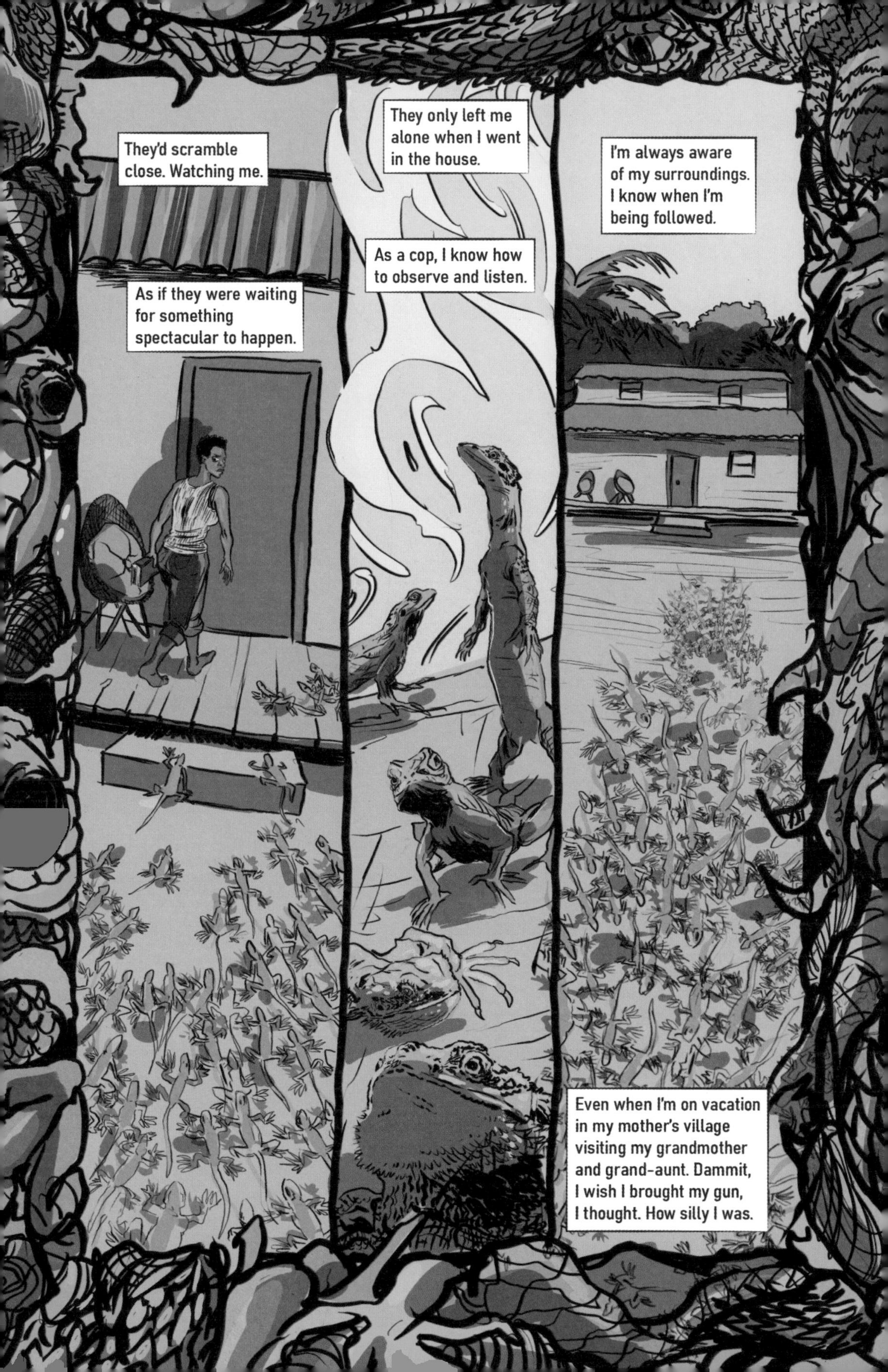
They'd scramble close. Watching me.
As if they were waiting for something spectacular to happen.
They only left me alone when I went in the house.
As a cop, I know how to observe and listen.
I'm always aware of my surroundings. I know when I'm being followed.
Even when I'm on vacation in my mother's village visiting my grandmother and grand-aunt. Dammit, I wish I brought my gun, I thought. How silly I was.

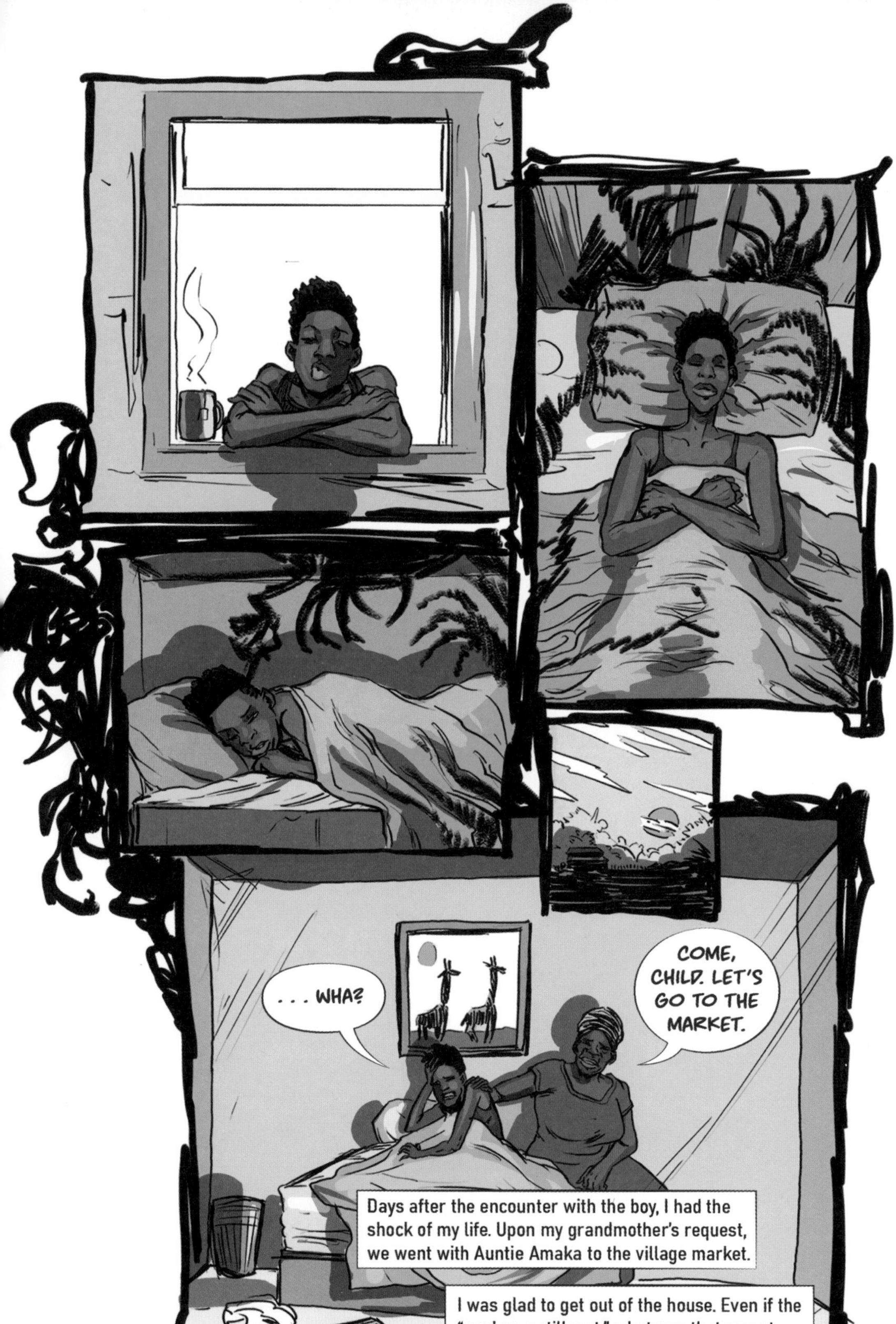
. . . WHA?
COME, CHILD. LET'S GO TO THE MARKET.
Days after the encounter with the boy, I had the shock of my life. Upon my grandmother's request, we went with Auntie Amaka to the village market.
I was glad to get out of the house. Even if the "mud was still wet," whatever that meant.

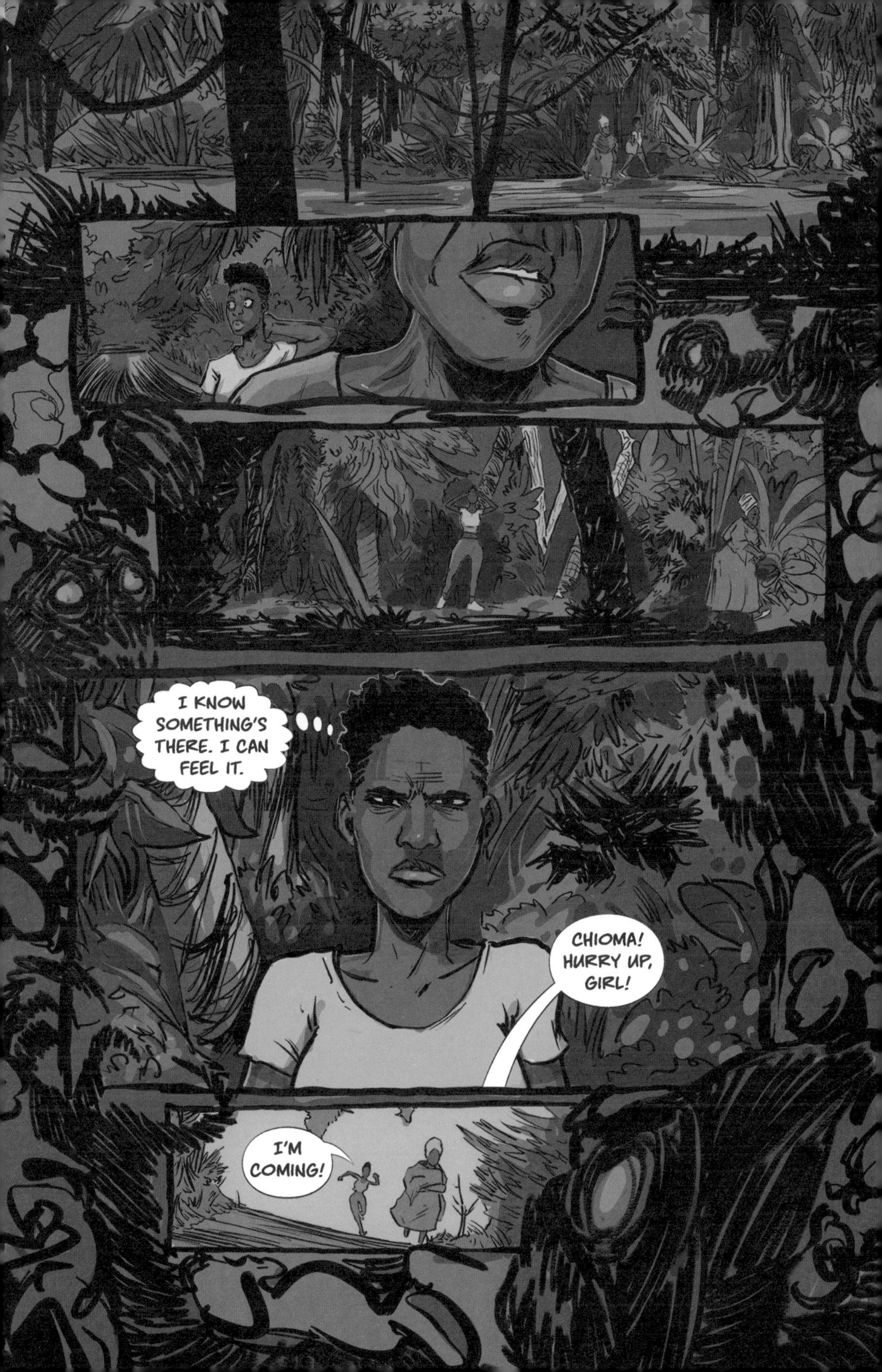
I KNOW SOMETHING'S THERE. I CAN FEEL IT.
CHIOMA! HURRY UP, GIRL!
I'M COMING!

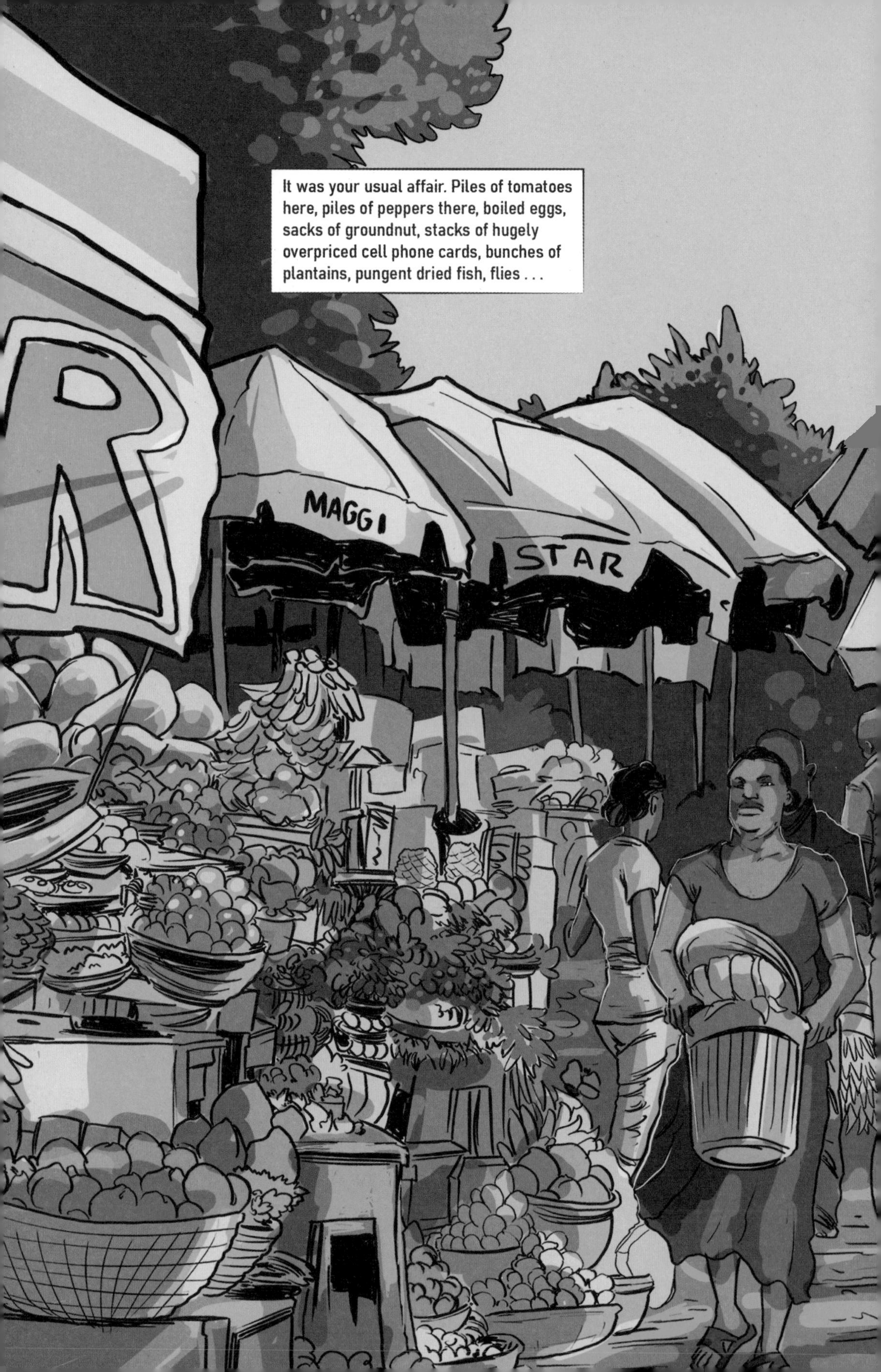
It was your usual affair. Piles of tomatoes here, piles of peppers there, boiled eggs, sacks of groundnut, stacks of hugely overpriced cell phone cards, bunches of plantains, pungent dried fish, flies . . .
MAGGI
STAR

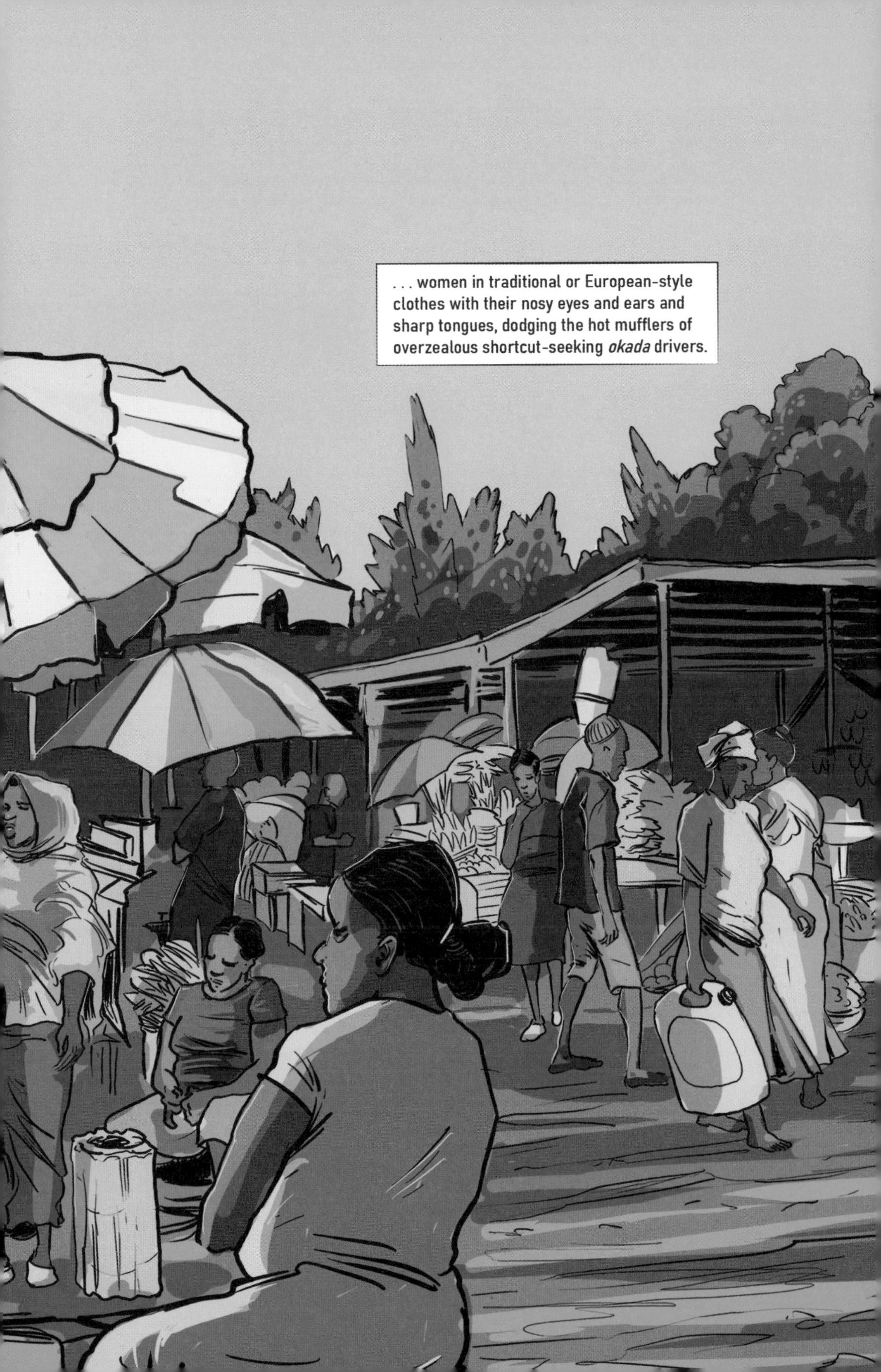
. . . women in traditional or European-style clothes with their nosy eyes and ears and sharp tongues, dodging the hot mufflers of overzealous shortcut-seeking *okada* drivers.

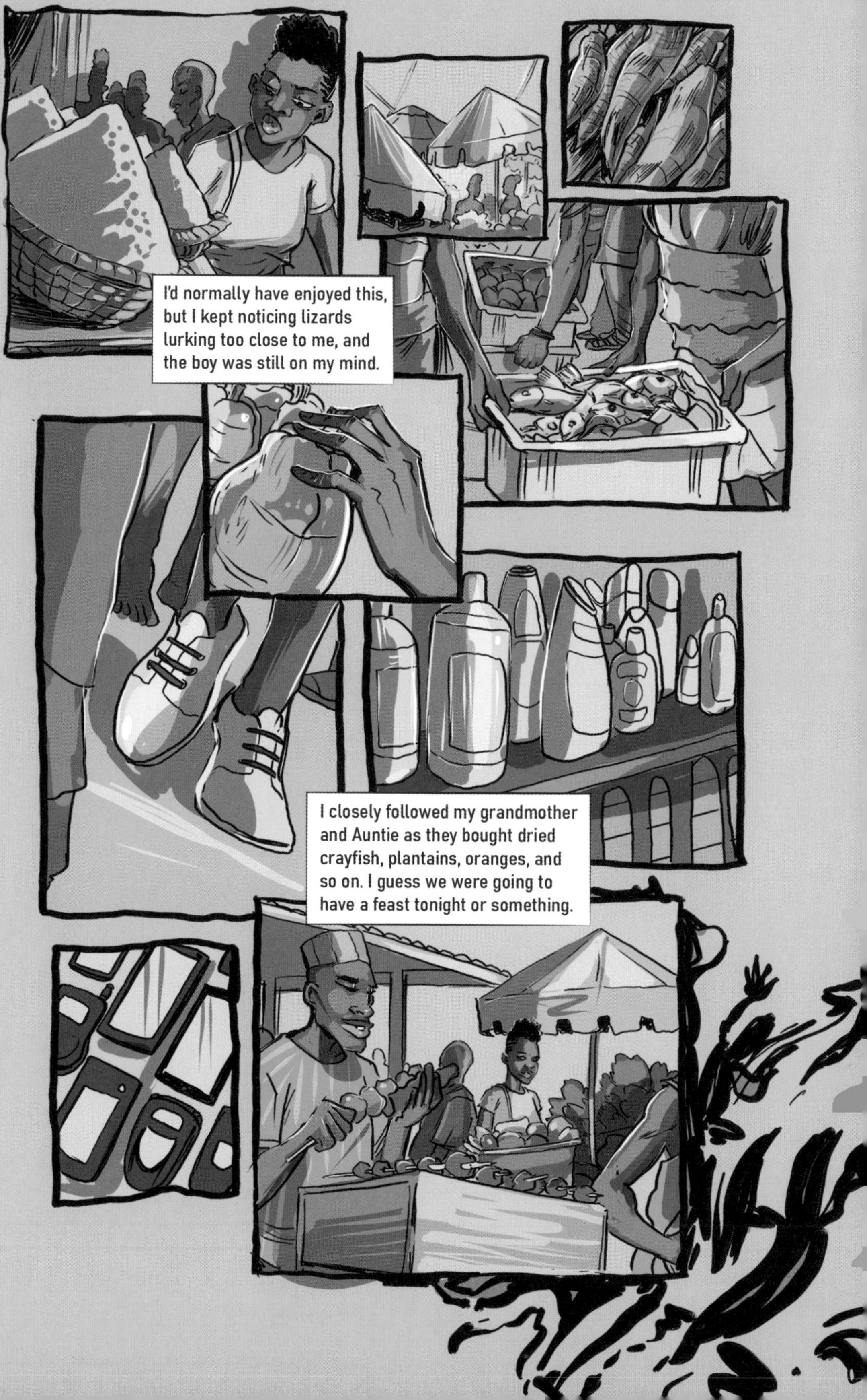
I'd normally have enjoyed this, but I kept noticing lizards lurking too close to me, and the boy was still on my mind.
I closely followed my grandmother and Auntie as they bought dried crayfish, plantains, oranges, and so on. I guess we were going to have a feast tonight or something.

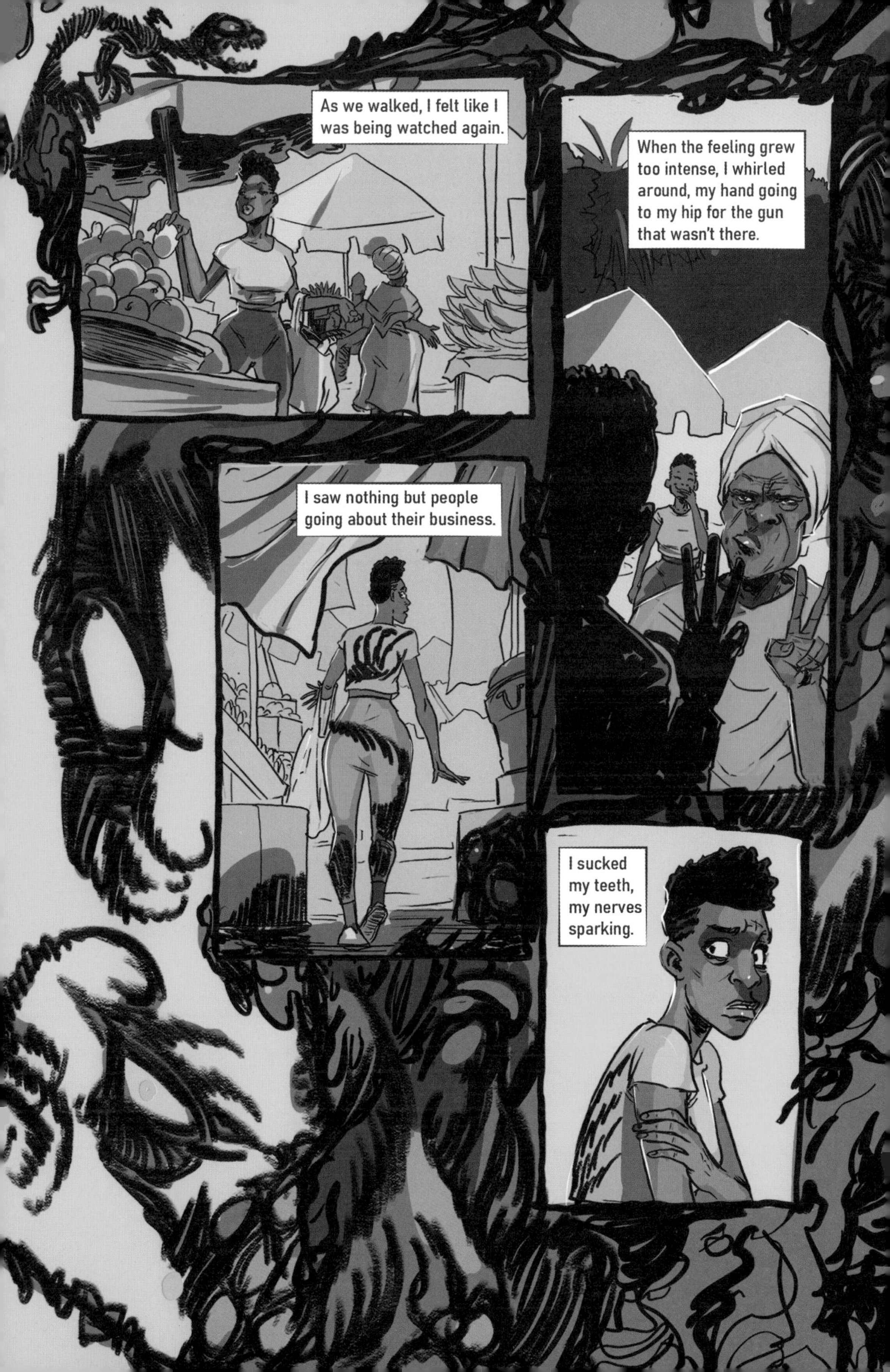
As we walked, I felt like I was being watched again.
When the feeling grew too intense, I whirled around, my hand going to my hip for the gun that wasn't there.
I saw nothing but people going about their business.
I sucked my teeth, my nerves sparking.

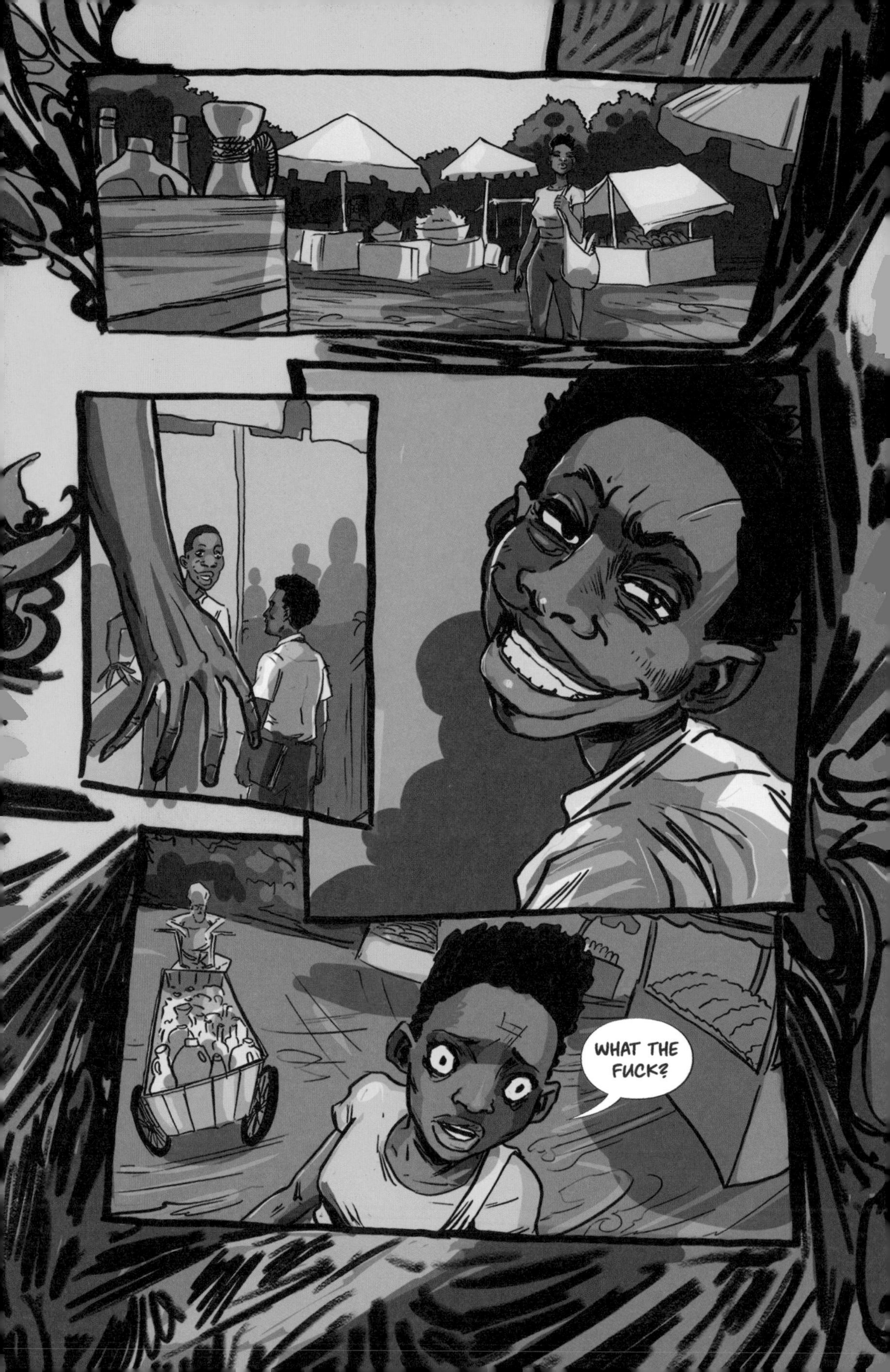
WHAT THE FUCK?

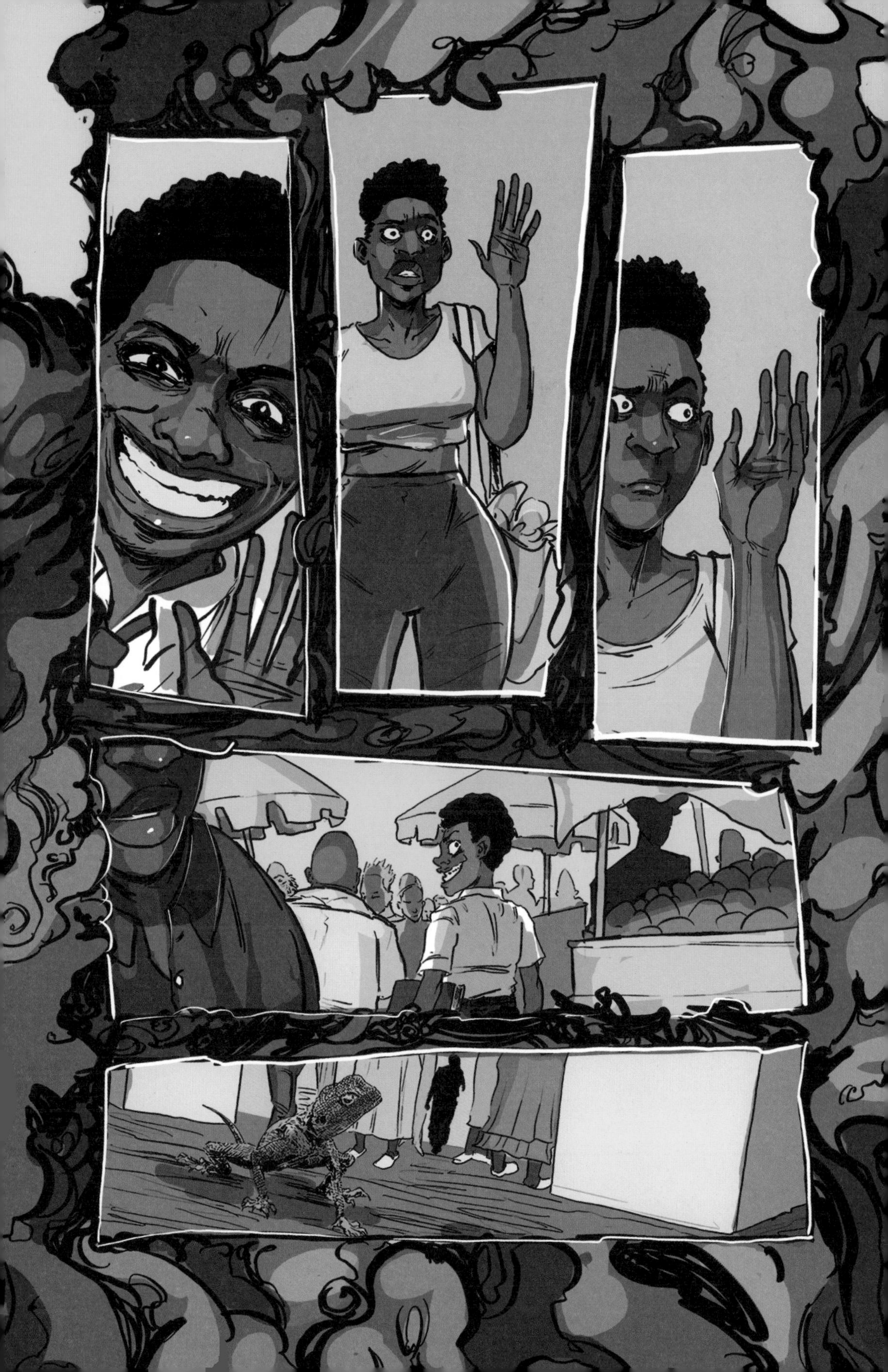

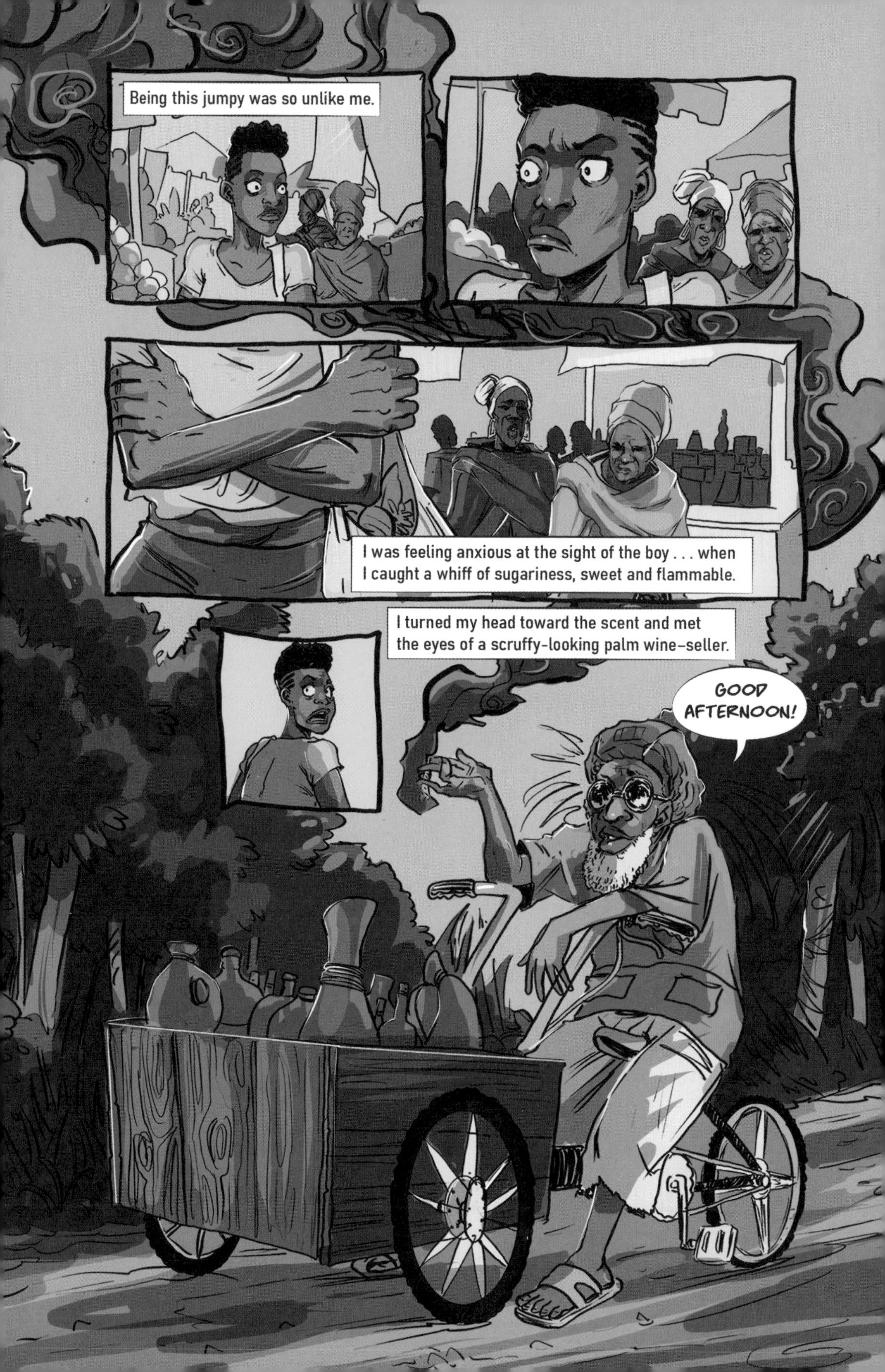
Being this jumpy was so unlike me.
I was feeling anxious at the sight of the boy . . . when I caught a whiff of sugariness, sweet and flammable.
I turned my head toward the scent and met the eyes of a scruffy-looking palm wine-seller.
GOOD AFTERNOON!

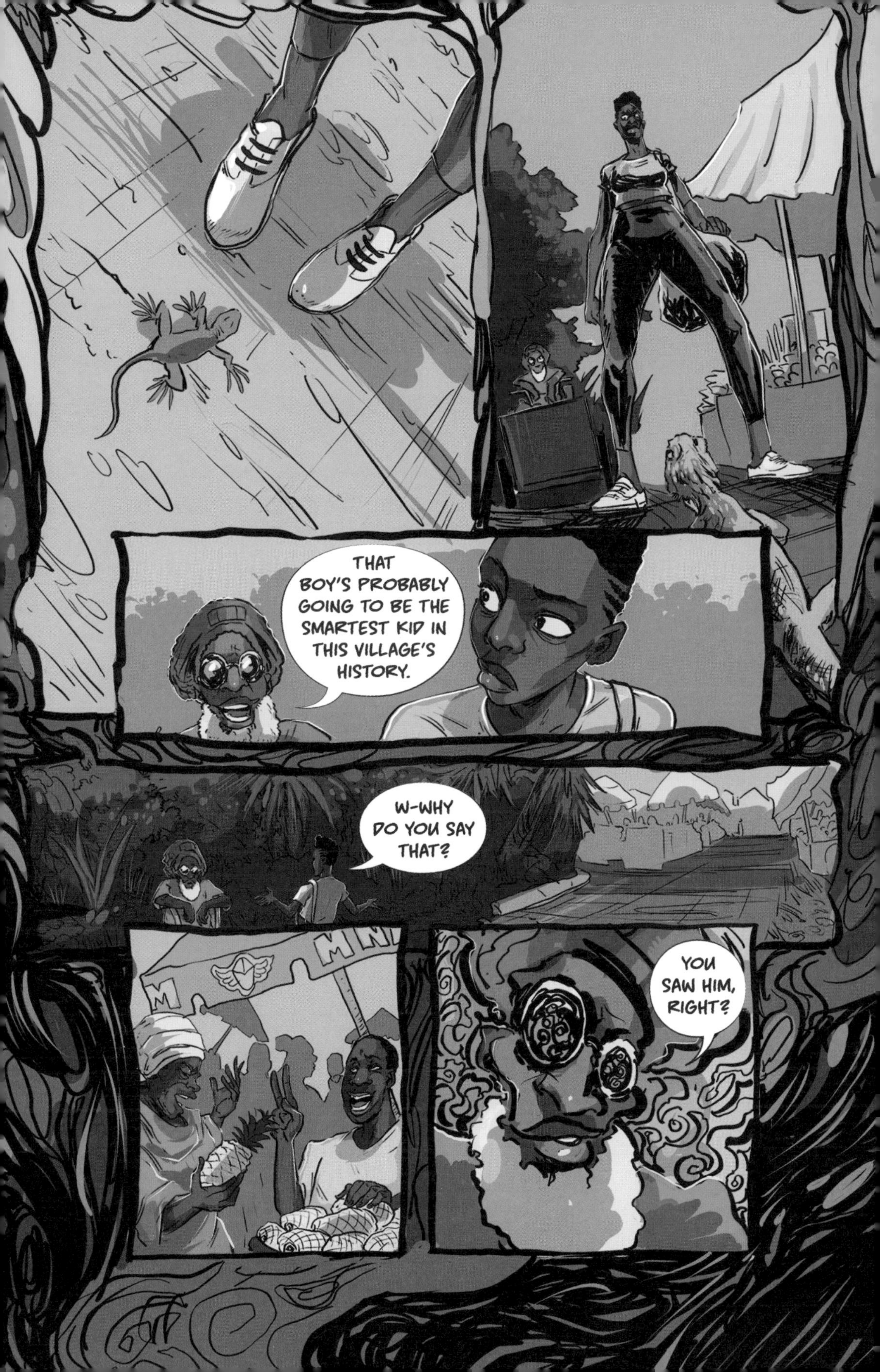
THAT BOY'S PROBABLY GOING TO BE THE SMARTEST KID IN THIS VILLAGE'S HISTORY.
W-WHY DO YOU SAY THAT?
YOU SAW HIM, RIGHT?

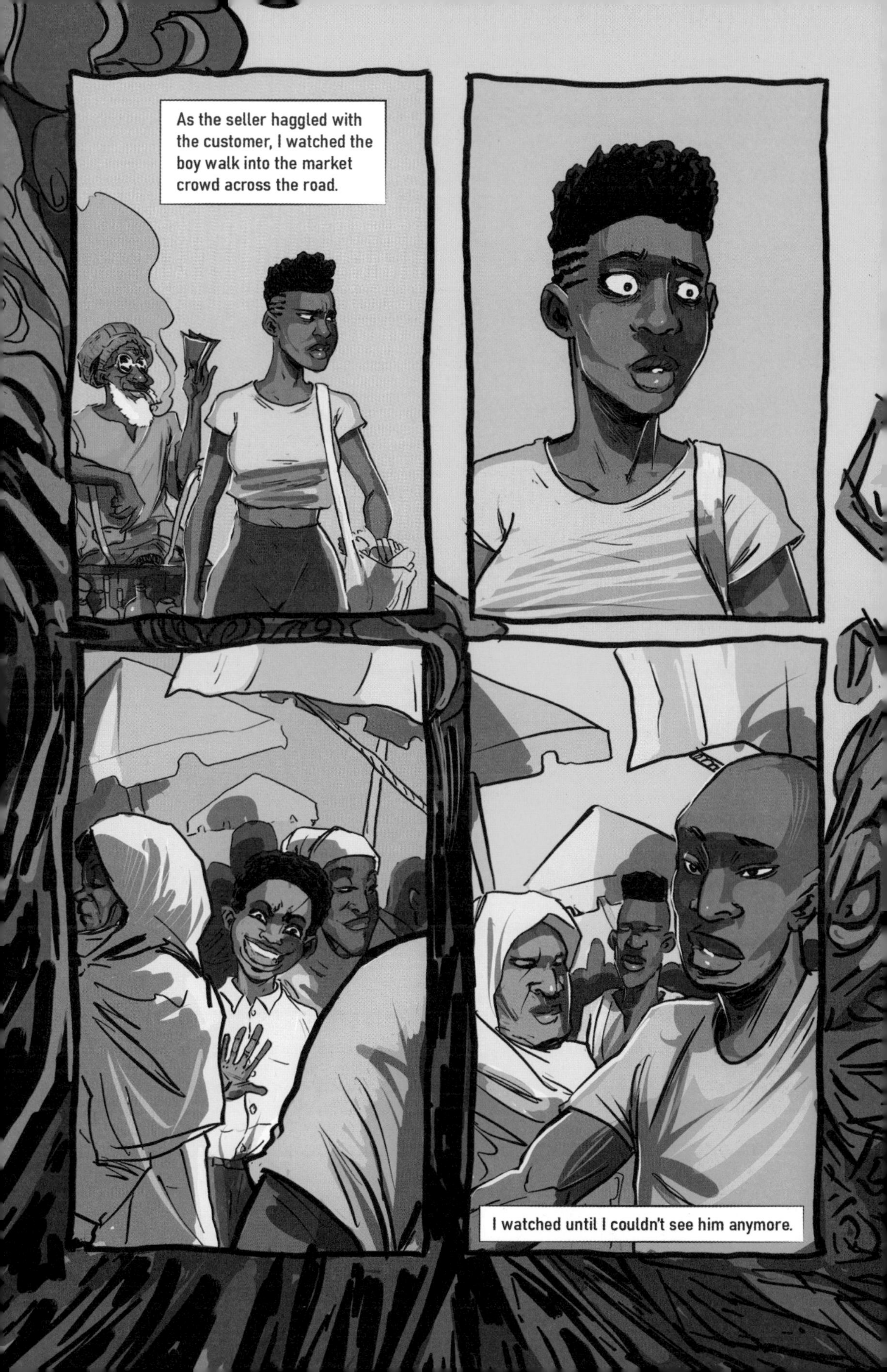
As the seller haggled with the customer, I watched the boy walk into the market crowd across the road.
I watched until I couldn't see him anymore.

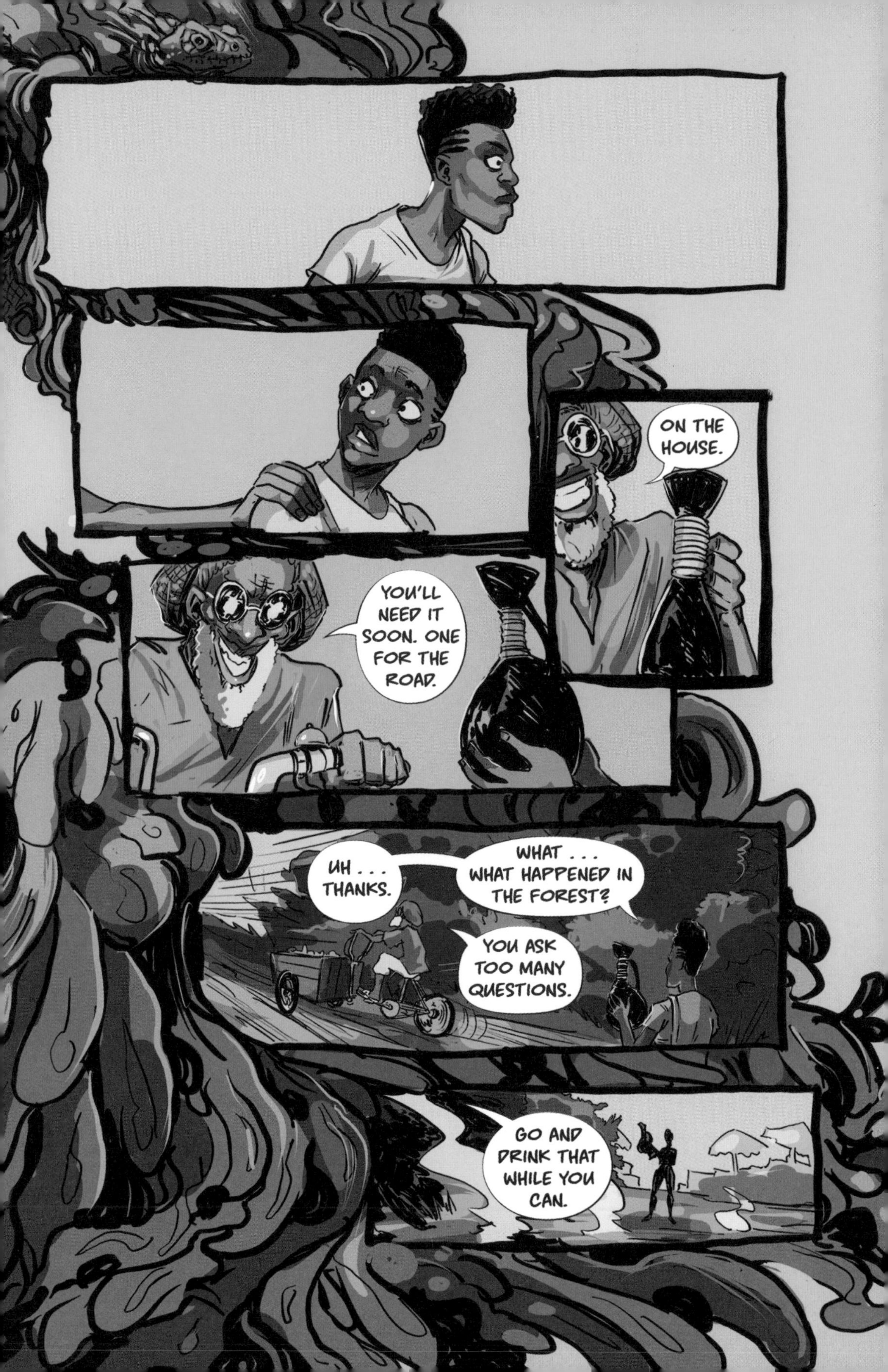
ON THE HOUSE.
YOU'LL NEED IT SOON. ONE FOR THE ROAD.
UH . . . THANKS.
WHAT . . . WHAT HAPPENED IN THE FOREST?
YOU ASK TOO MANY QUESTIONS.
GO AND DRINK THAT WHILE YOU CAN.

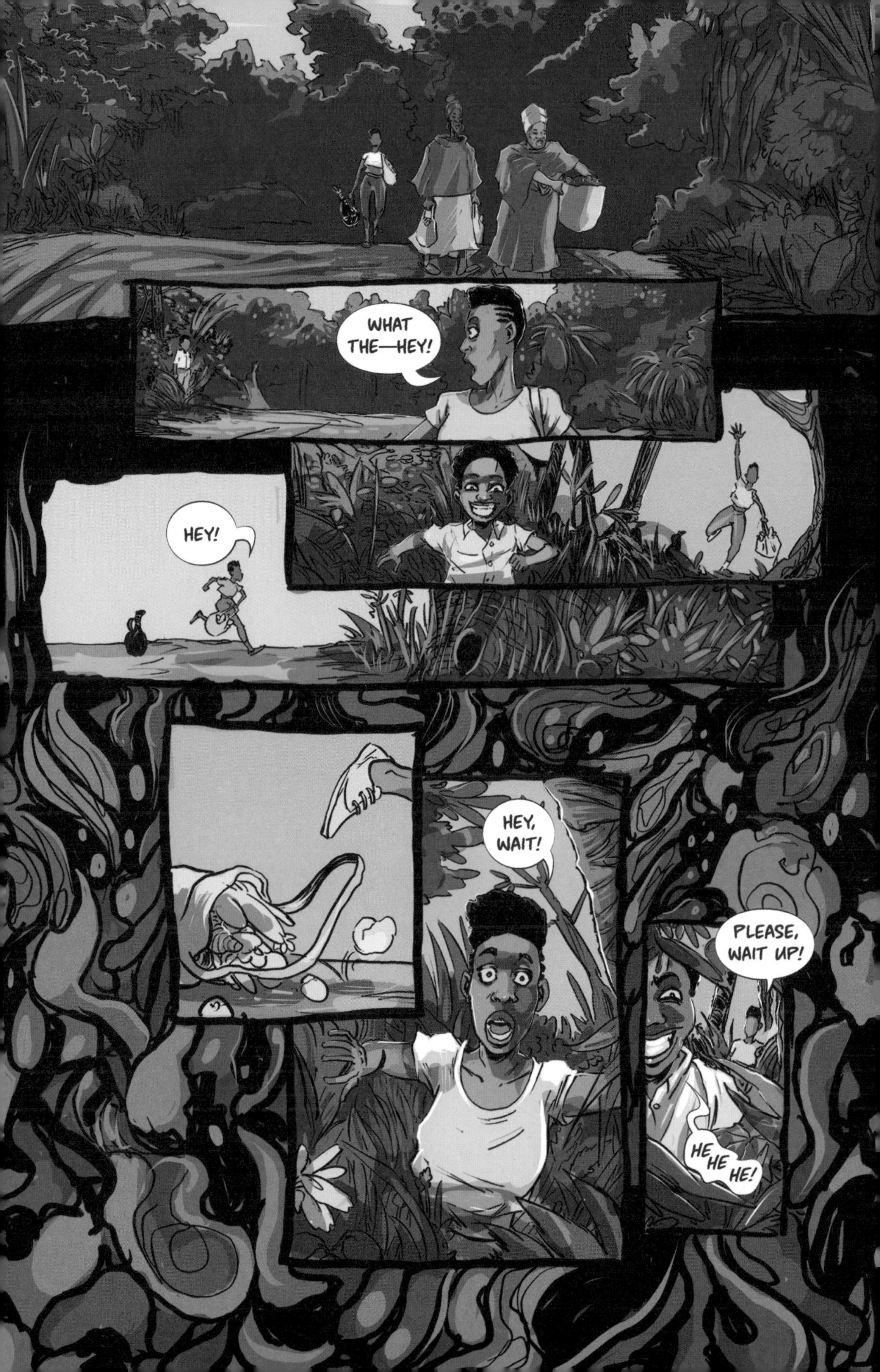
WHAT THE—HEY!
HEY!
HEY, WAIT!
PLEASE, WAIT UP!
HE HE HE!

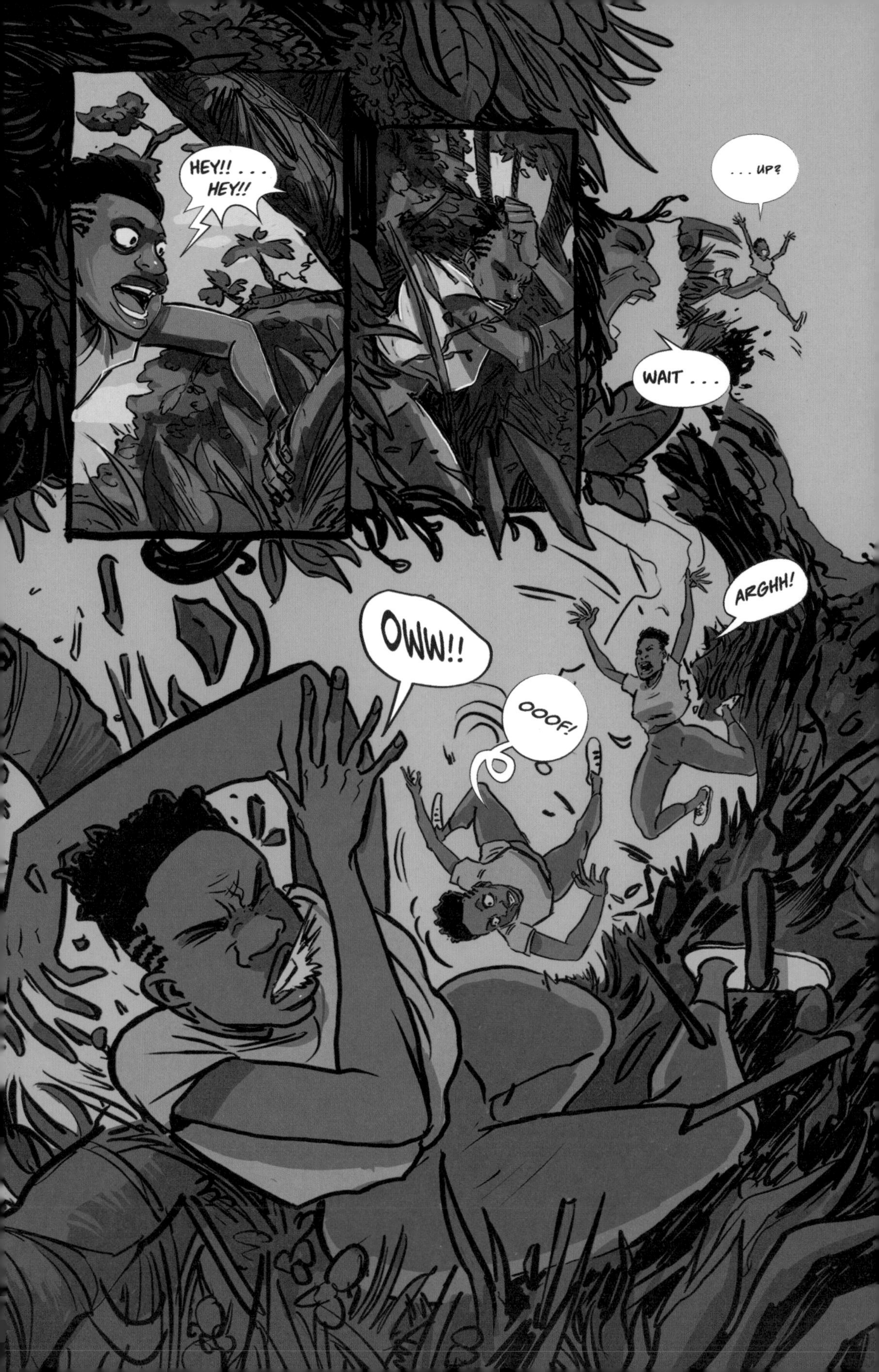
HEY!! . . .
HEY!!
. . . UP?
WAIT . . .
ARGHH!
OWW!!
OOOF!

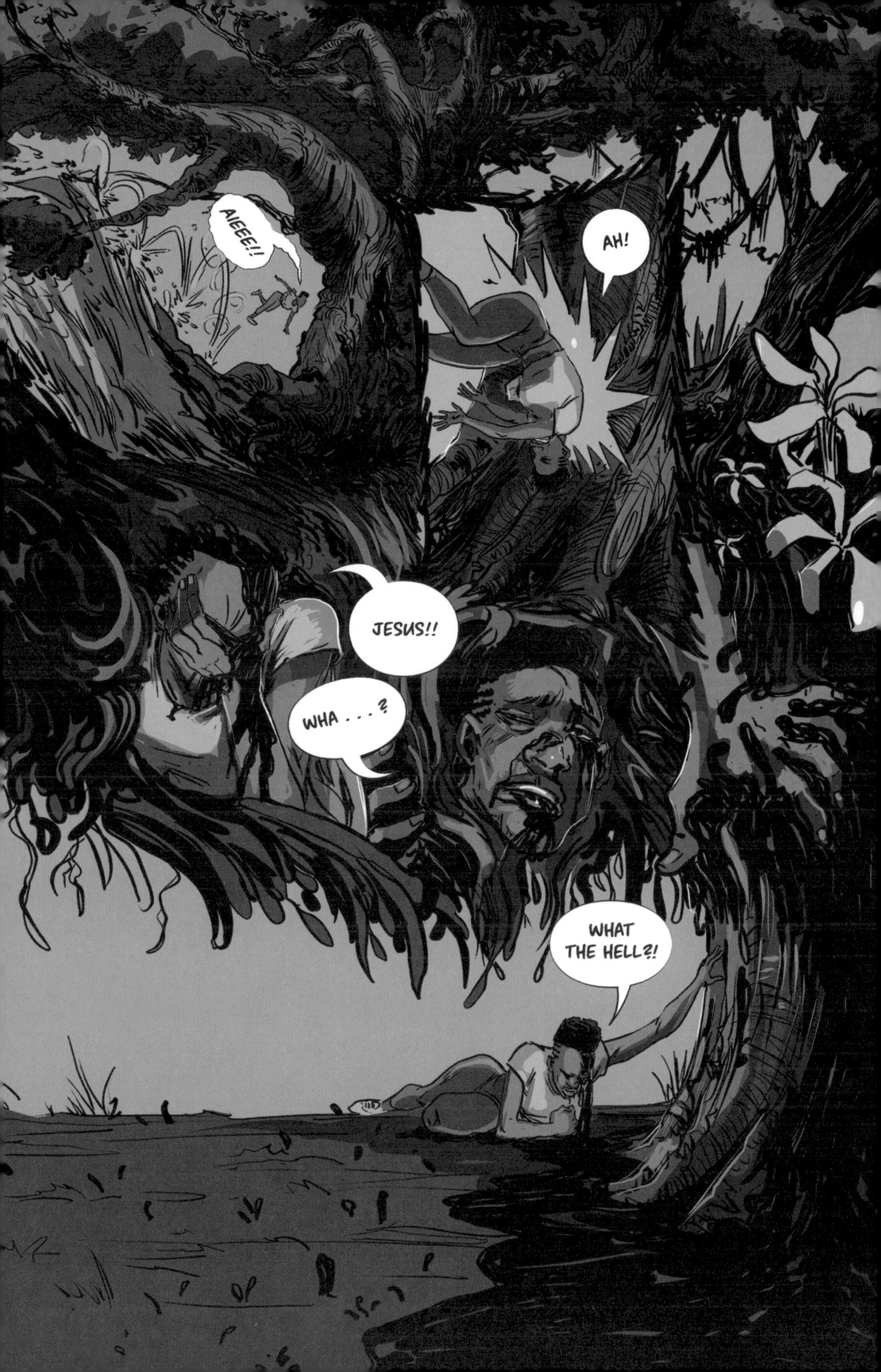
AIEEE!!
AH!
JESUS!!
WHA . . . ?
WHAT THE HELL?!

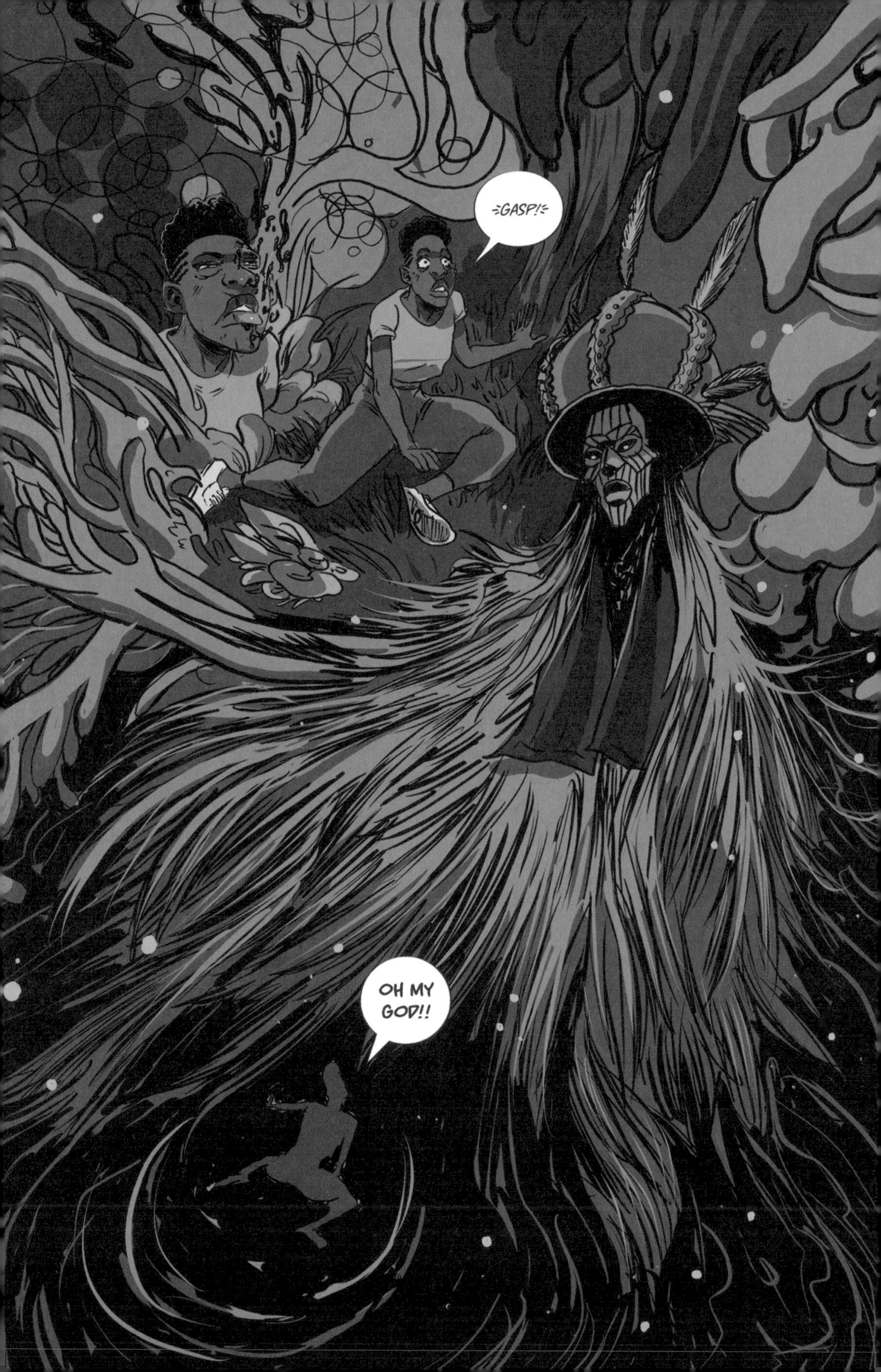
GASP!
OH MY GOD!!

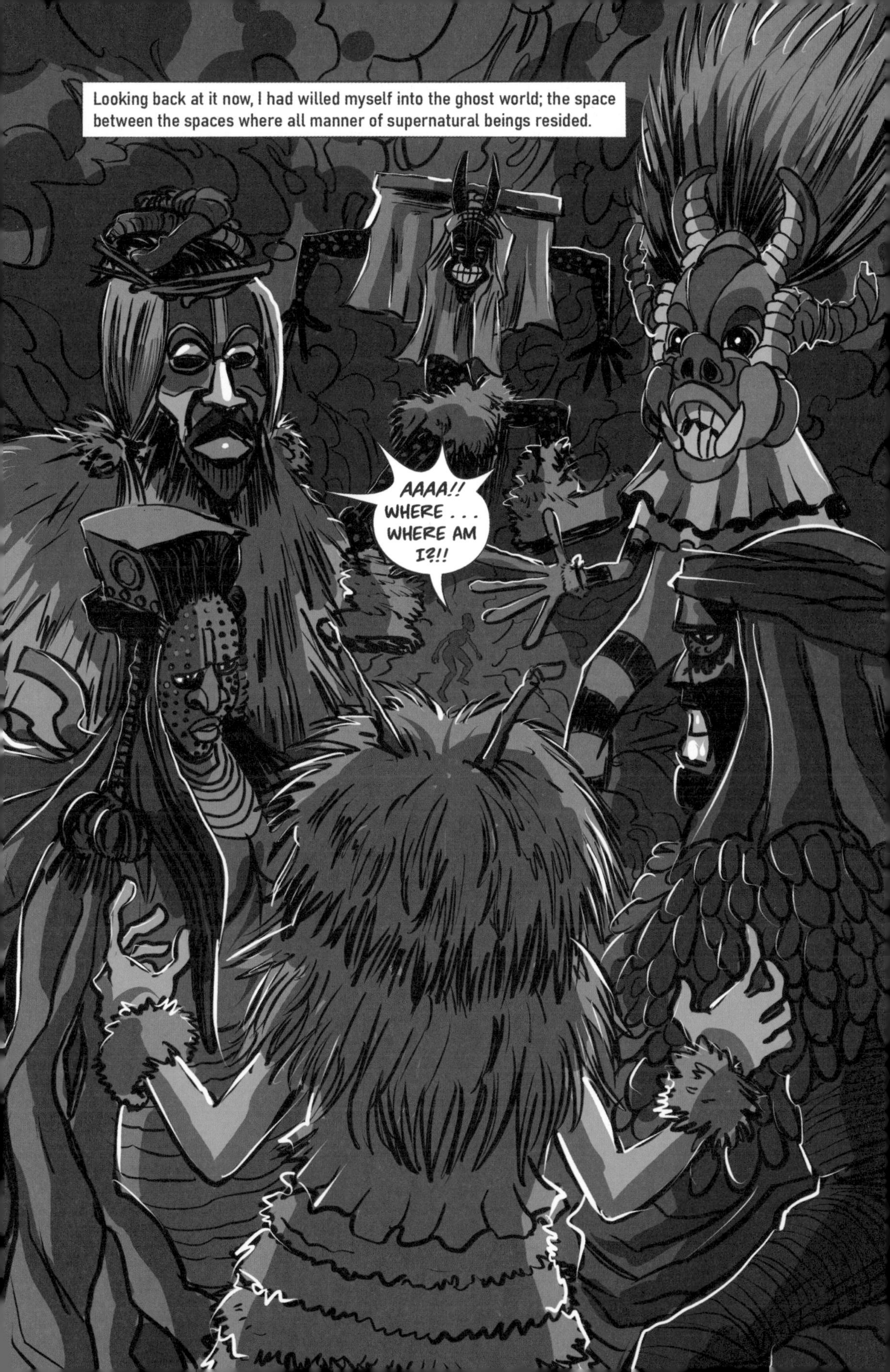
Looking back at it now, I had willed myself into the ghost world; the space between the spaces where all manner of supernatural beings resided.
AAAA!! WHERE . . . WHERE AM I?!!

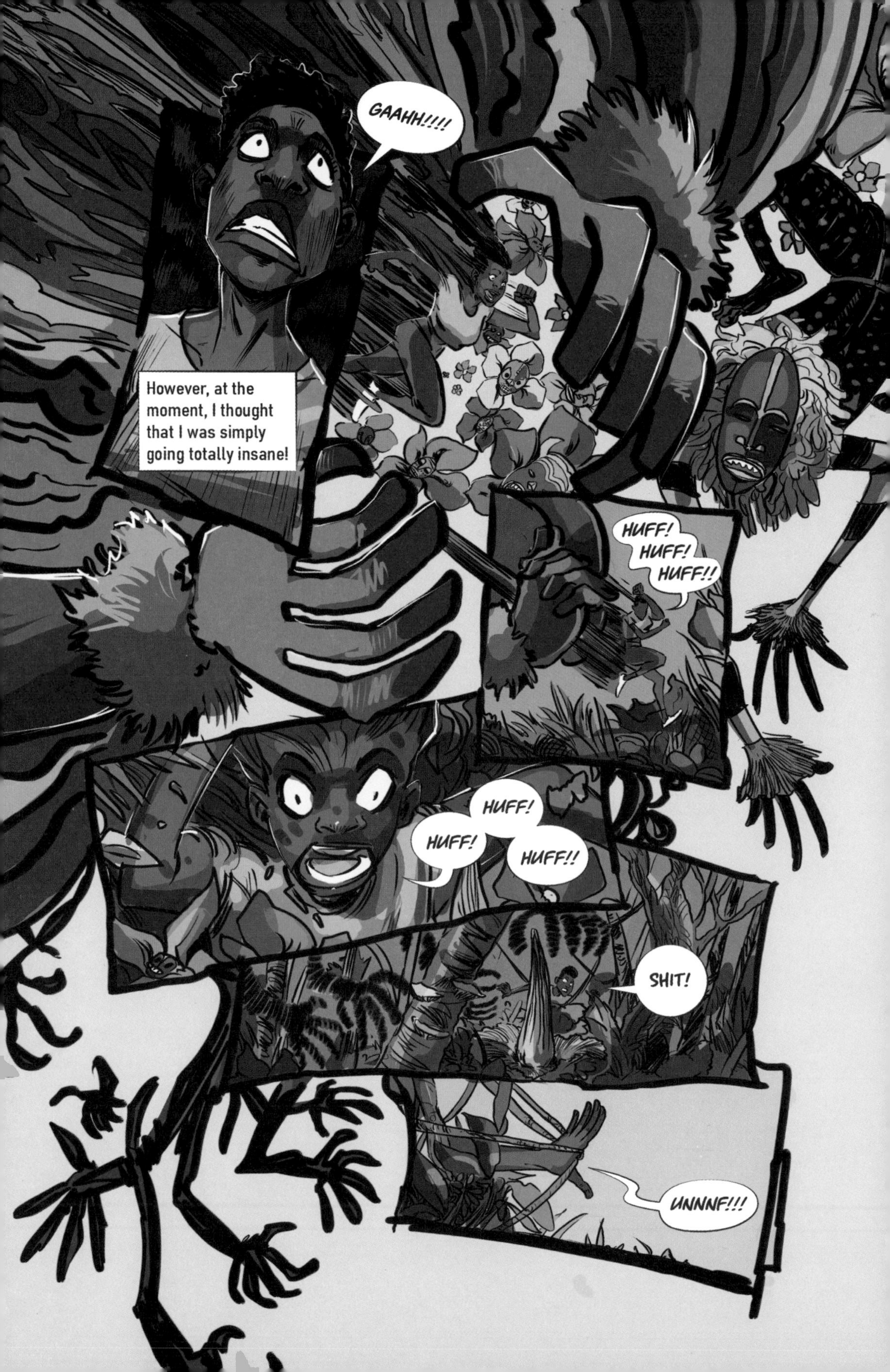
GAAHH!!!!
However, at the moment, I thought that I was simply going totally insane!
HUFF! HUFF! HUFF!!
HUFF! HUFF! HUFF!!
SHIT!
UNNNF!!!

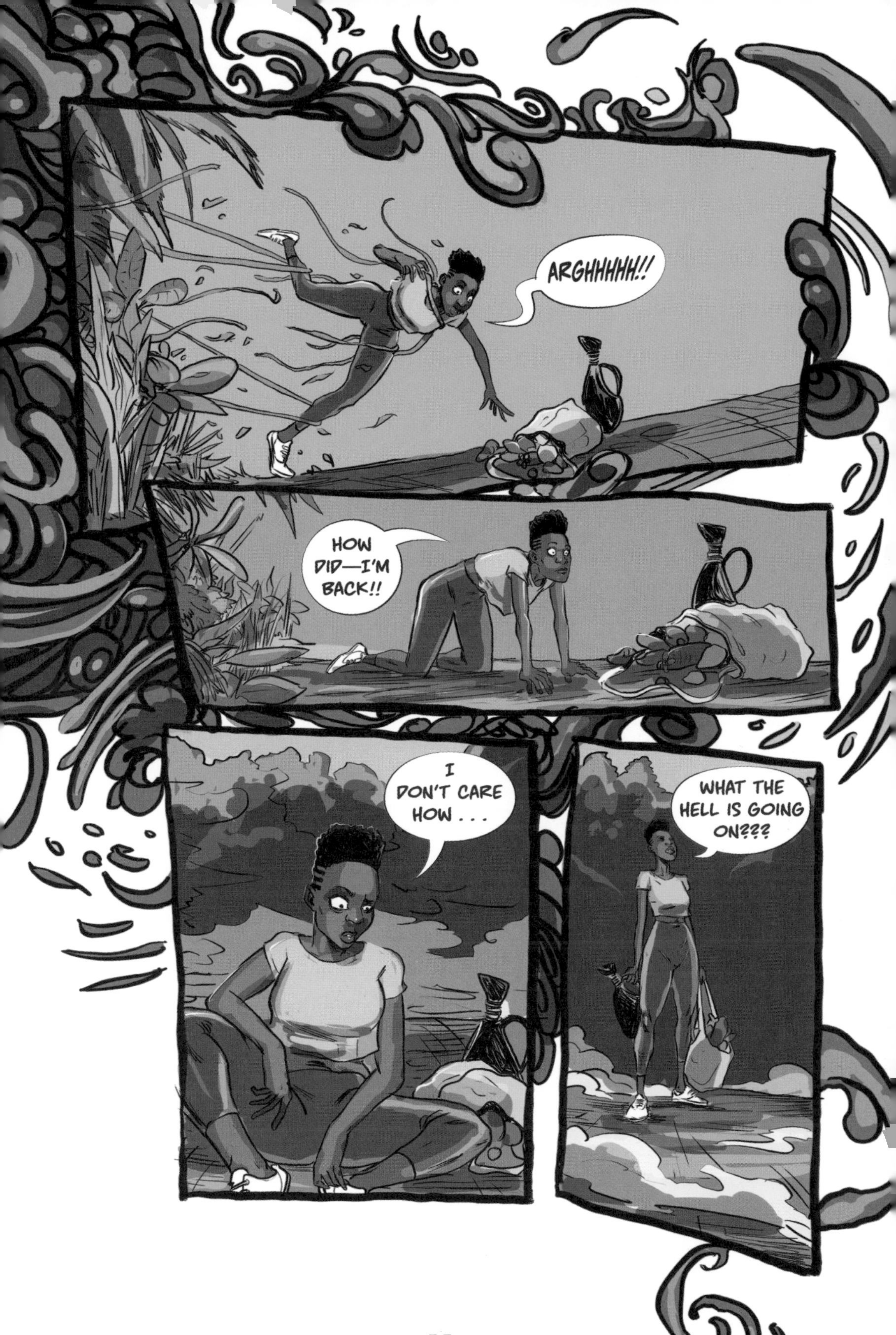
ARGHHHHH!!
HOW DID—I'M BACK!!
I DON'T CARE HOW . . .
WHAT THE HELL IS GOING ON???

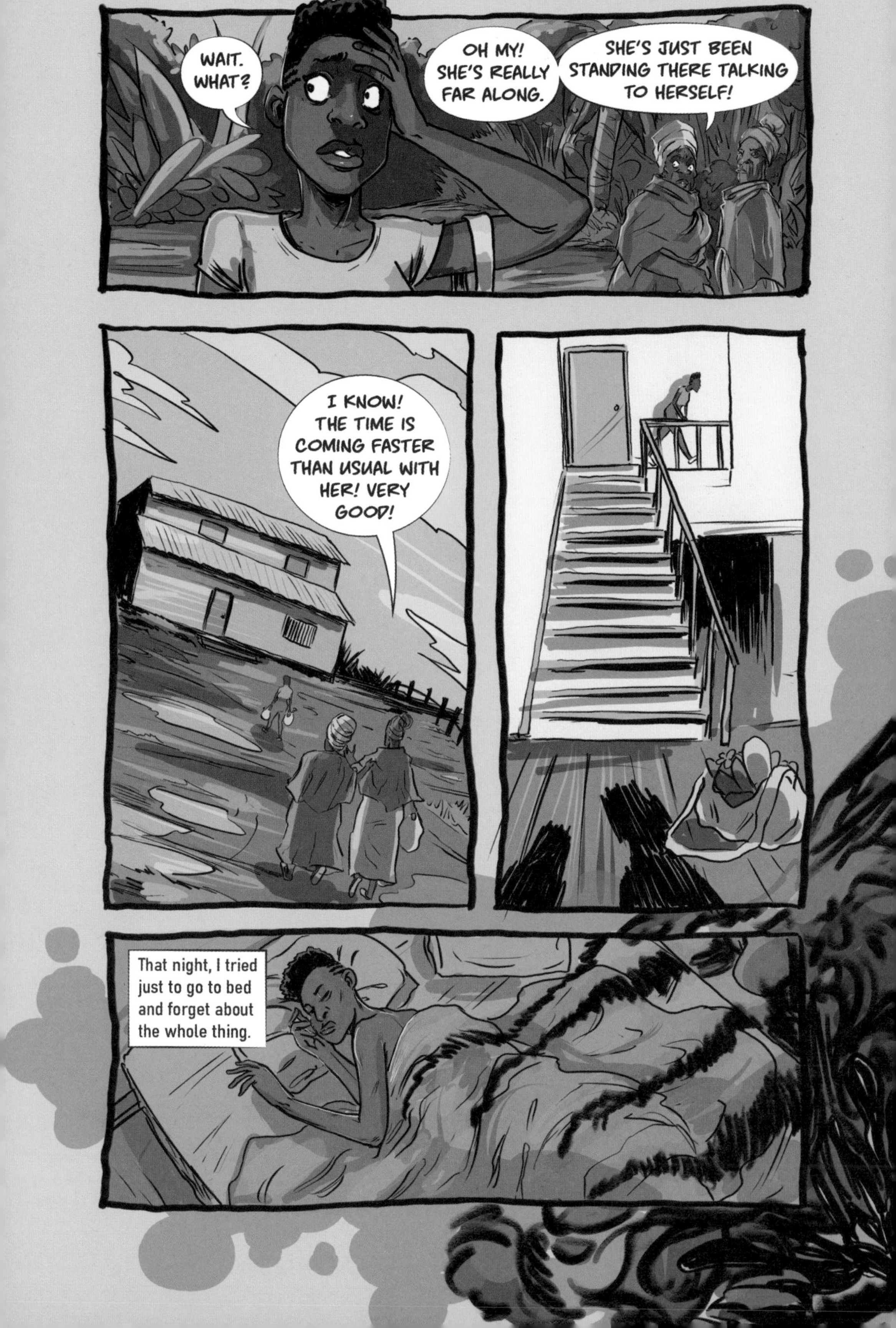
WAIT. WHAT?
OH MY! SHE'S REALLY FAR ALONG.
SHE'S JUST BEEN STANDING THERE TALKING TO HERSELF!
I KNOW! THE TIME IS COMING FASTER THAN USUAL WITH HER! VERY GOOD!
That night, I tried just to go to bed and forget about the whole thing.

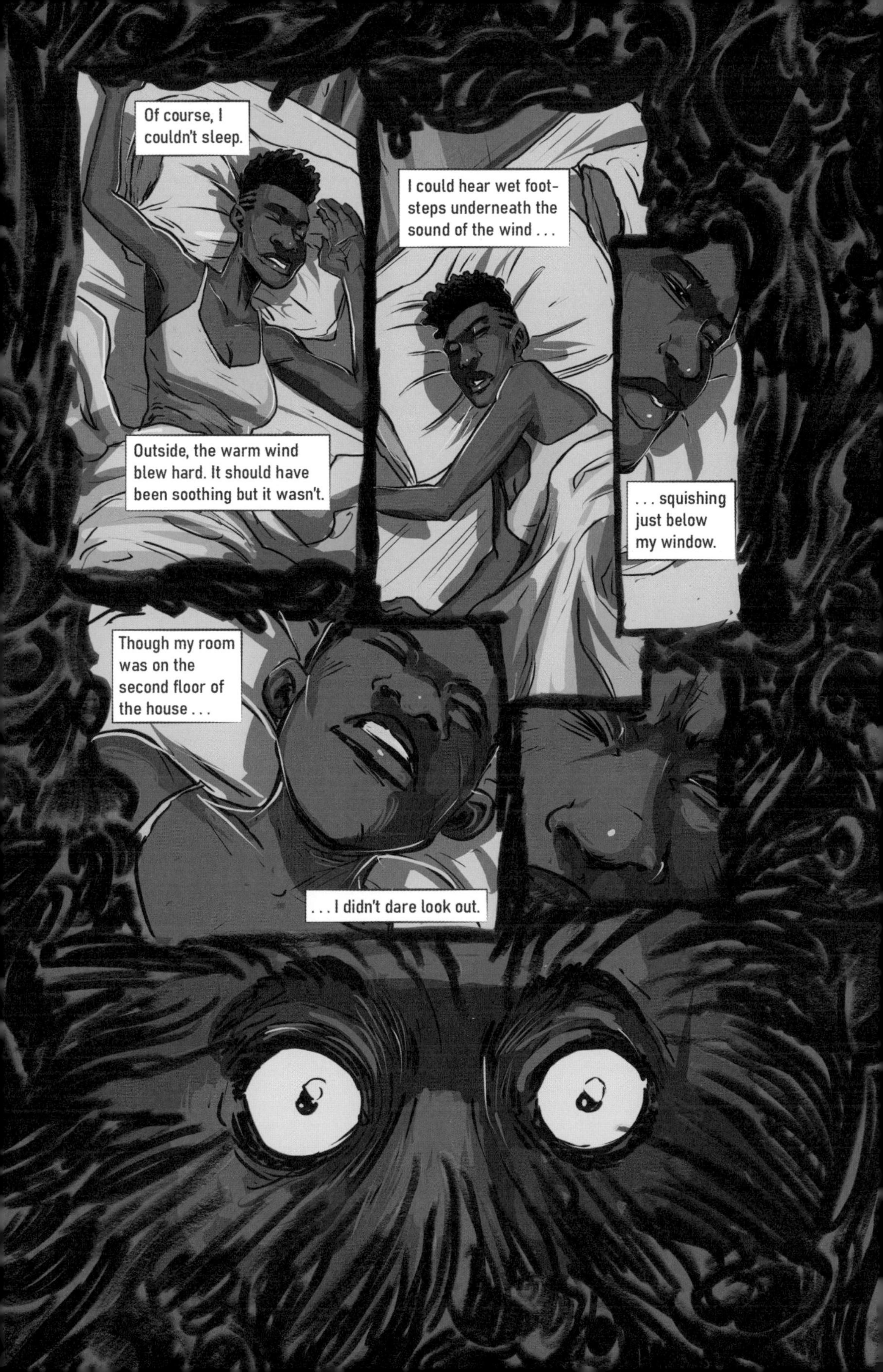

Of course, I couldn't sleep.
Outside, the warm wind blew hard. It should have been soothing but it wasn't.
I could hear wet foot-steps underneath the sound of the wind . . .
. . . squishing just below my window.
Though my room was on the second floor of the house . . .
. . . I didn't dare look out.

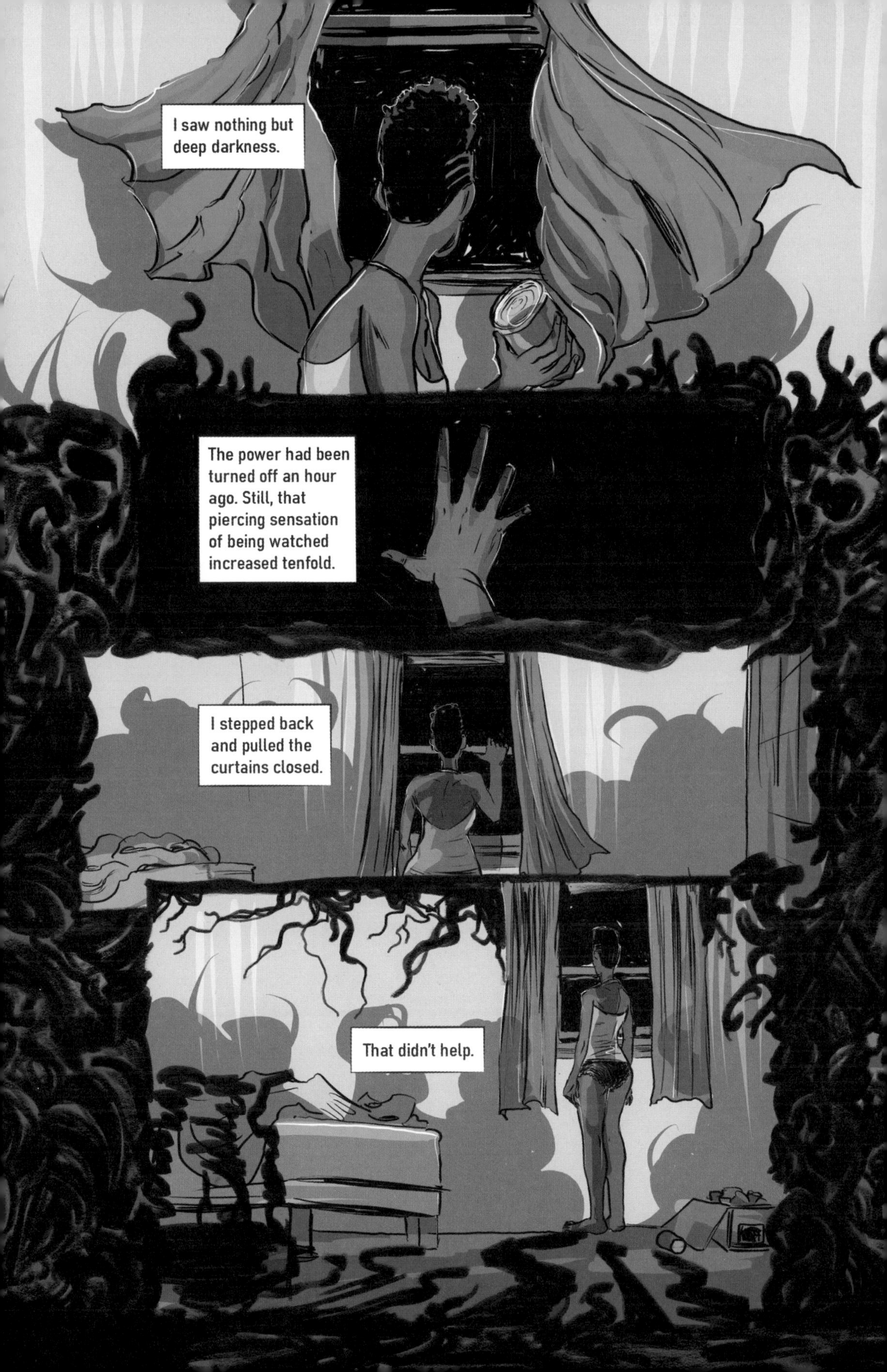
I saw nothing but deep darkness.
The power had been turned off an hour ago. Still, that piercing sensation of being watched increased tenfold.
I stepped back and pulled the curtains closed.
That didn't help.

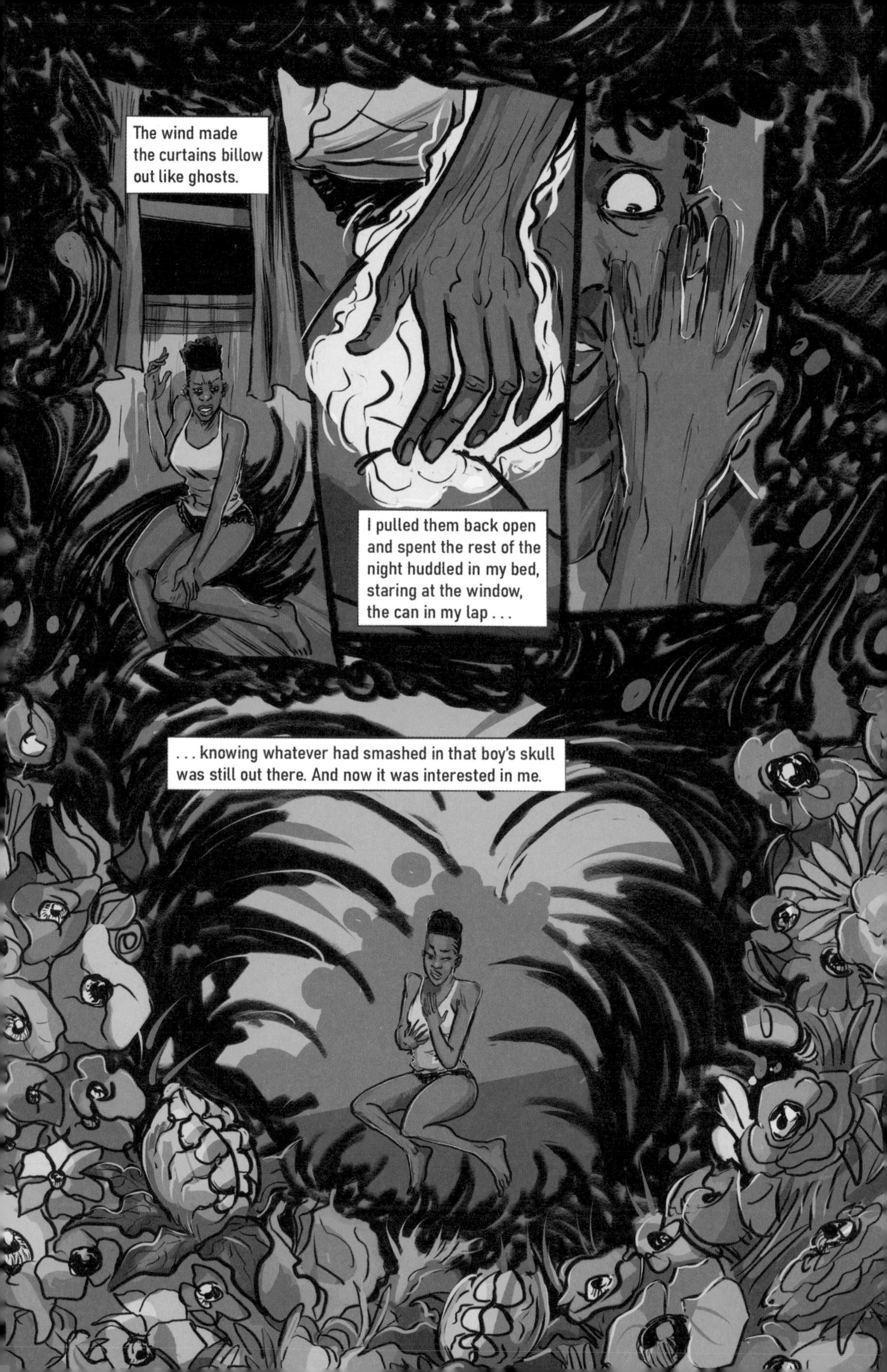
The wind made the curtains billow out like ghosts.
I pulled them back open and spent the rest of the night huddled in my bed, staring at the window, the can in my lap . . .
. . . knowing whatever had smashed in that boy's skull was still out there. And now it was interested in me.

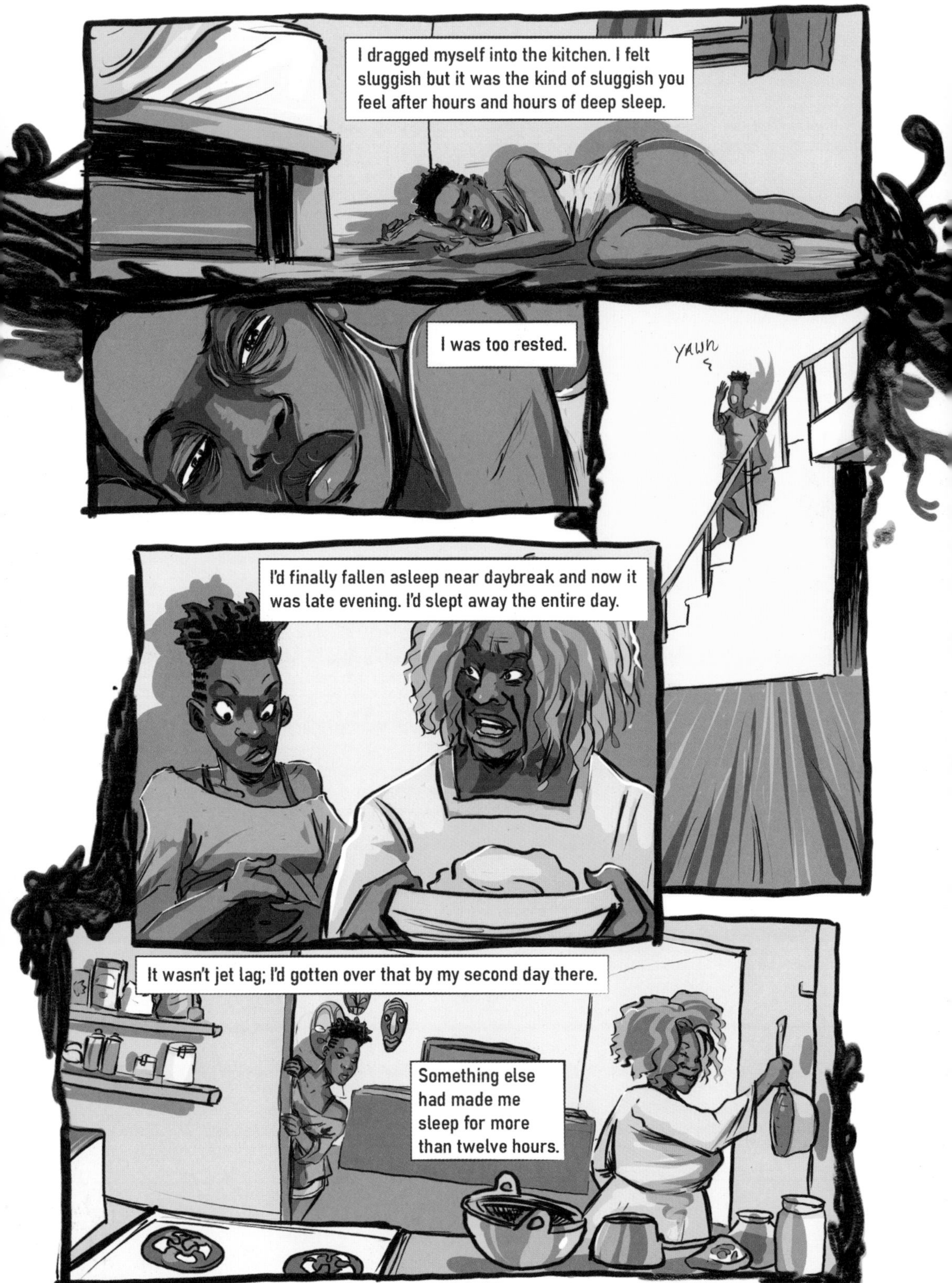

I dragged myself into the kitchen. I felt sluggish but it was the kind of sluggish you feel after hours and hours of deep sleep.
I was too rested.
YAWN
I'd finally fallen asleep near daybreak and now it was late evening. I'd slept away the entire day.
It wasn't jet lag; I'd gotten over that by my second day there.
Something else had made me sleep for more than twelve hours.

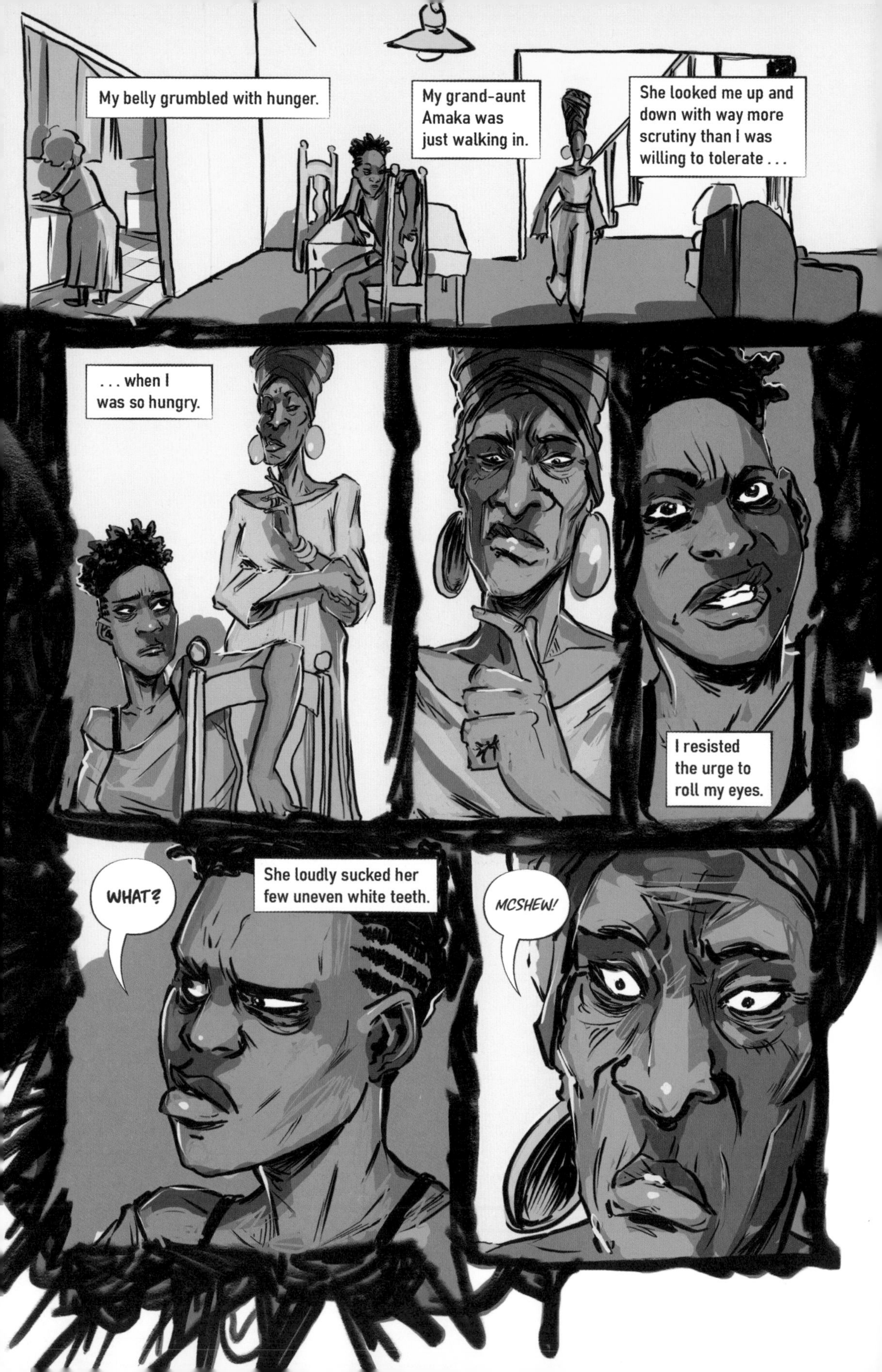

My belly grumbled with hunger.
My grand-aunt Amaka was just walking in.
She looked me up and down with way more scrutiny than I was willing to tolerate . . .
. . . when I was so hungry.
I resisted the urge to roll my eyes.
WHAT?
She loudly sucked her few uneven white teeth.
MCSHEW!

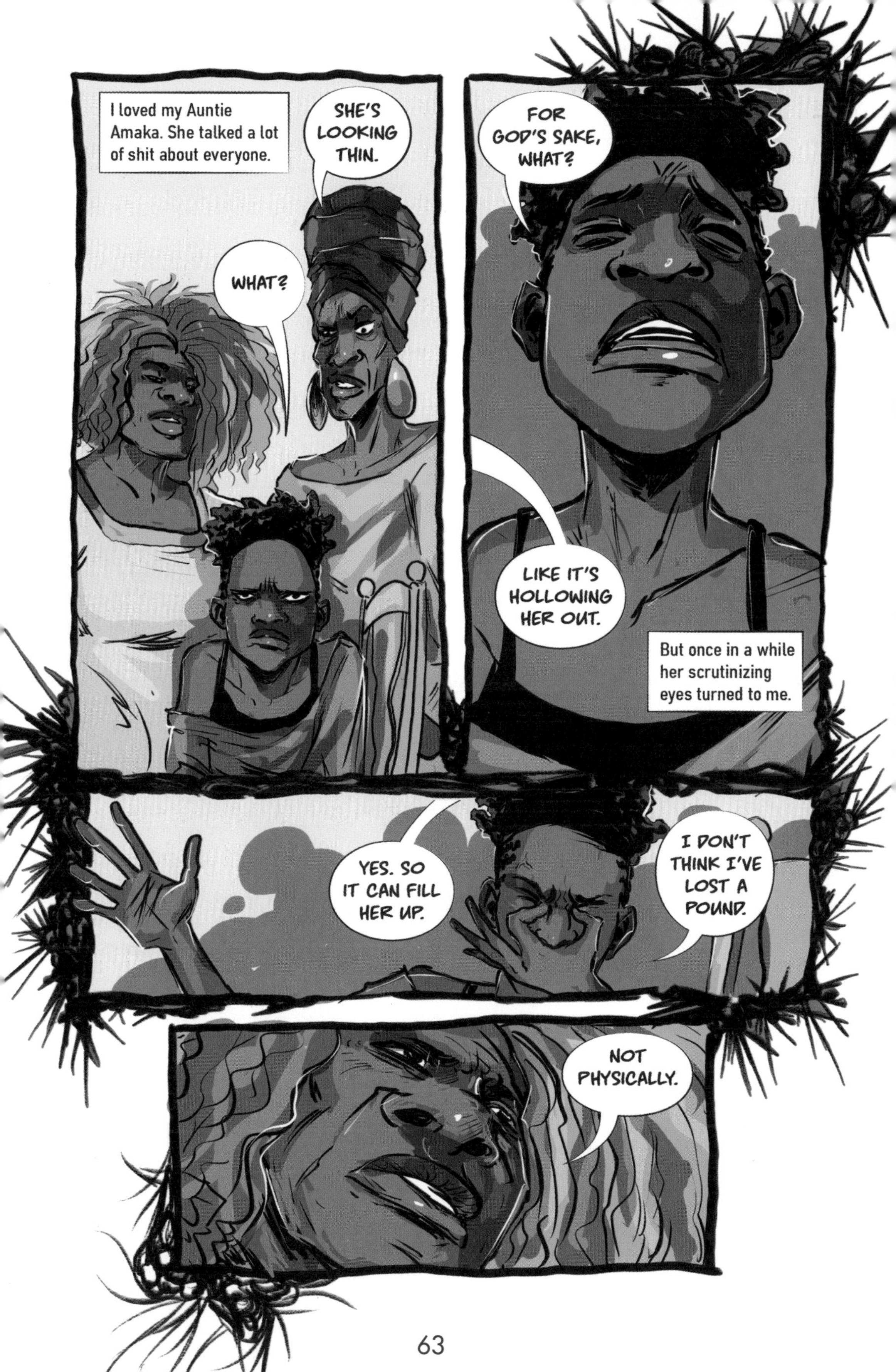
I loved my Auntie Amaka. She talked a lot of shit about everyone.
SHE'S LOOKING THIN.
WHAT?
FOR GOD'S SAKE, WHAT?
LIKE IT'S HOLLOWING HER OUT.
But once in a while her scrutinizing eyes turned to me.
YES. SO IT CAN FILL HER UP.
I DON'T THINK I'VE LOST A POUND.
NOT PHYSICALLY.

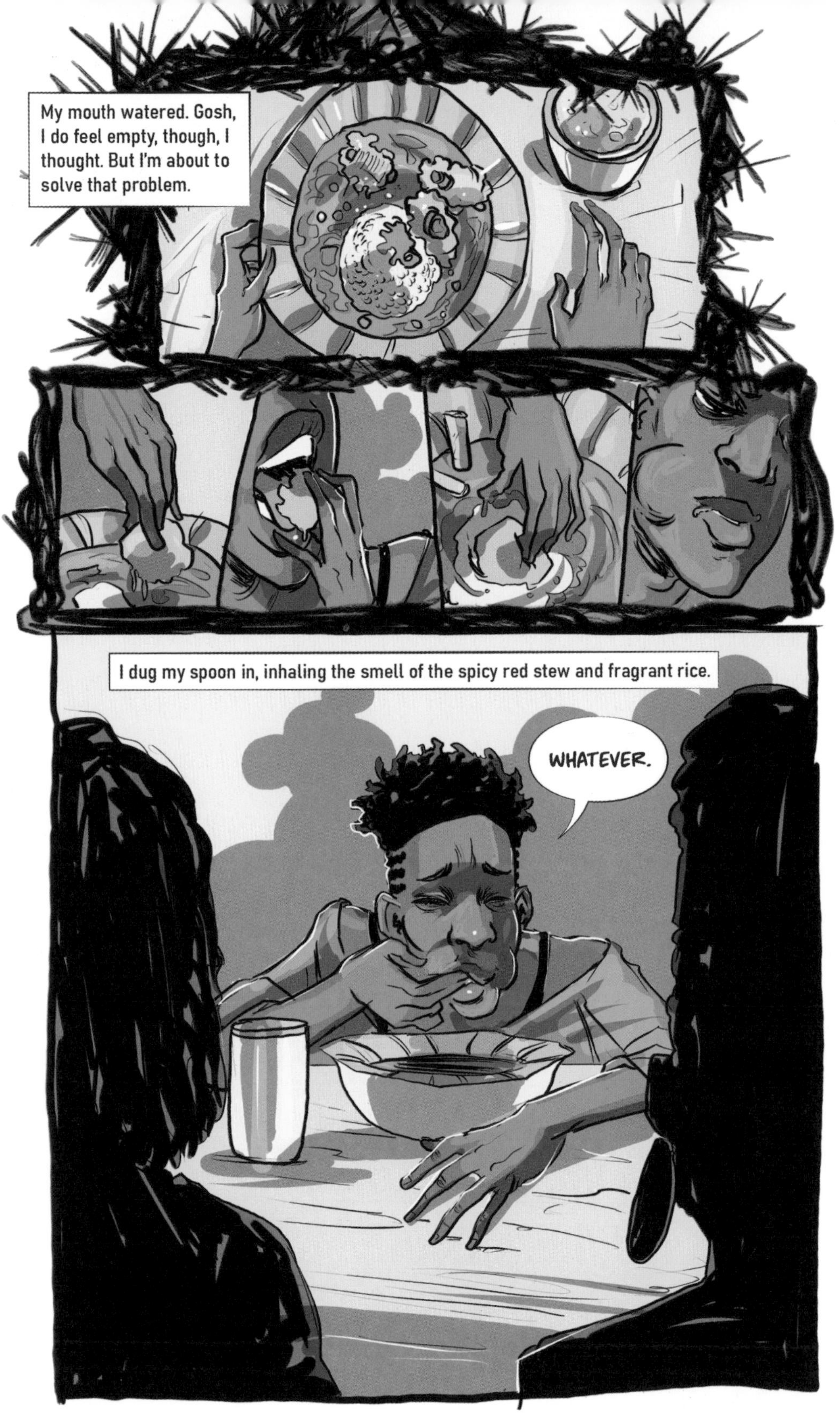
My mouth watered. Gosh, I do feel empty, though, I thought. But I'm about to solve that problem.
I dug my spoon in, inhaling the smell of the spicy red stew and fragrant rice.
WHATEVER.

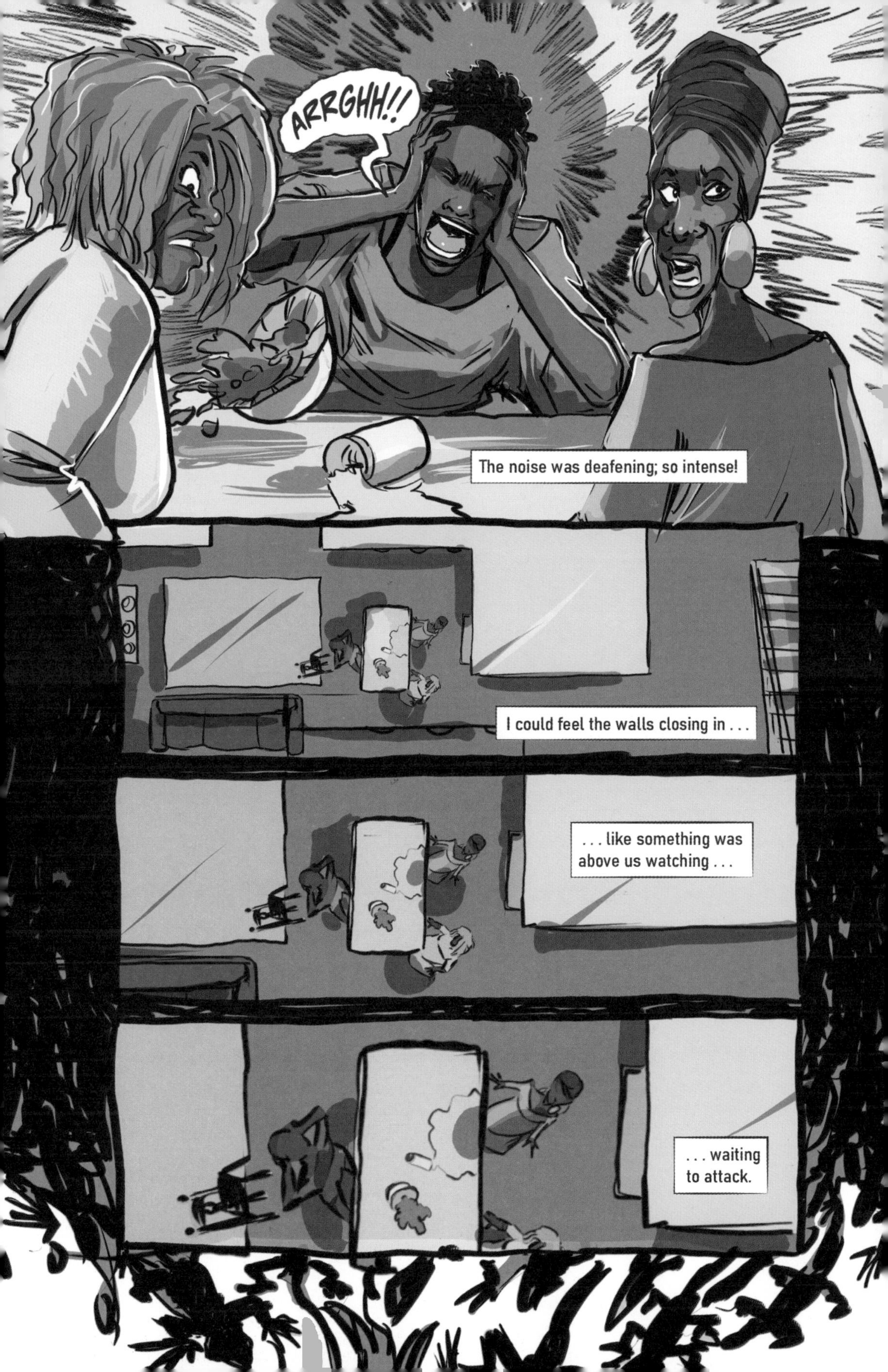
ARRGHH!!
The noise was deafening; so intense!
I could feel the walls closing in . . .
. . . like something was above us watching . . .
. . . waiting to attack.

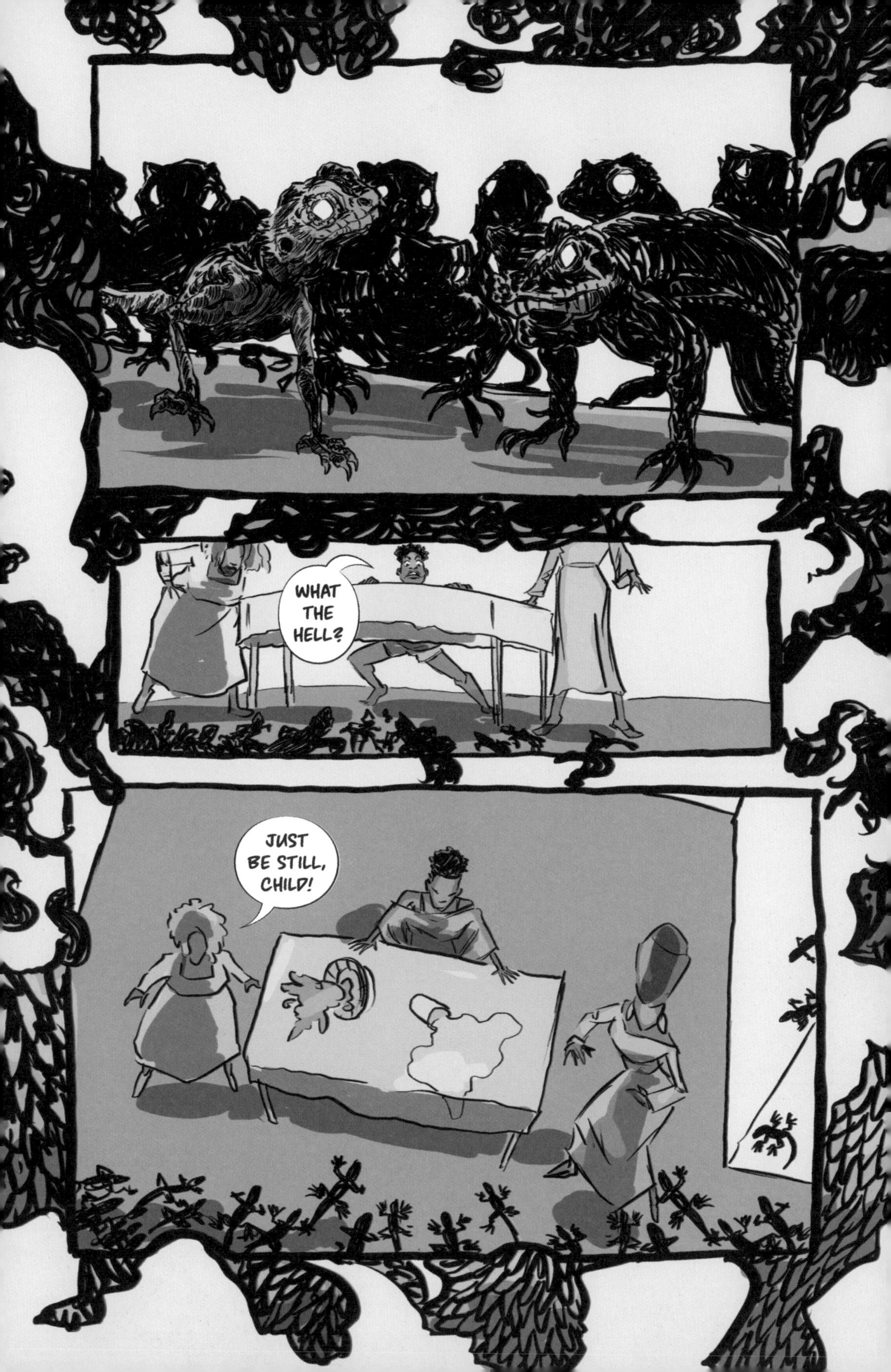
WHAT THE HELL?
JUST BE STILL, CHILD!

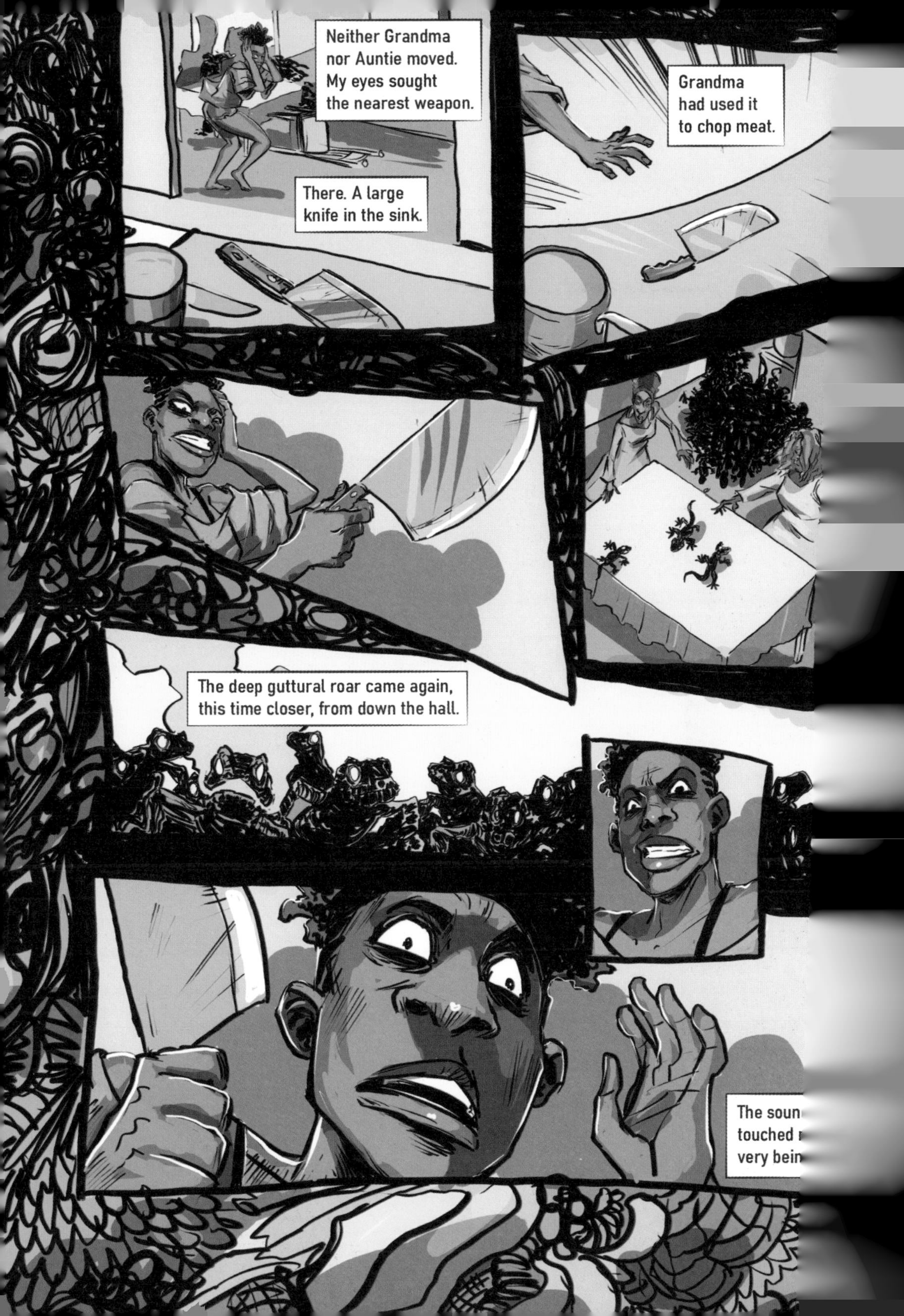
Neither Grandma nor Auntie moved. My eyes sought the nearest weapon.
There. A large knife in the sink.
Grandma had used it to chop meat.
The deep guttural roar came again, this time closer, from down the hall.
The soun touched very bein

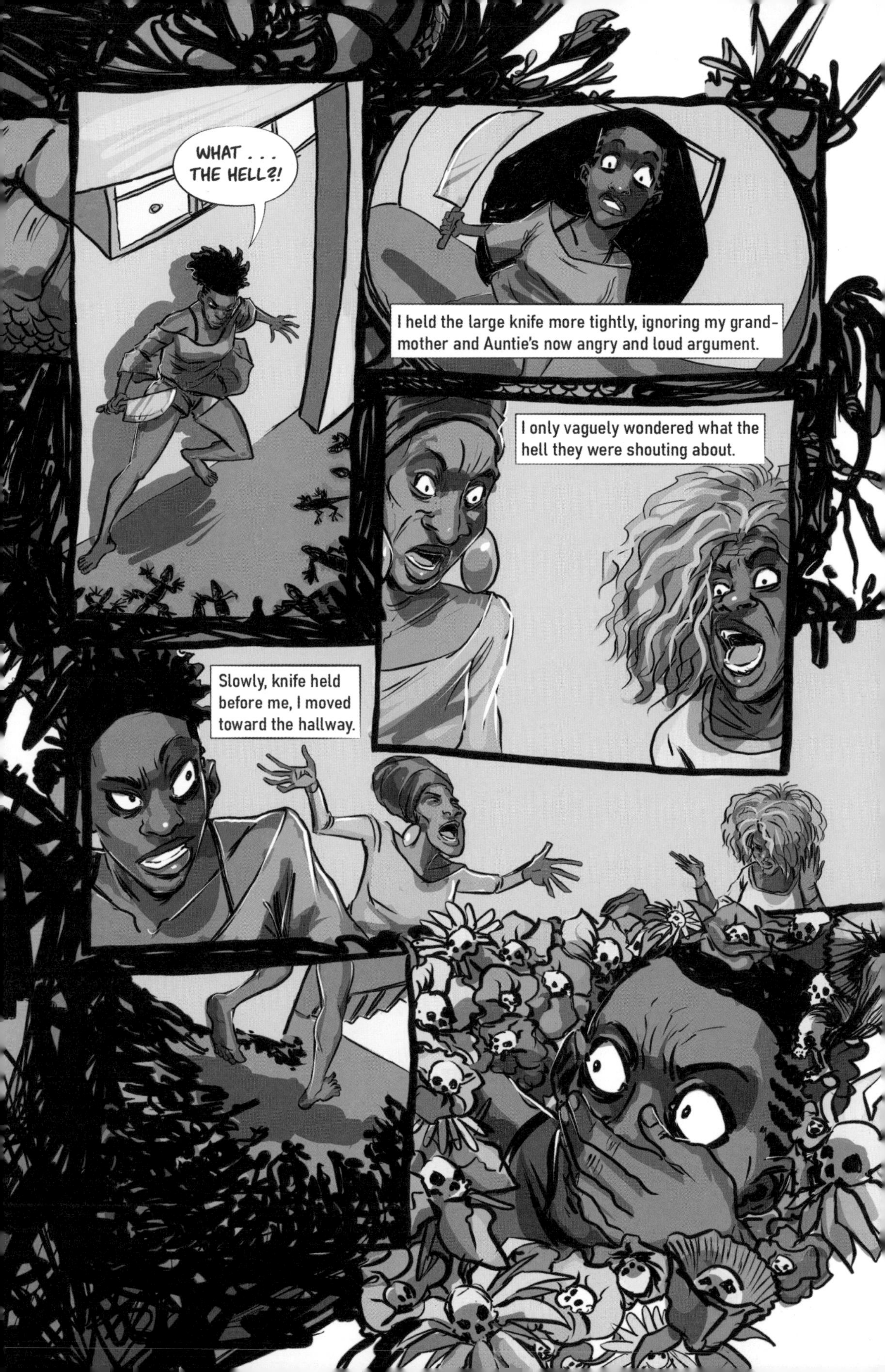
WHAT . . . THE HELL?!
I held the large knife more tightly, ignoring my grand-mother and Auntie's now angry and loud argument.
I only vaguely wondered what the hell they were shouting about.
Slowly, knife held before me, I moved toward the hallway.

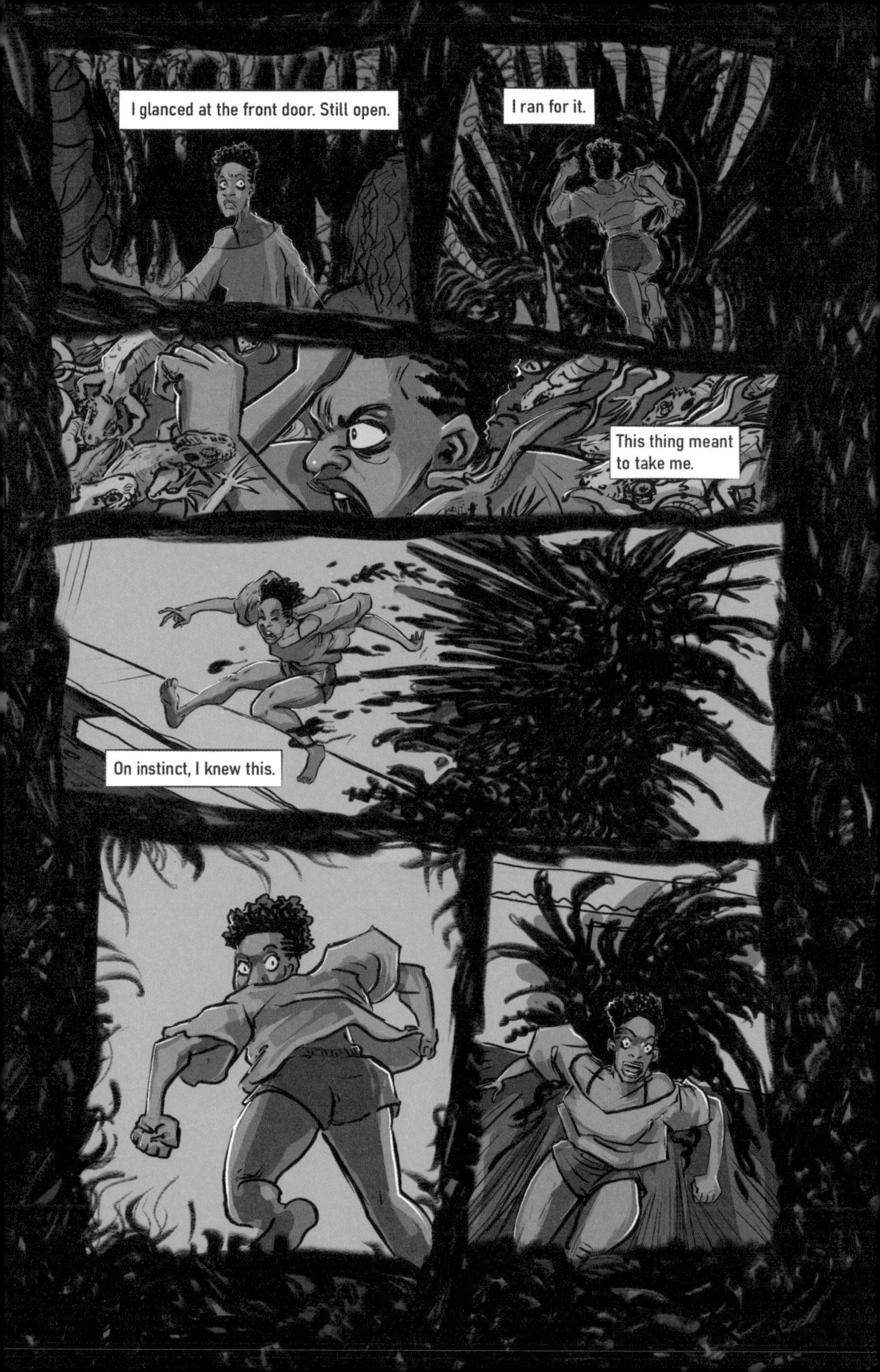
I glanced at the front door. Still open.
I ran for it.
This thing meant to take me.
On instinct, I knew this.

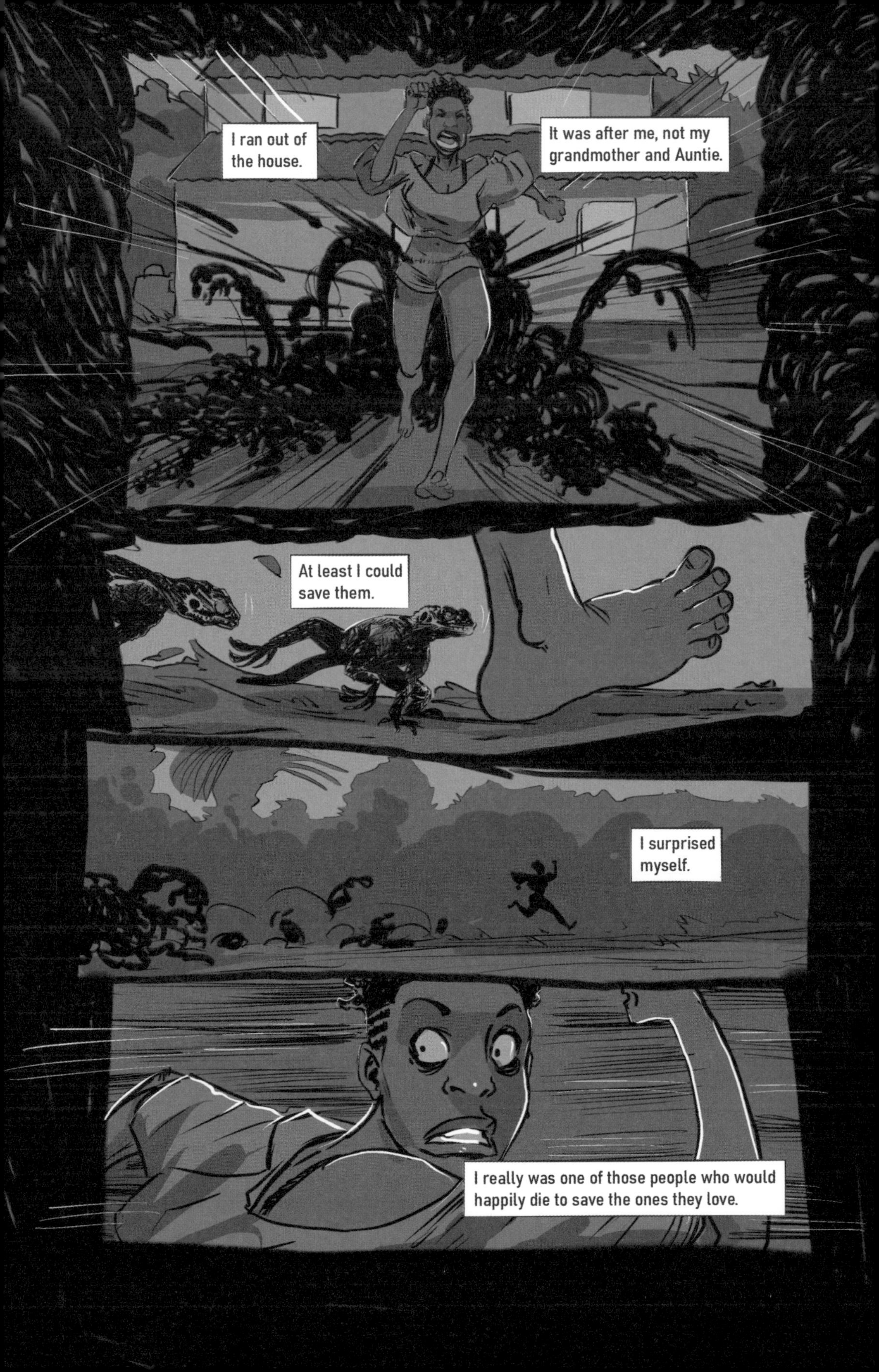
I ran out of the house.
It was after me, not my grandmother and Auntie.
At least I could save them.
I surprised myself.
I really was one of those people who would happily die to save the ones they love.

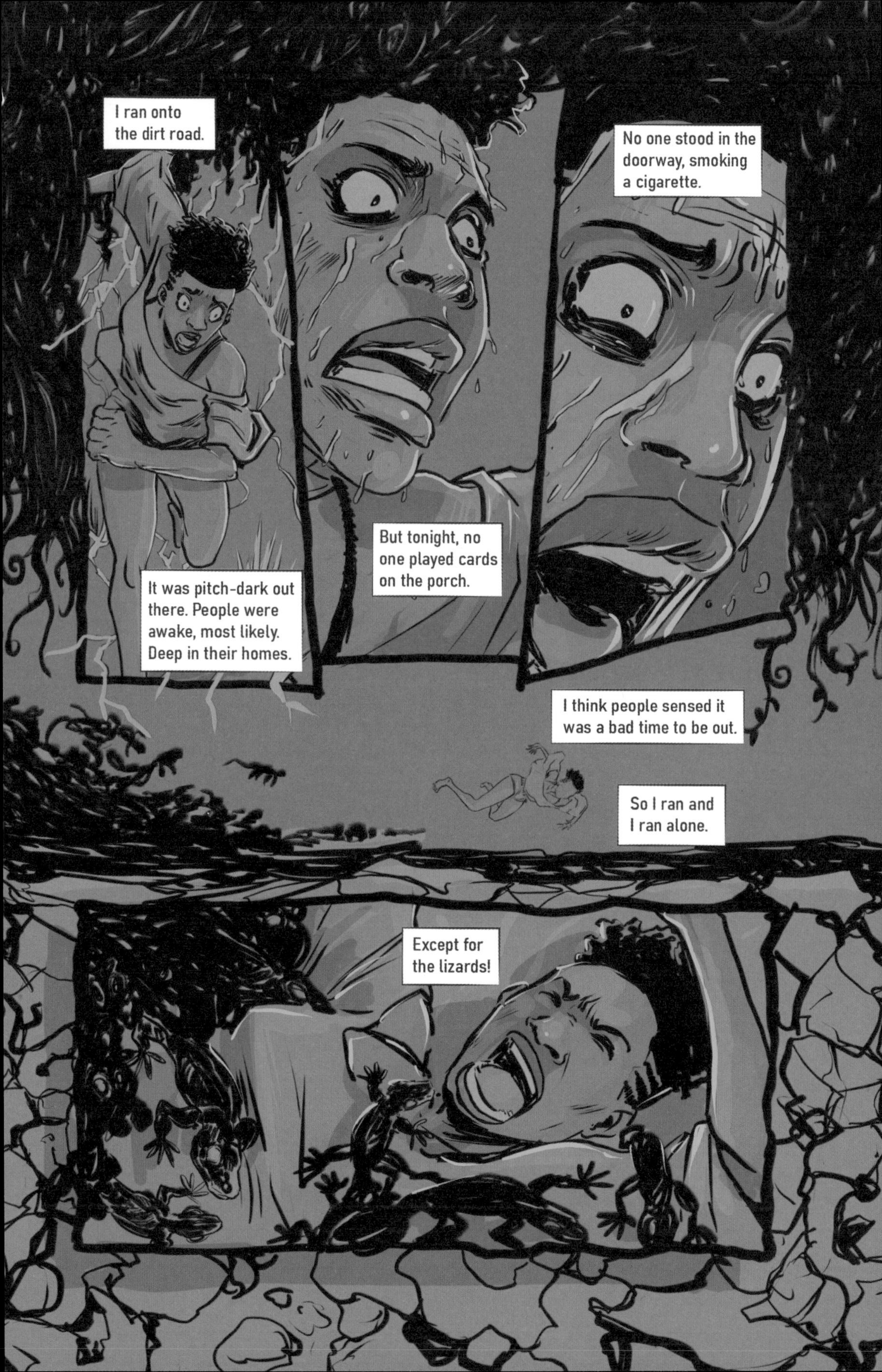
I ran onto the dirt road.
But tonight, no one played cards on the porch.
No one stood in the doorway, smoking a cigarette.
It was pitch-dark out there. People were awake, most likely. Deep in their homes.
I think people sensed it was a bad time to be out.
So I ran and I ran alone.
Except for the lizards!

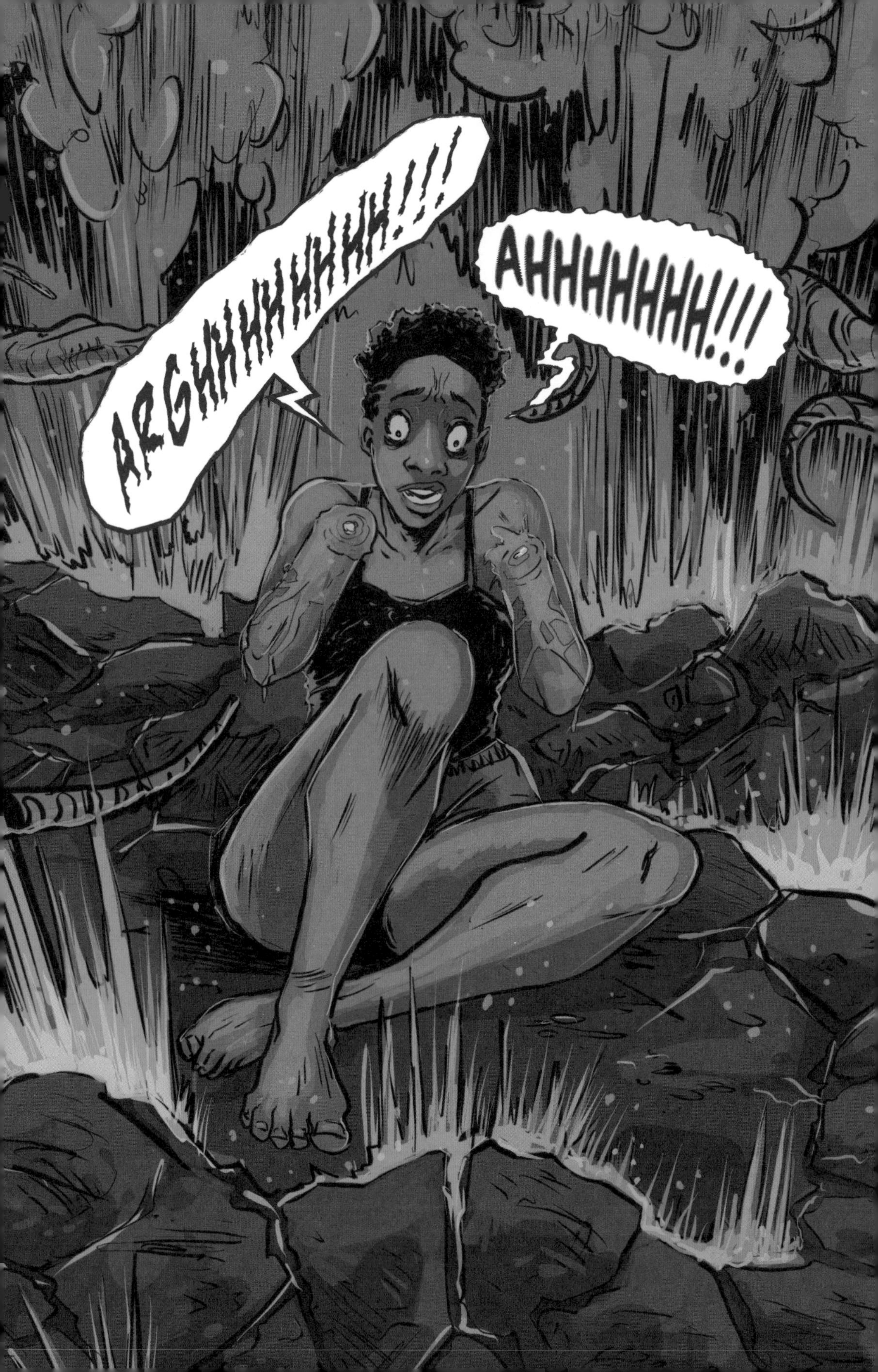
ARGHHHHHHH!!!
AHHHHHHH!!!

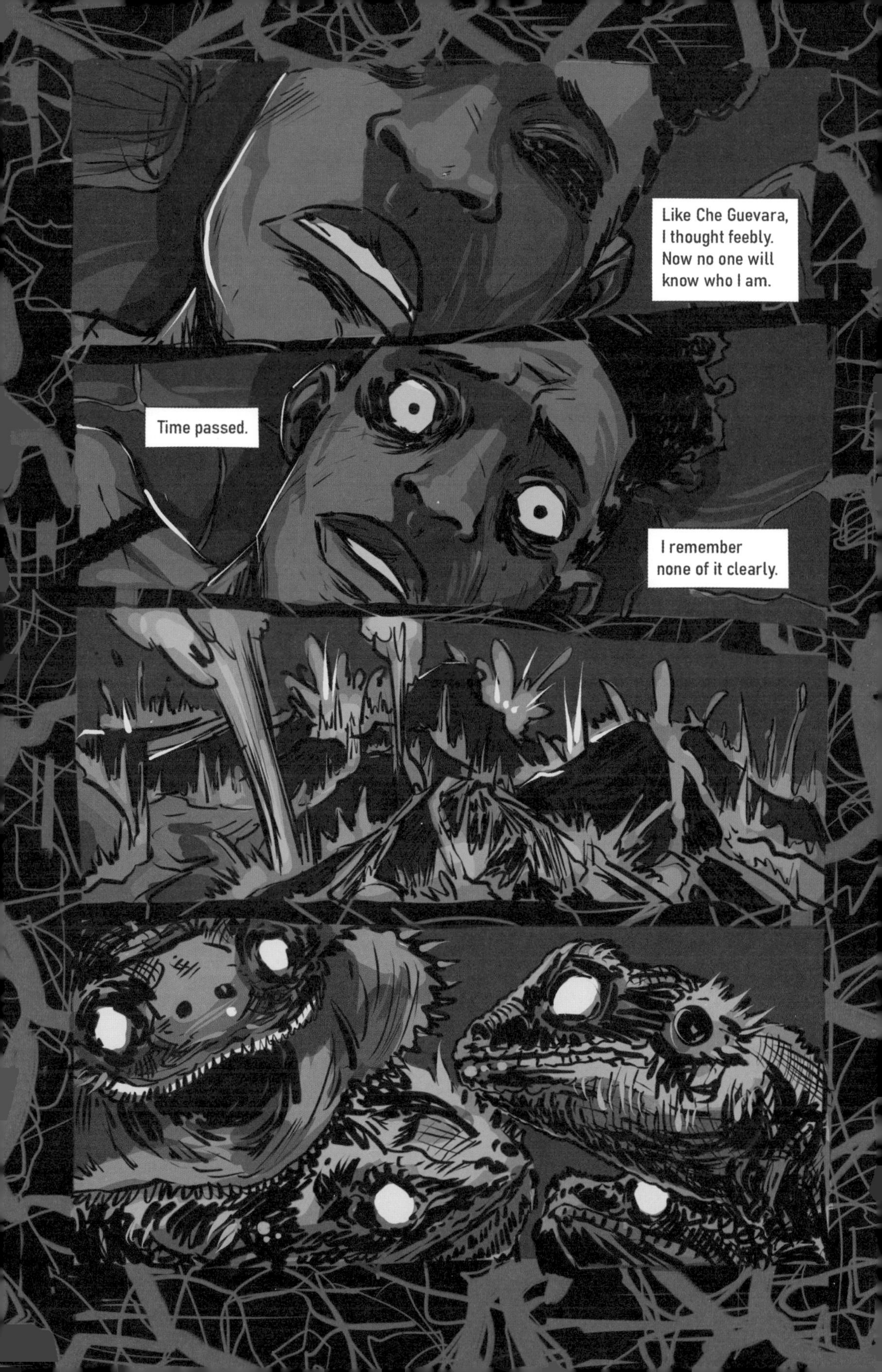
Like Che Guevara, I thought feebly. Now no one will know who I am.
Time passed.
I remember none of it clearly.

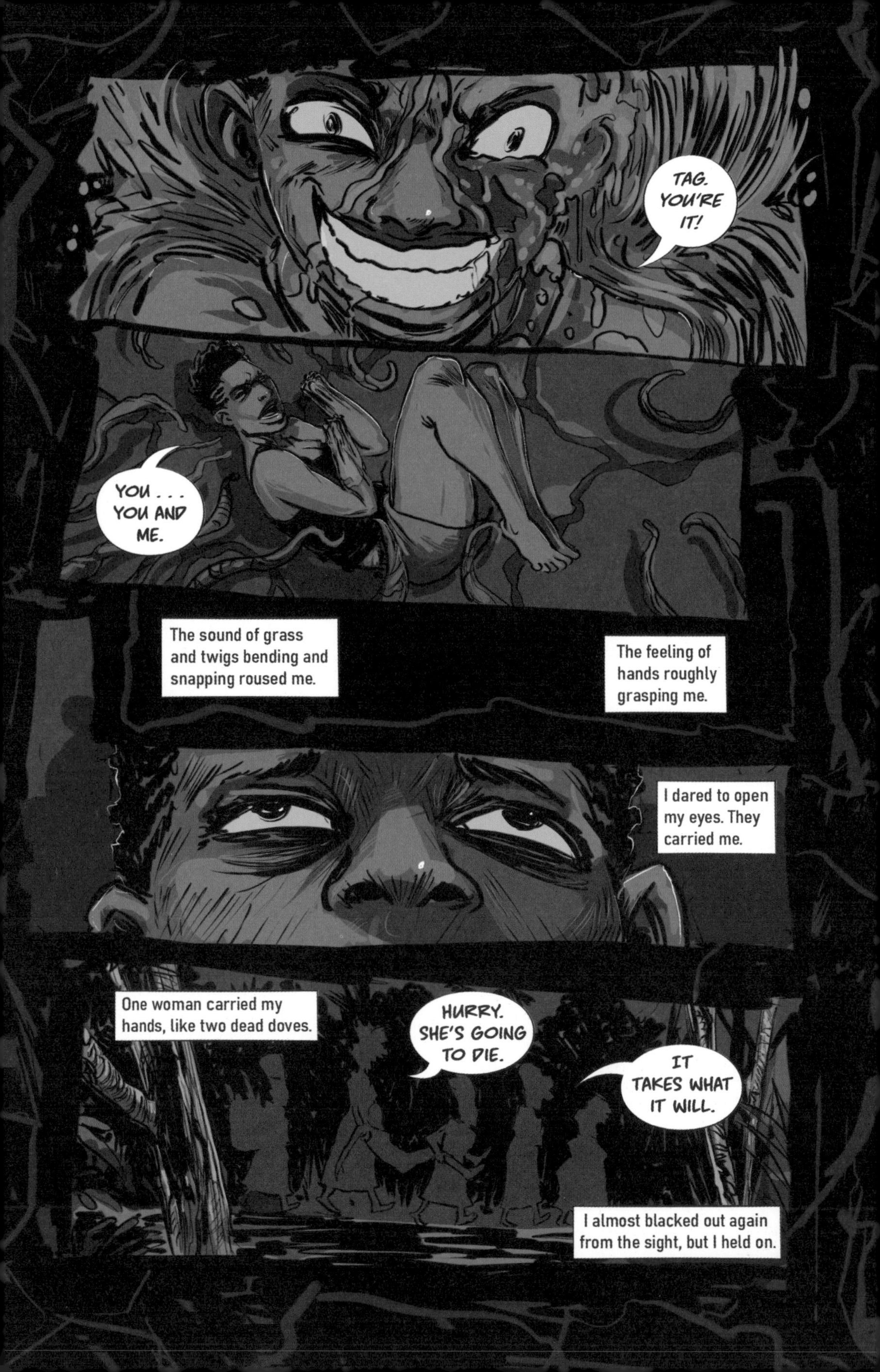
TAG. YOU'RE IT!
YOU . . . YOU AND ME.
The sound of grass and twigs bending and snapping roused me.
The feeling of hands roughly grasping me.
I dared to open my eyes. They carried me.
One woman carried my hands, like two dead doves.
HURRY. SHE'S GOING TO DIE.
IT TAKES WHAT IT WILL.
I almost blacked out again from the sight, but I held on.

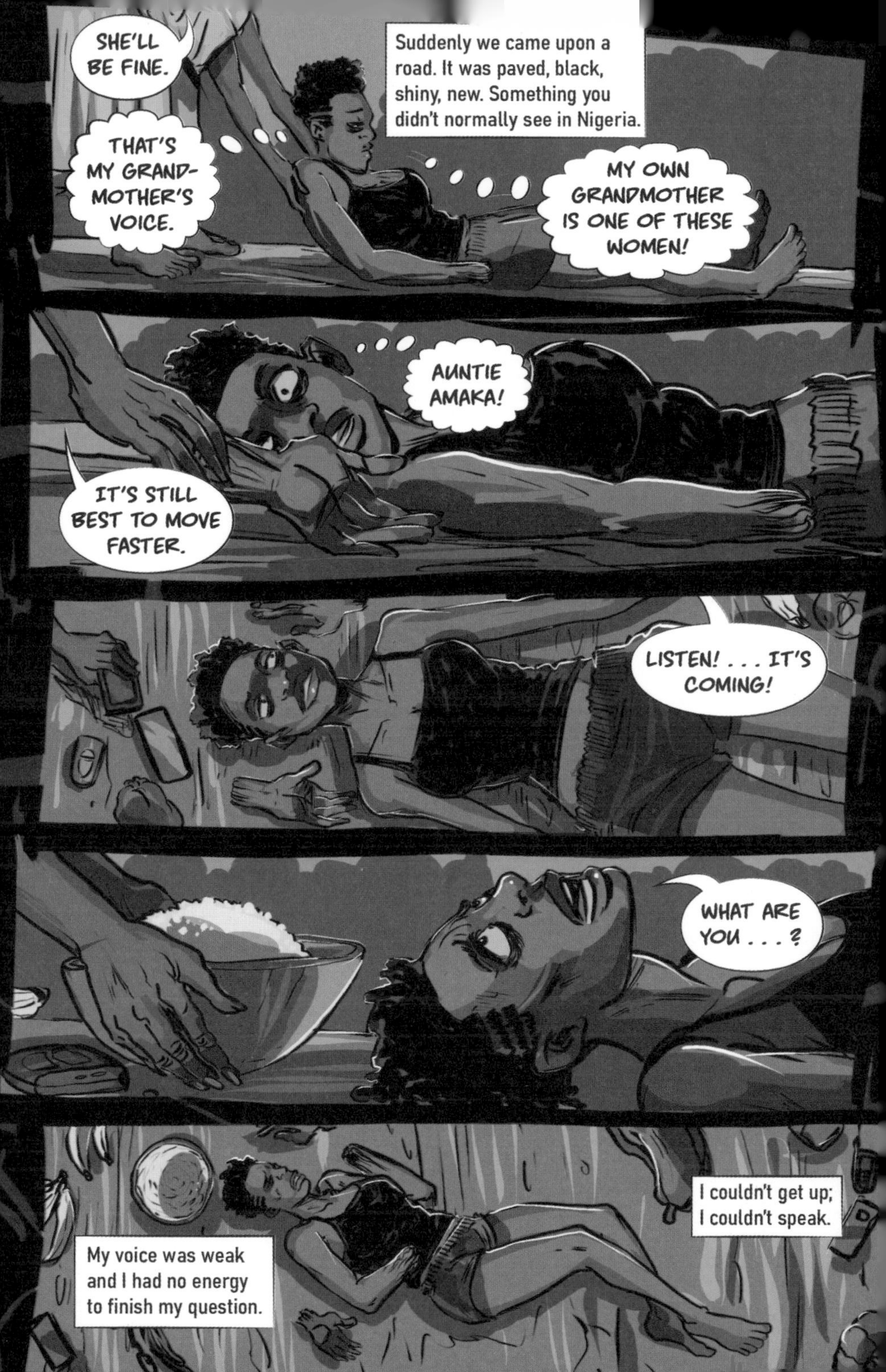
SHE'LL BE FINE.
Suddenly we came upon a road. It was paved, black, shiny, new. Something you didn't normally see in Nigeria.
THAT'S MY GRAND-MOTHER'S VOICE.
MY OWN GRANDMOTHER IS ONE OF THESE WOMEN!
AUNTIE AMAKA!
IT'S STILL BEST TO MOVE FASTER.
LISTEN! . . . IT'S COMING!
WHAT ARE YOU . . . ?
I couldn't get up; I couldn't speak.
My voice was weak and I had no energy to finish my question.

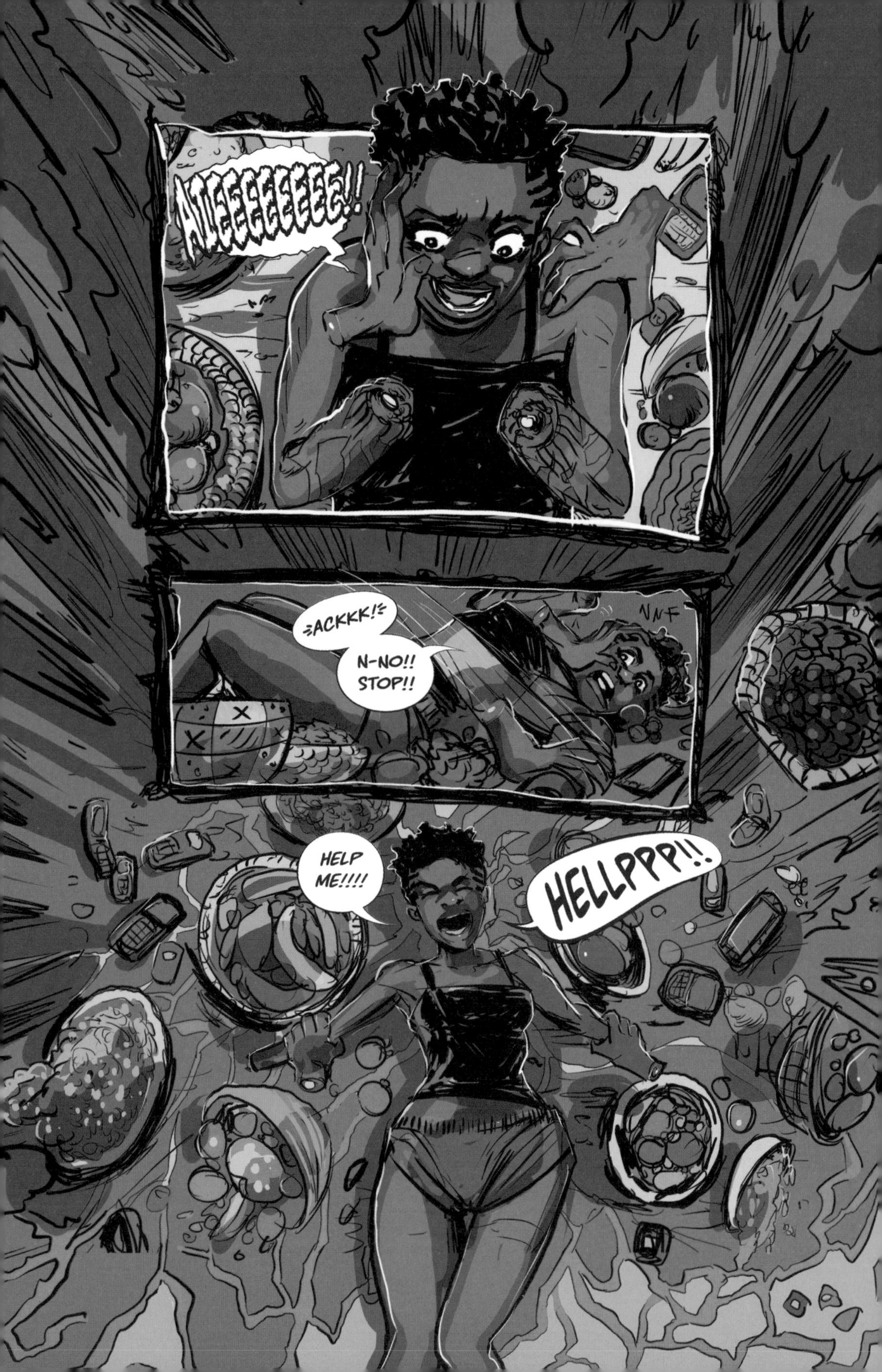
AIIEEEEEEEEEE!!
ACKKK!
N-NO!! STOP!!
NNF
HELP ME!!!!
HELLPPP!!

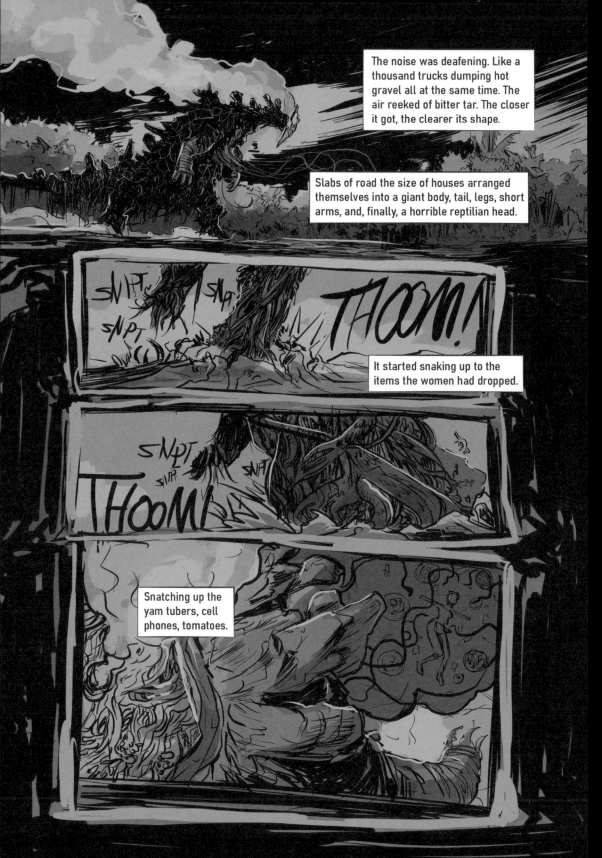

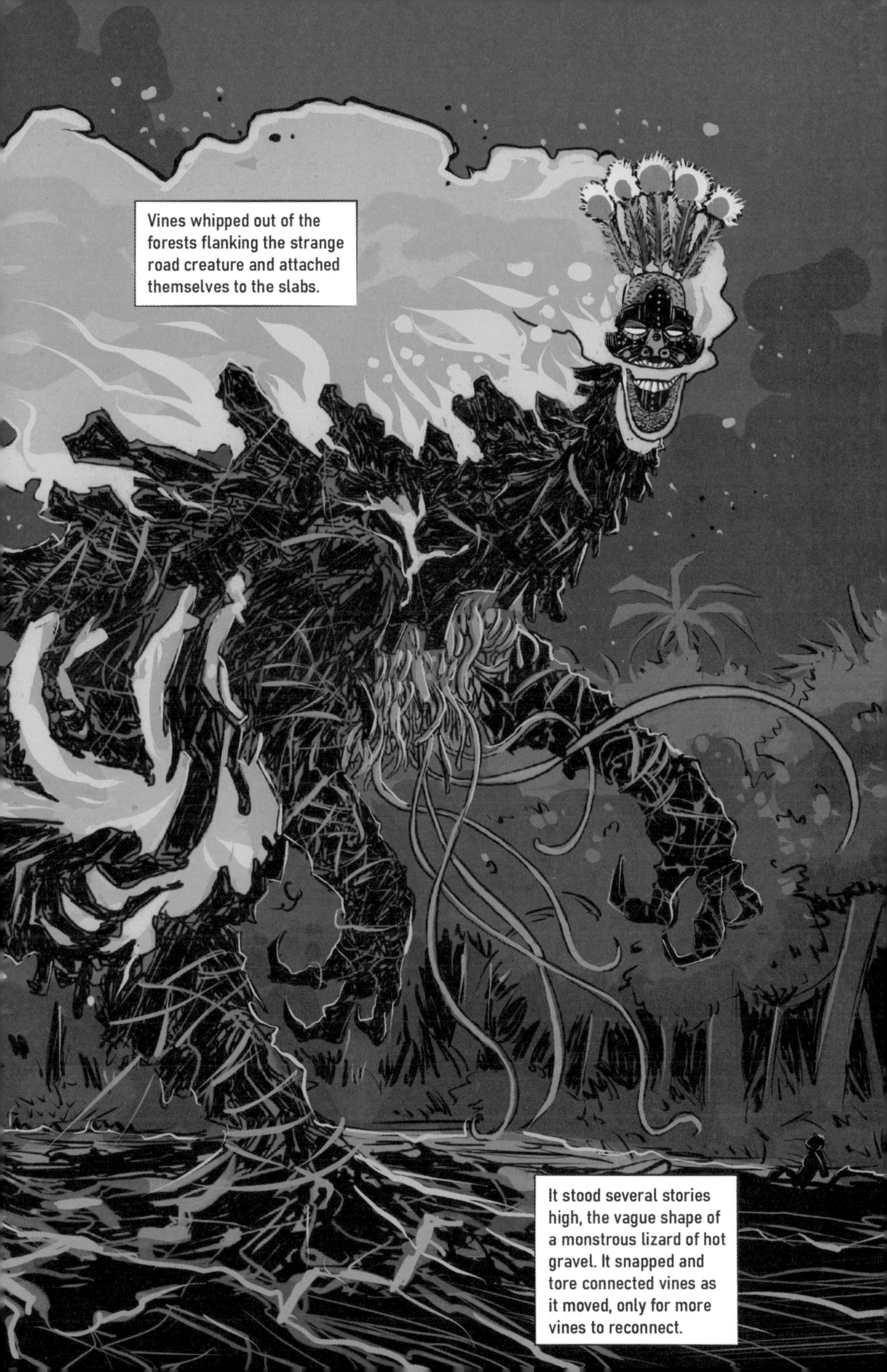
Vines whipped out of the forests flanking the strange road creature and attached themselves to the slabs.
It stood several stories high, the vague shape of a monstrous lizard of hot gravel. It snapped and tore connected vines as it moved, only for more vines to reconnect.

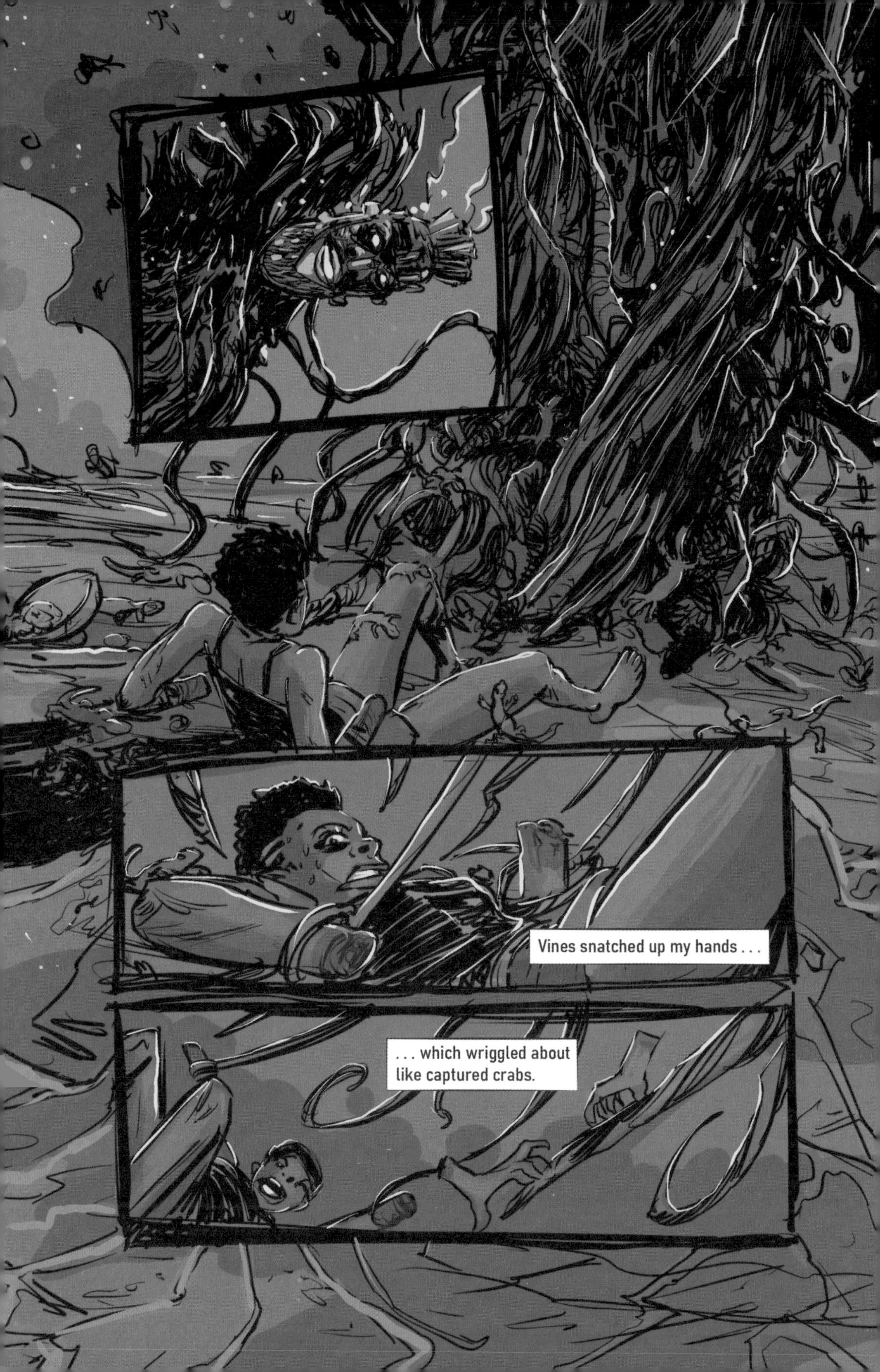
Vines snatched up my hands . . .
. . . which wriggled about like captured crabs.

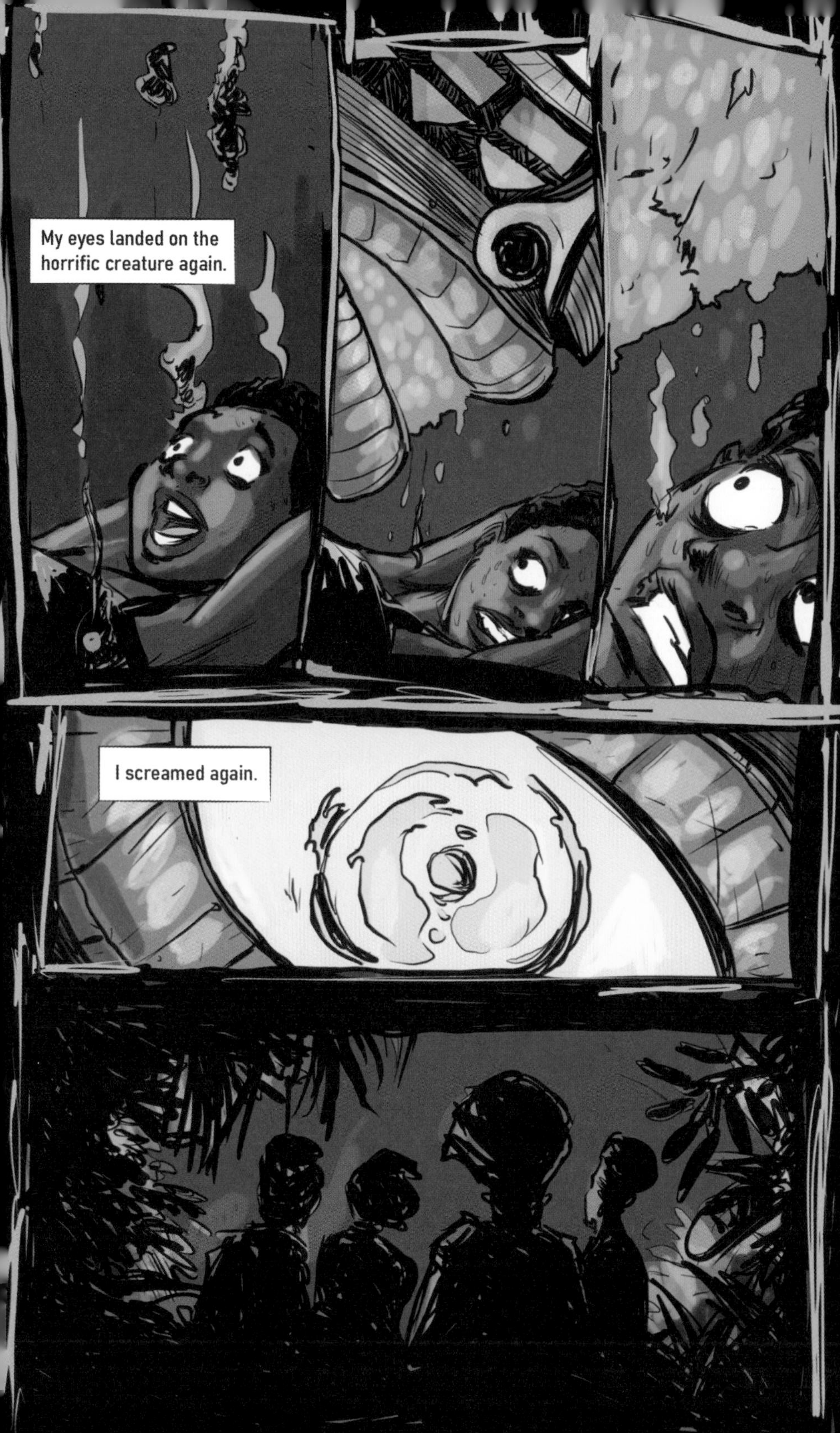
My eyes landed on the horrific creature again.
I screamed again.

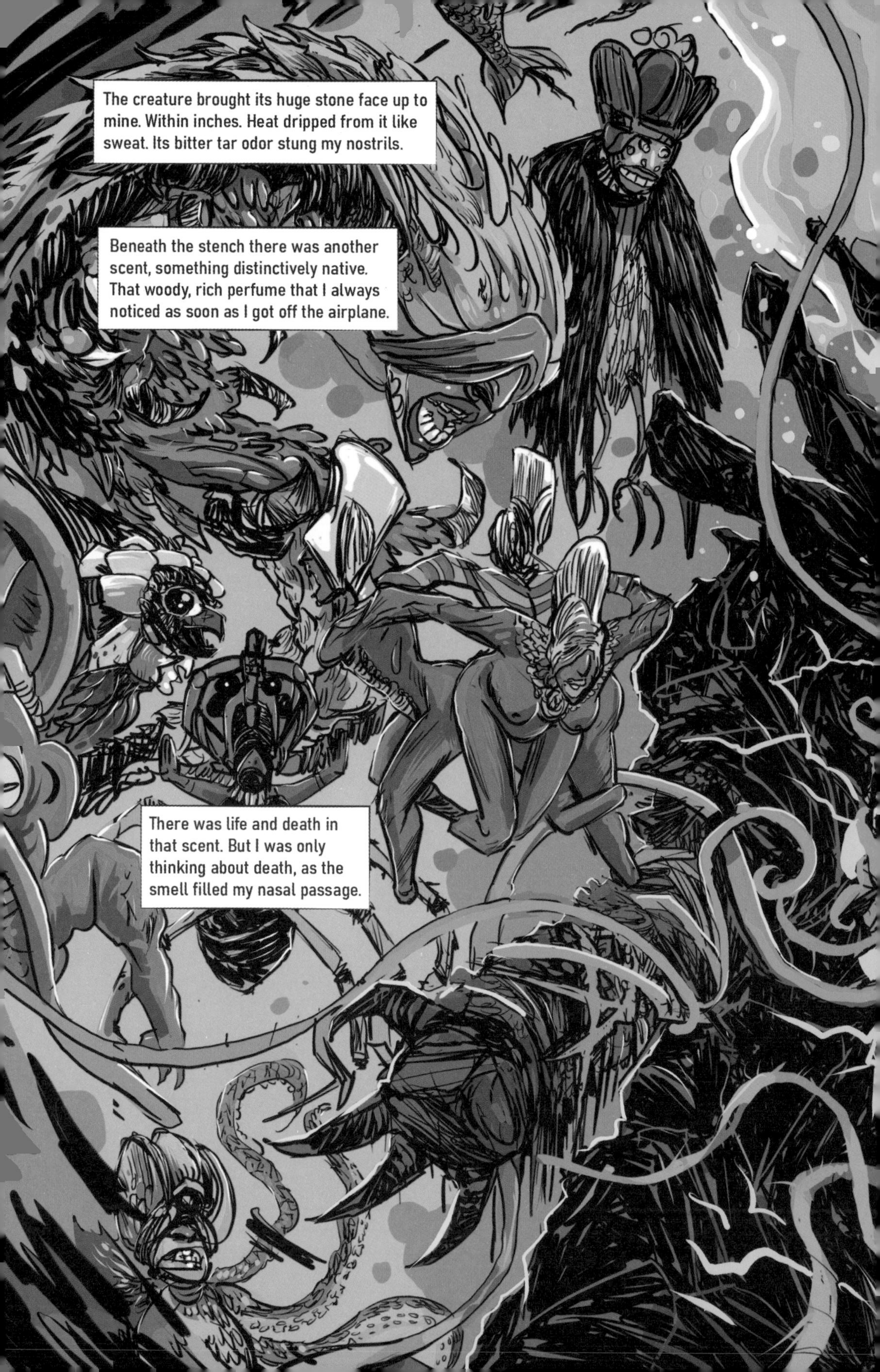
The creature brought its huge stone face up to mine. Within inches. Heat dripped from it like sweat. Its bitter tar odor stung my nostrils.
Beneath the stench there was another scent, something distinctively native. That woody, rich perfume that I always noticed as soon as I got off the airplane.
There was life and death in that scent. But I was only thinking about death, as the smell filled my nasal passage.

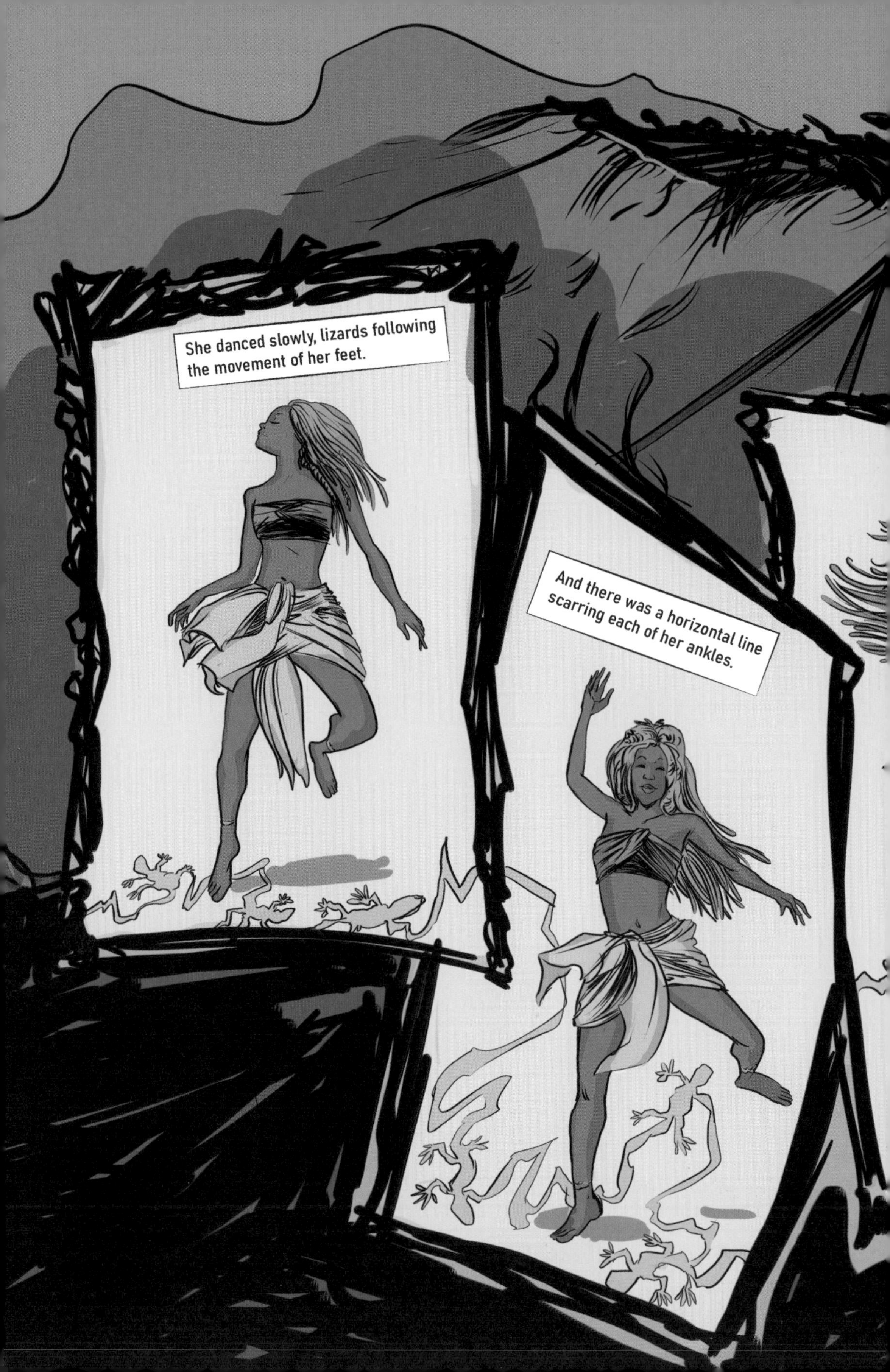
She danced slowly, lizards following the movement of her feet.
And there was a horizontal line scarring each of her ankles.

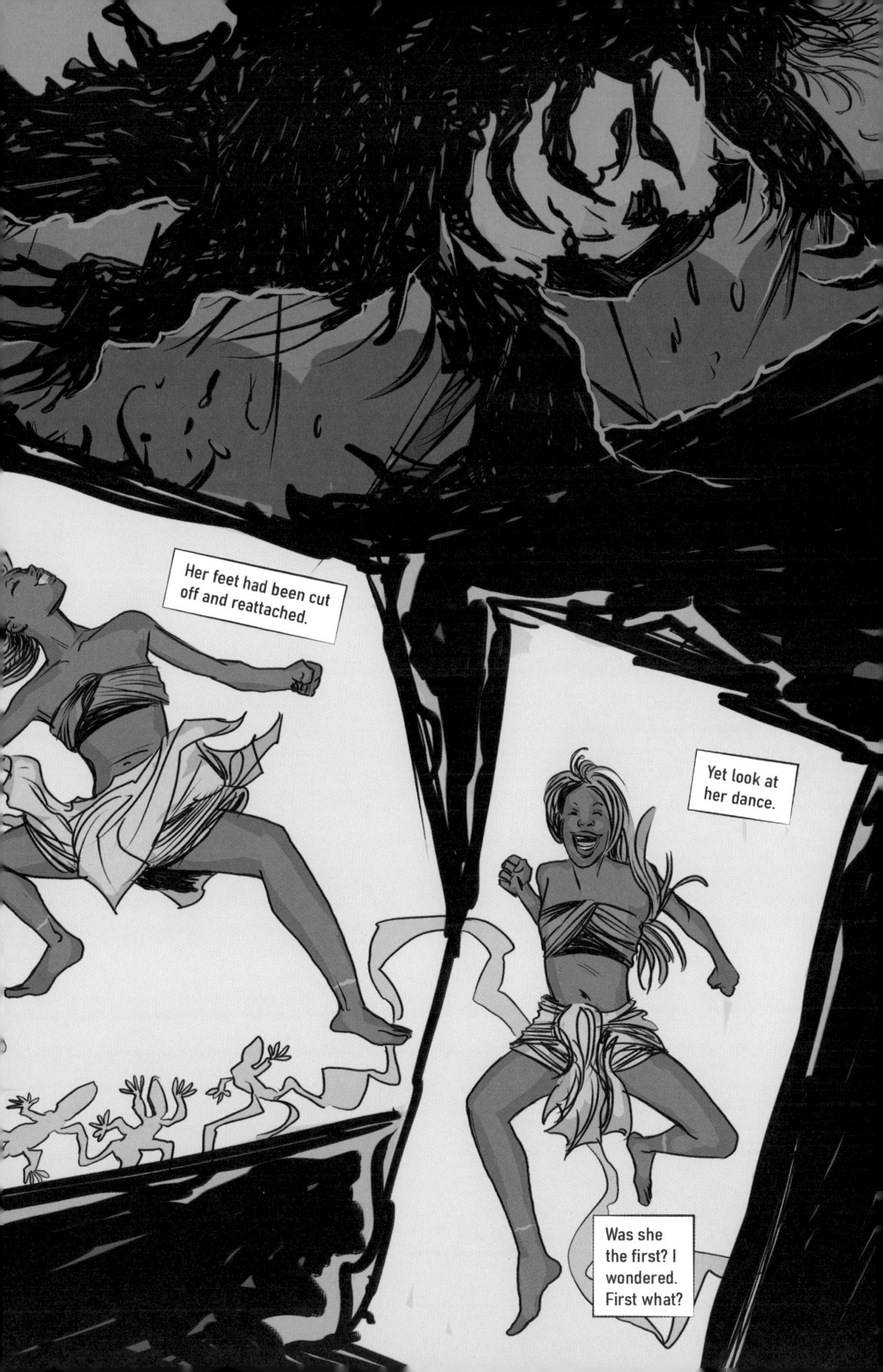
Her feet had been cut off and reattached.
Yet look at her dance.
Was she the first? I wondered. First what?

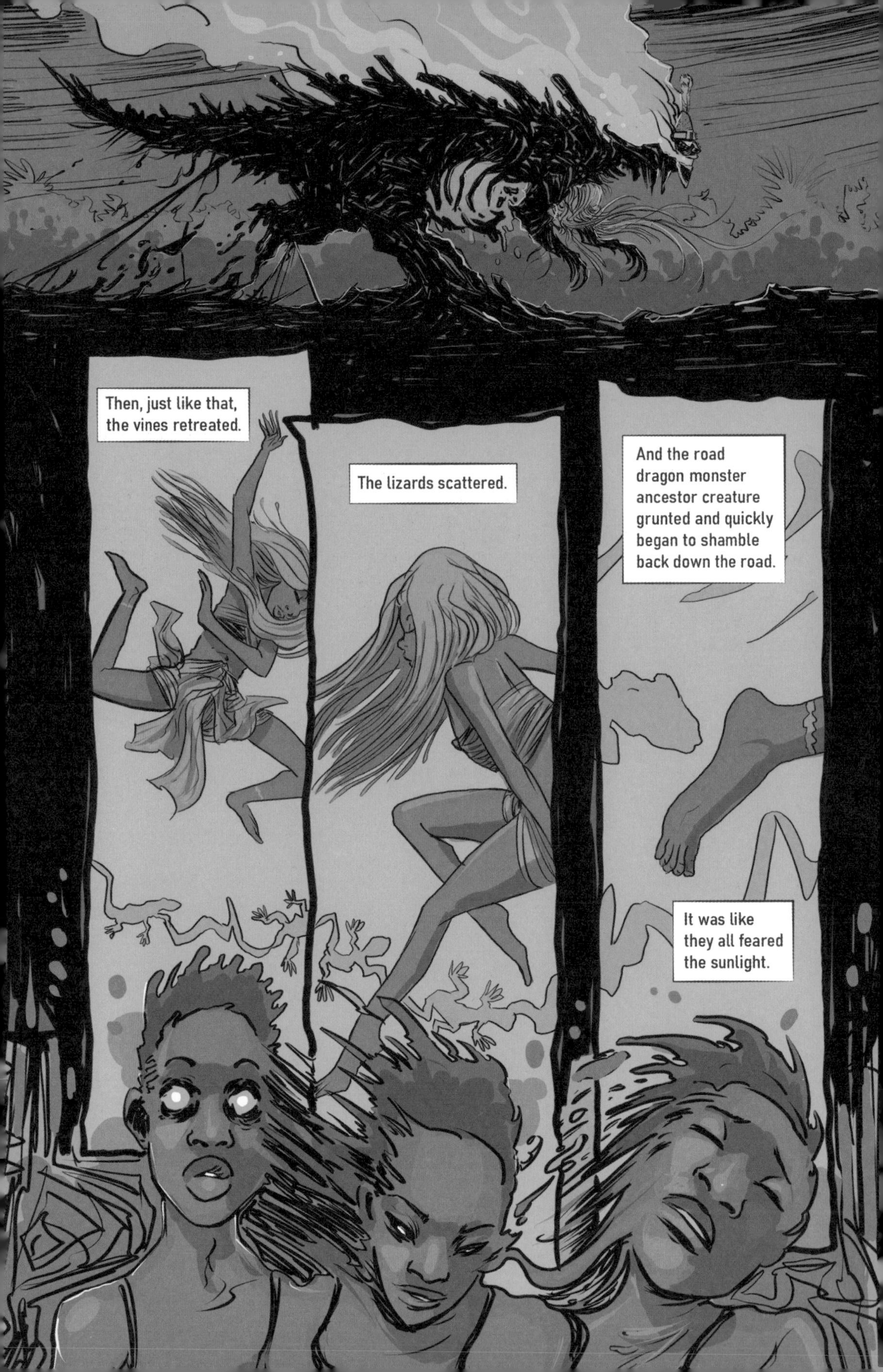
Then, just like that, the vines retreated.
The lizards scattered.
And the road dragon monster ancestor creature grunted and quickly began to shamble back down the road.
It was like they all feared the sunlight.

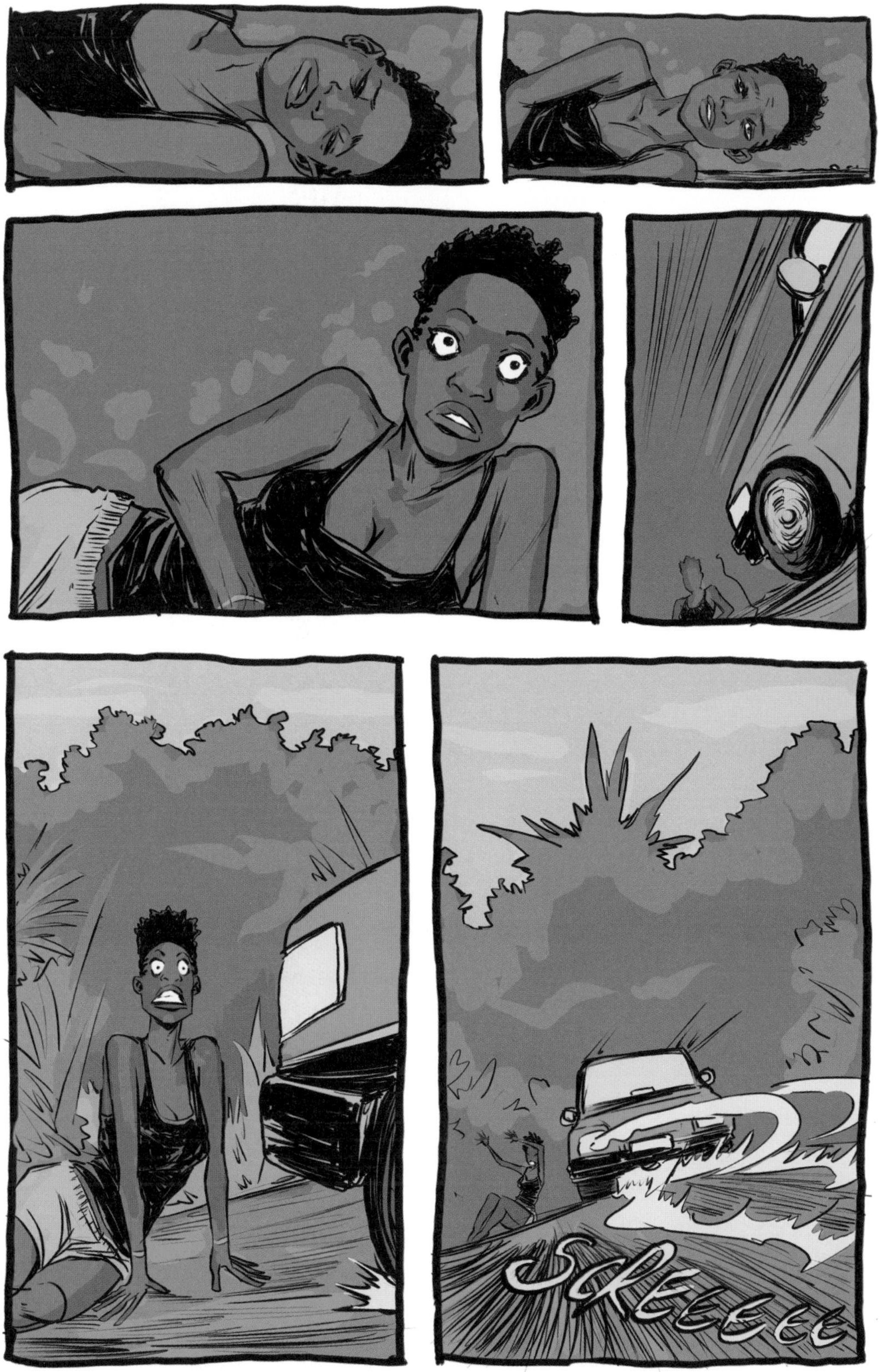
SKREEEEEE

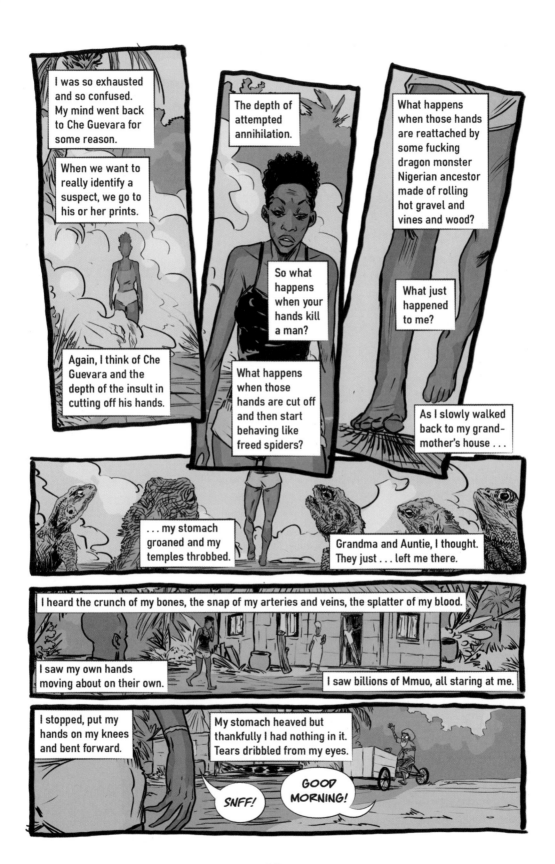

I was so exhausted and so confused. My mind went back to Che Guevara for some reason.

When we want to really identify a suspect, we go to his or her prints.

Again, I think of Che Guevara and the depth of the insult in cutting off his hands.

The depth of attempted annihilation.

So what happens when your hands kill a man?

What happens when those hands are cut off and then start behaving like freed spiders?

What happens when those hands are reattached by some fucking dragon monster Nigerian ancestor made of rolling hot gravel and vines and wood?

What just happened to me?

As I slowly walked back to my grand-mother's house . . .

. . . my stomach groaned and my temples throbbed.

Grandma and Auntie, I thought. They just . . . left me there.

I heard the crunch of my bones, the snap of my arteries and veins, the splatter of my blood.

I saw my own hands moving about on their own.

I saw billions of Mmuo, all staring at me.

I stopped, put my hands on my knees and bent forward.

My stomach heaved but thankfully I had nothing in it. Tears dribbled from my eyes.

SNFF!

GOOD MORNING!

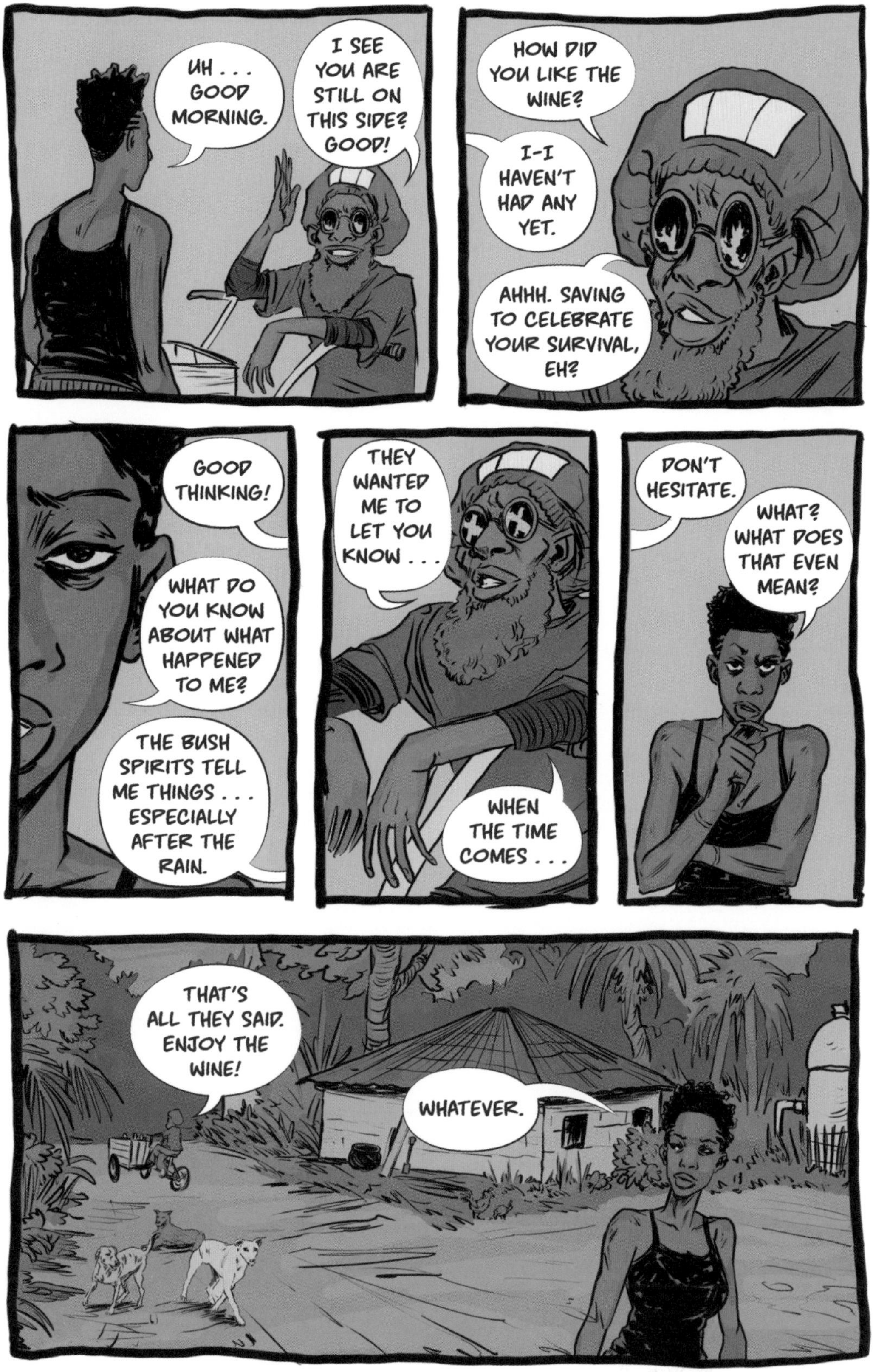
UH . . . GOOD MORNING.
I SEE YOU ARE STILL ON THIS SIDE? GOOD!
HOW DID YOU LIKE THE WINE?
I-I HAVEN'T HAD ANY YET.
AHHH. SAVING TO CELEBRATE YOUR SURVIVAL, EH?
GOOD THINKING!
WHAT DO YOU KNOW ABOUT WHAT HAPPENED TO ME?
THE BUSH SPIRITS TELL ME THINGS . . . ESPECIALLY AFTER THE RAIN.
THEY WANTED ME TO LET YOU KNOW . . .
WHEN THE TIME COMES . . .
DON'T HESITATE.
WHAT? WHAT DOES THAT EVEN MEAN?
THAT'S ALL THEY SAID. ENJOY THE WINE!
WHATEVER.

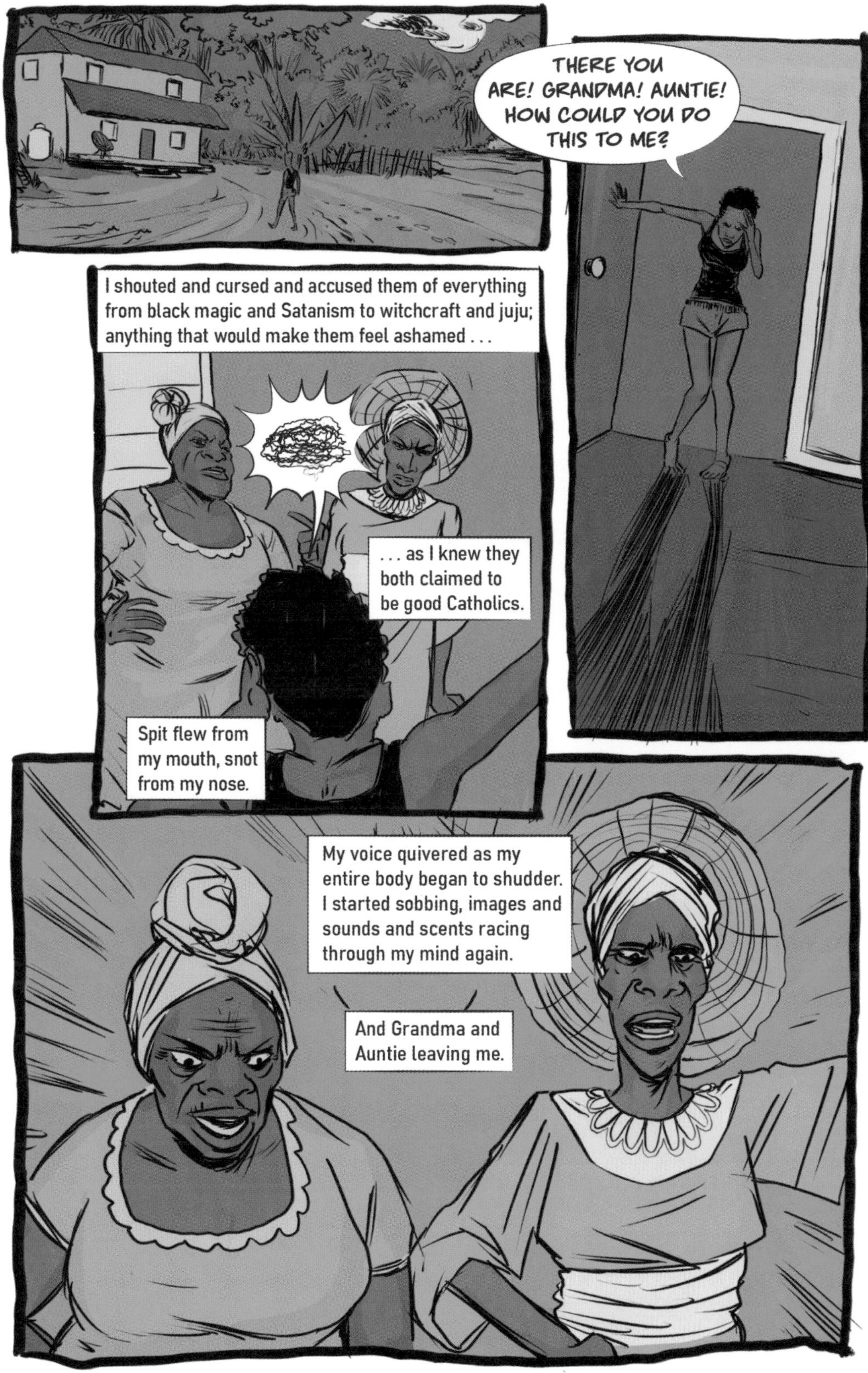

THERE YOU ARE! GRANDMA! AUNTIE! HOW COULD YOU DO THIS TO ME?
I shouted and cursed and accused them of everything from black magic and Satanism to witchcraft and juju; anything that would make them feel ashamed . . .
. . . as I knew they both claimed to be good Catholics.
Spit flew from my mouth, snot from my nose.
My voice quivered as my entire body began to shudder. I started sobbing, images and sounds and scents racing through my mind again.
And Grandma and Auntie leaving me.

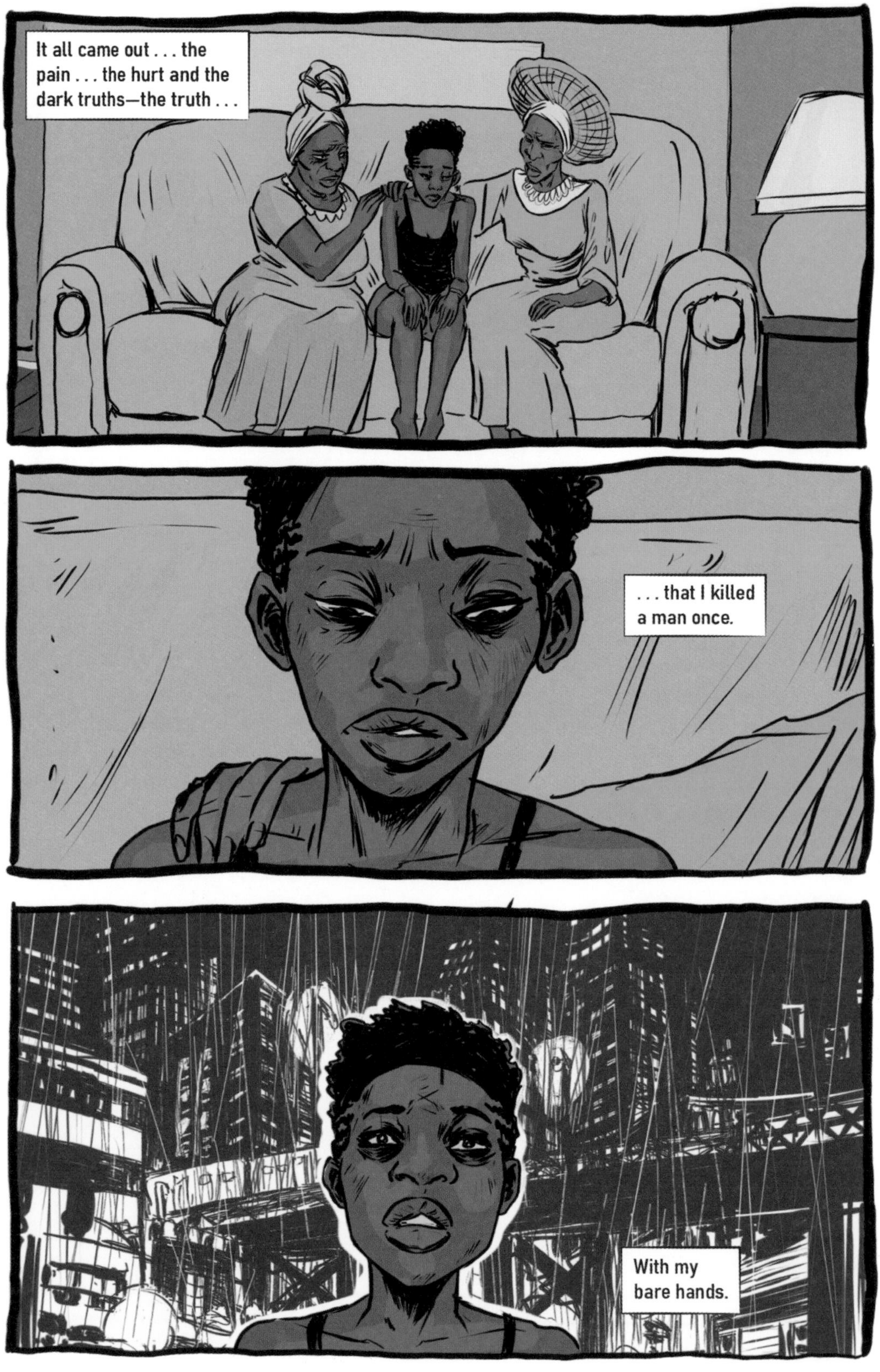
It all came out . . . the pain . . . the hurt and the dark truths—the truth . . .
. . . that I killed a man once.
With my bare hands.

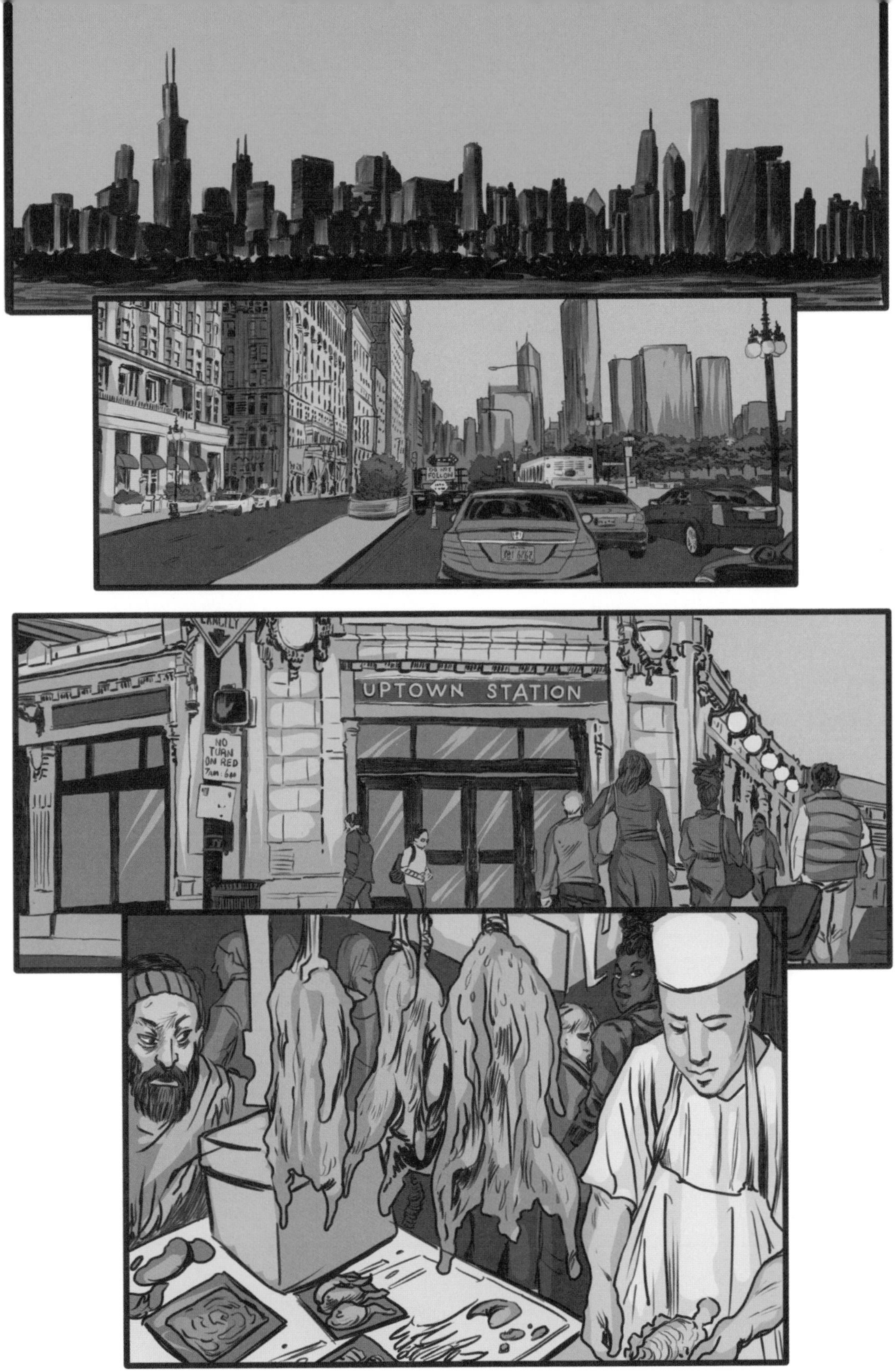
UPTOWN STATION
NO TURN ON RED

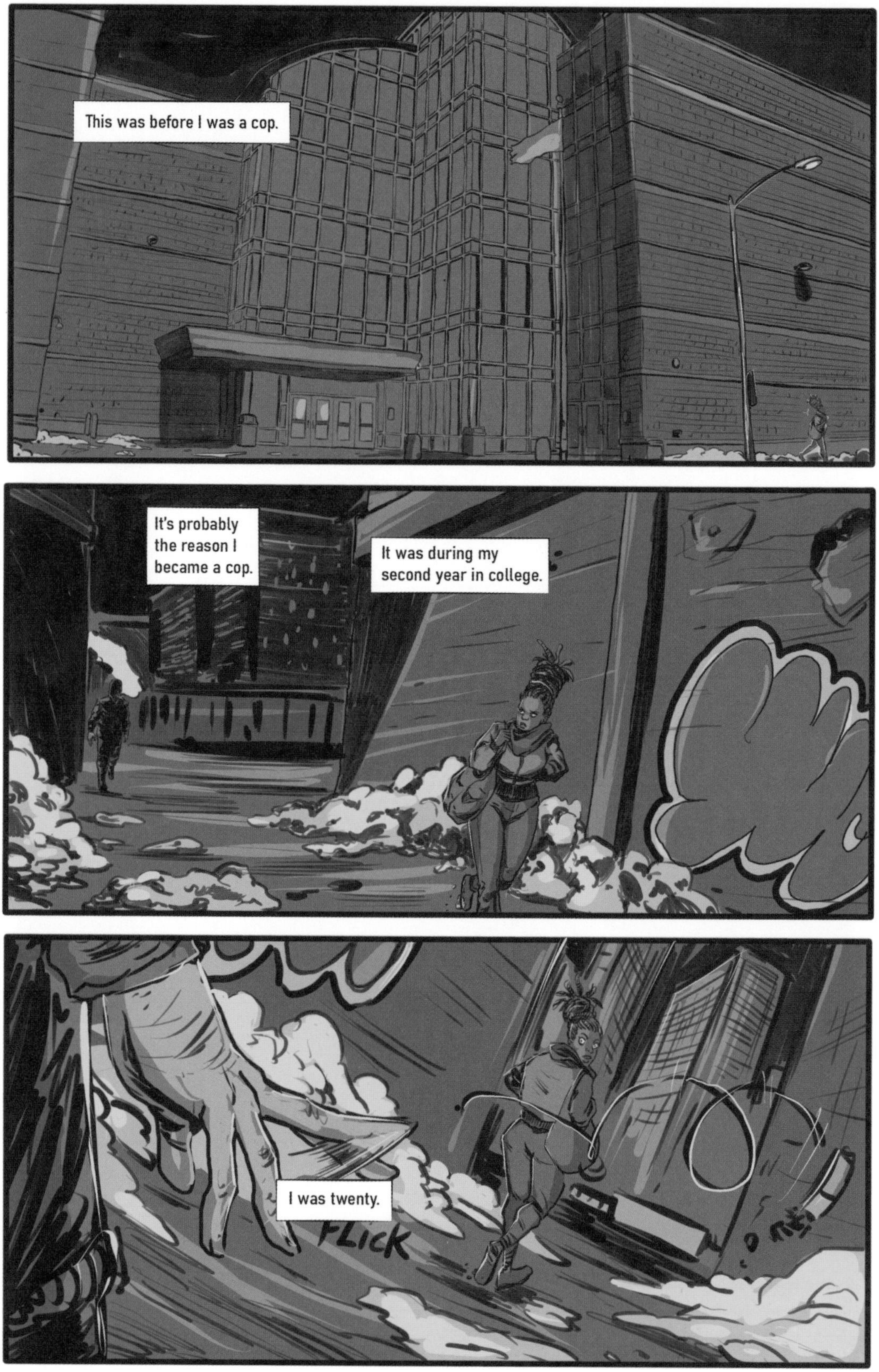
This was before I was a cop.
It's probably the reason I became a cop.
It was during my second year in college.
I was twenty.
FLICK

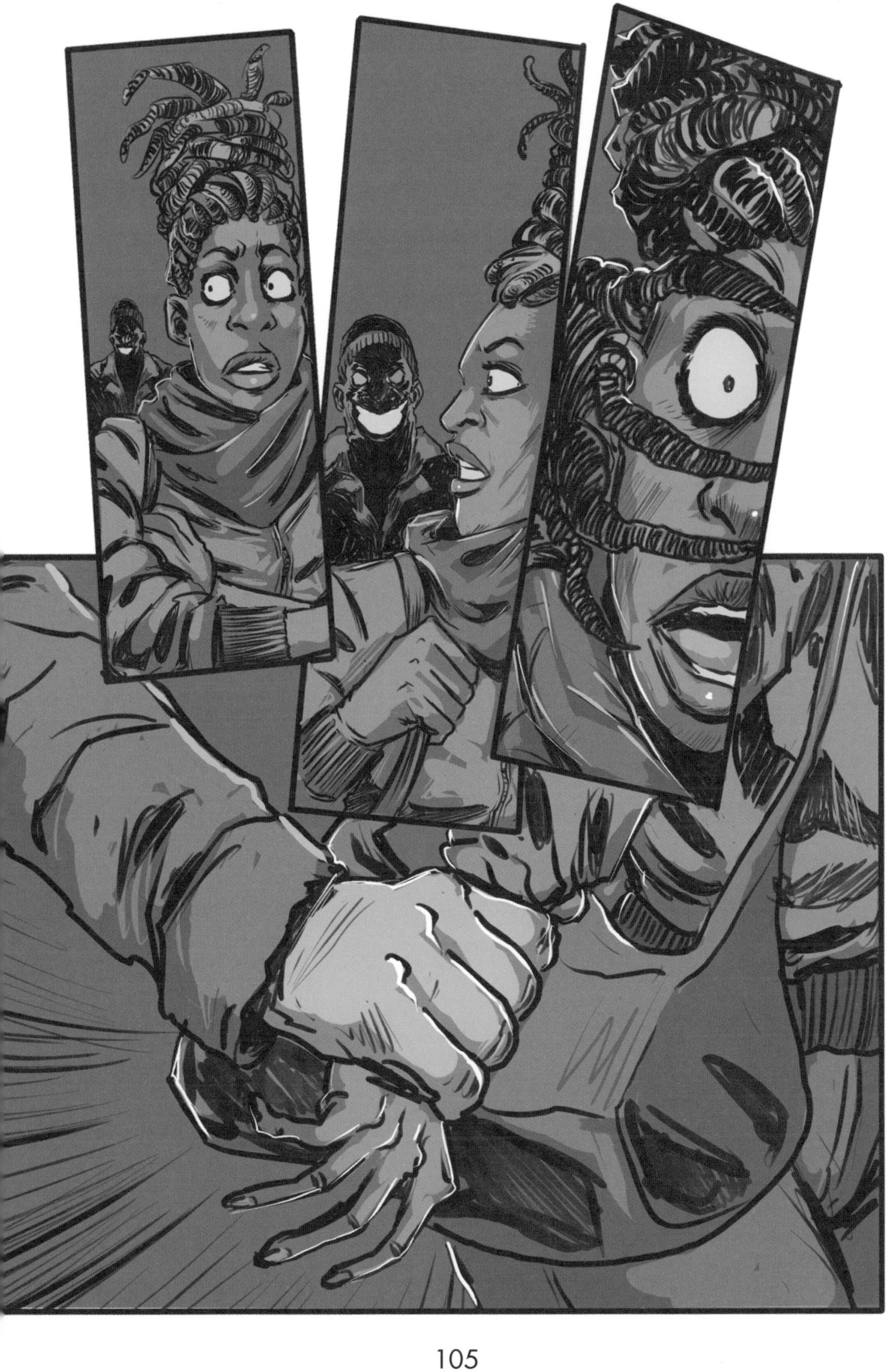

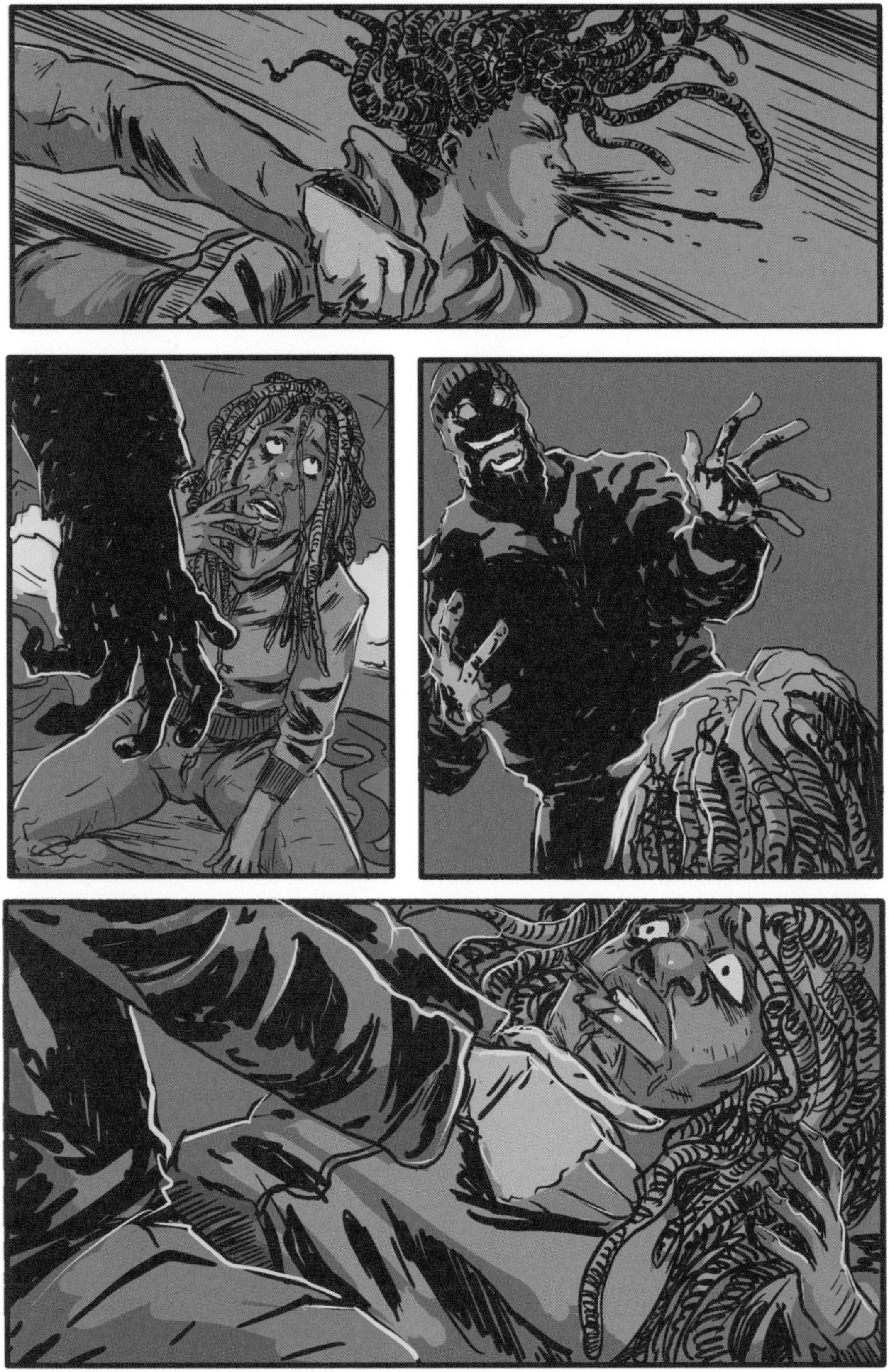

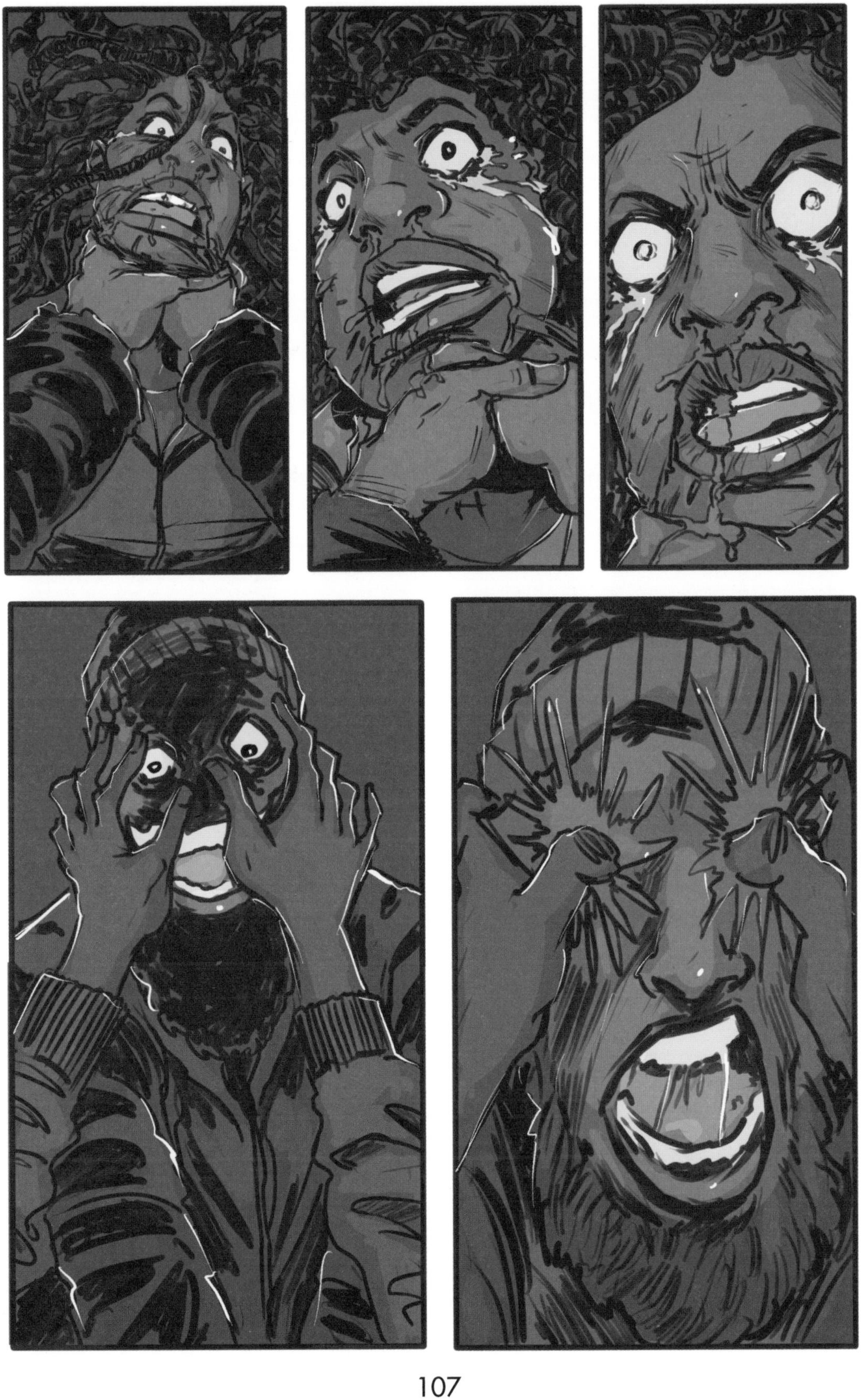

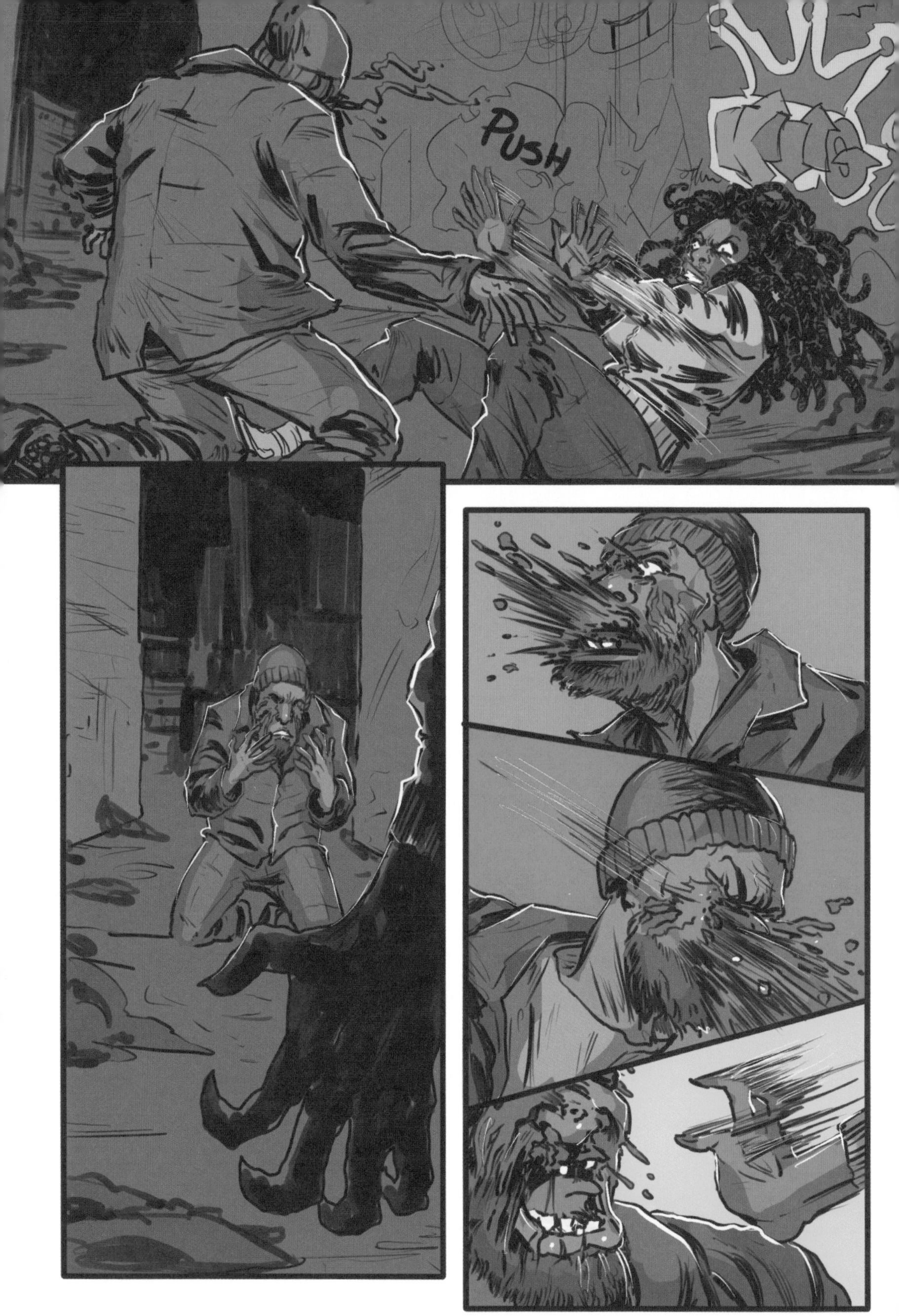
PUSH

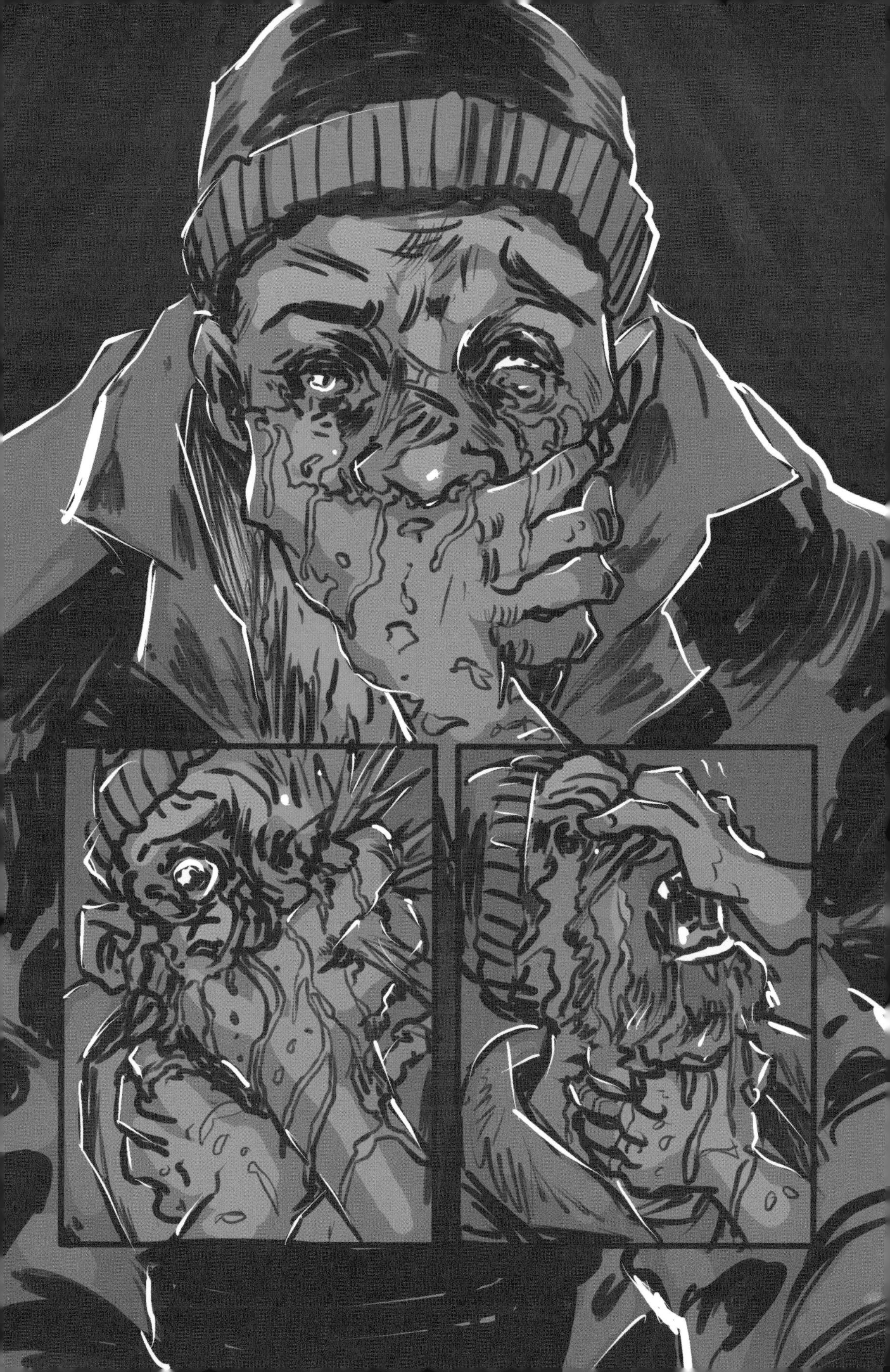

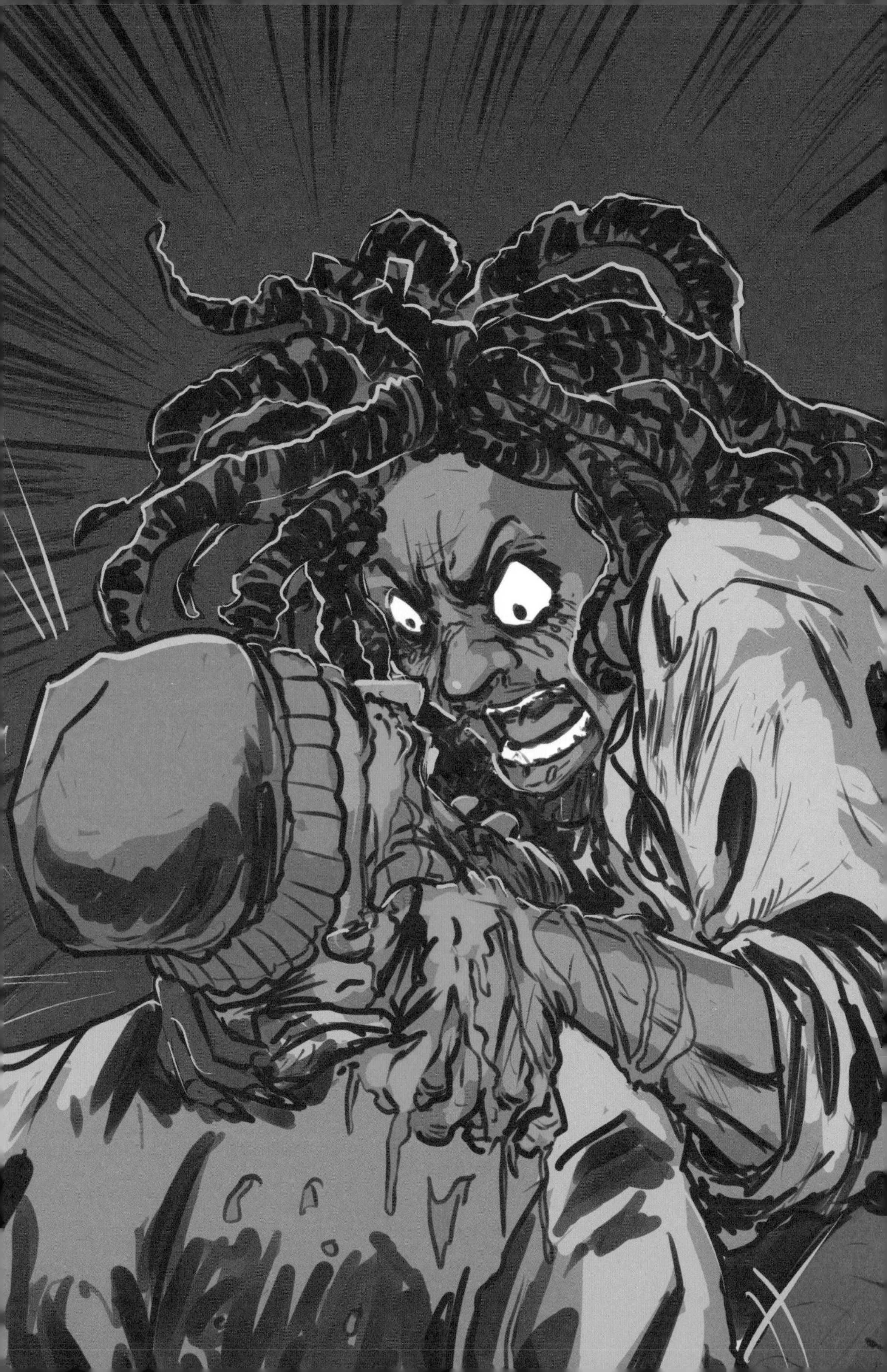

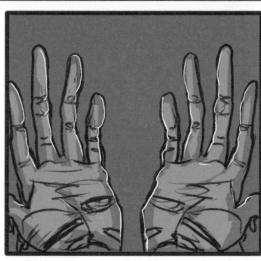

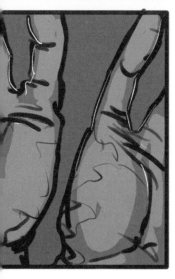

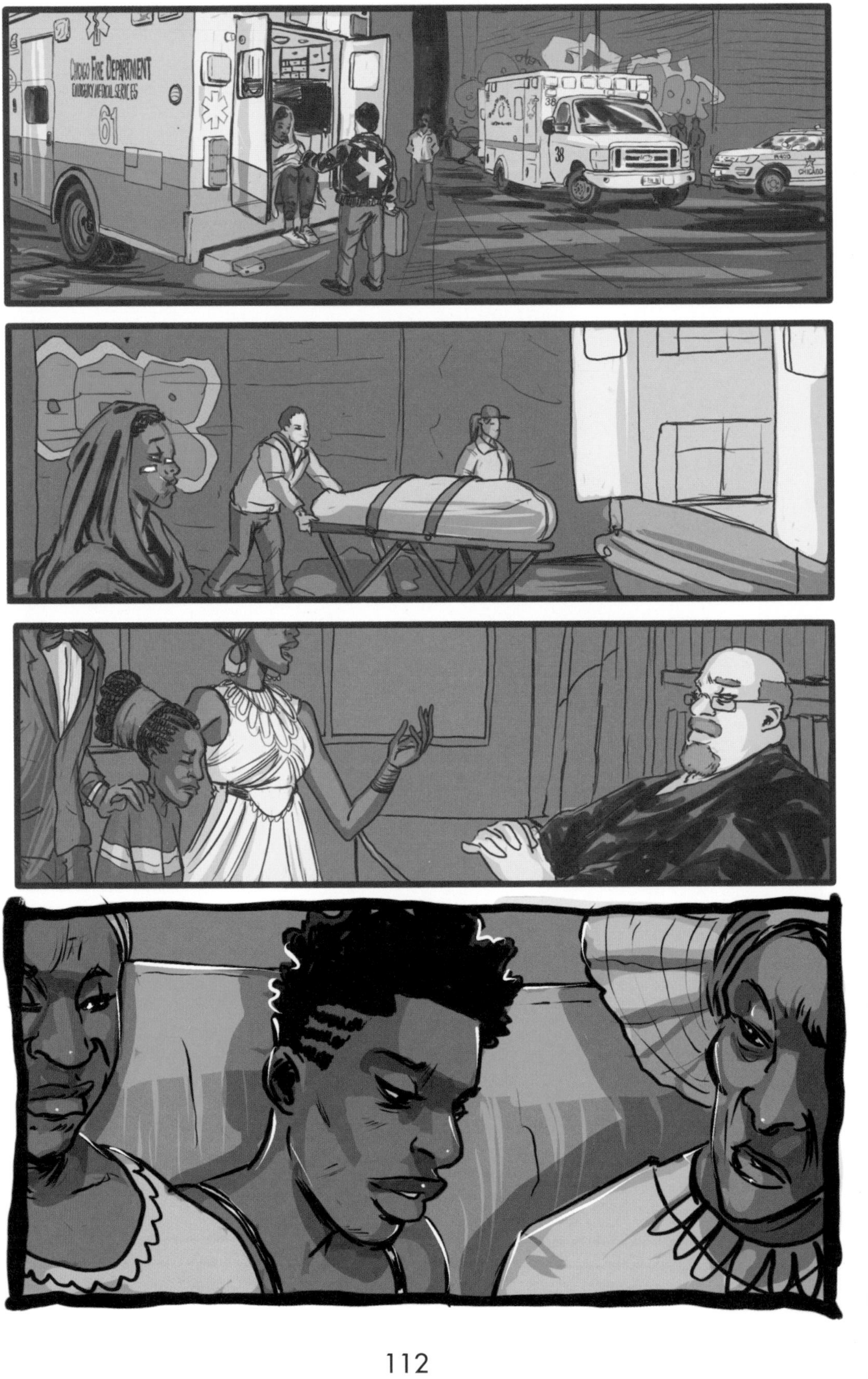
CHICAGO FIRE DEPARTMENT
EMERGENCY MEDICAL SERVICES
61
38
CHICAGO

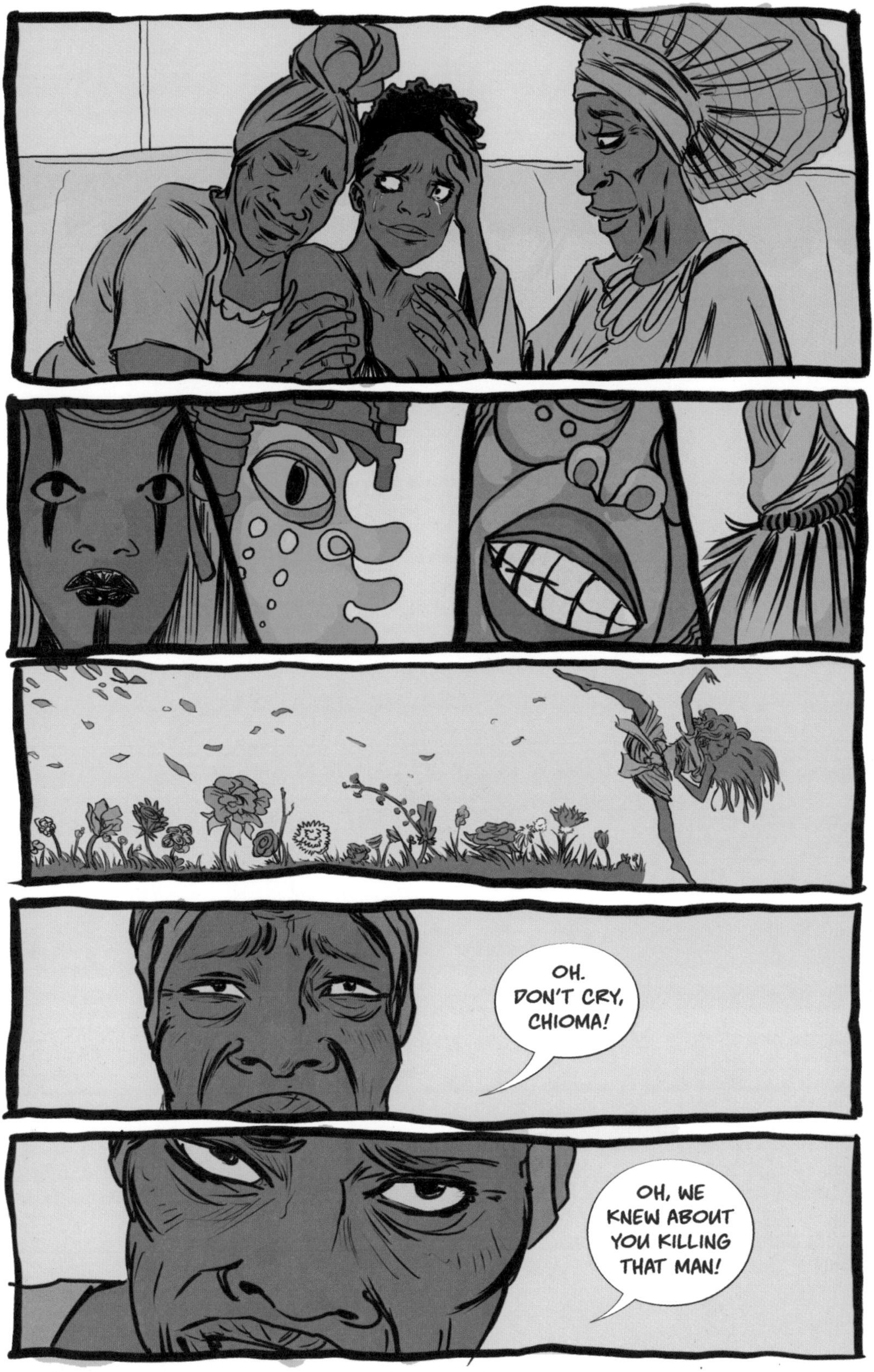
OH.
DON'T CRY,
CHIOMA!
OH, WE
KNEW ABOUT
YOU KILLING
THAT MAN!

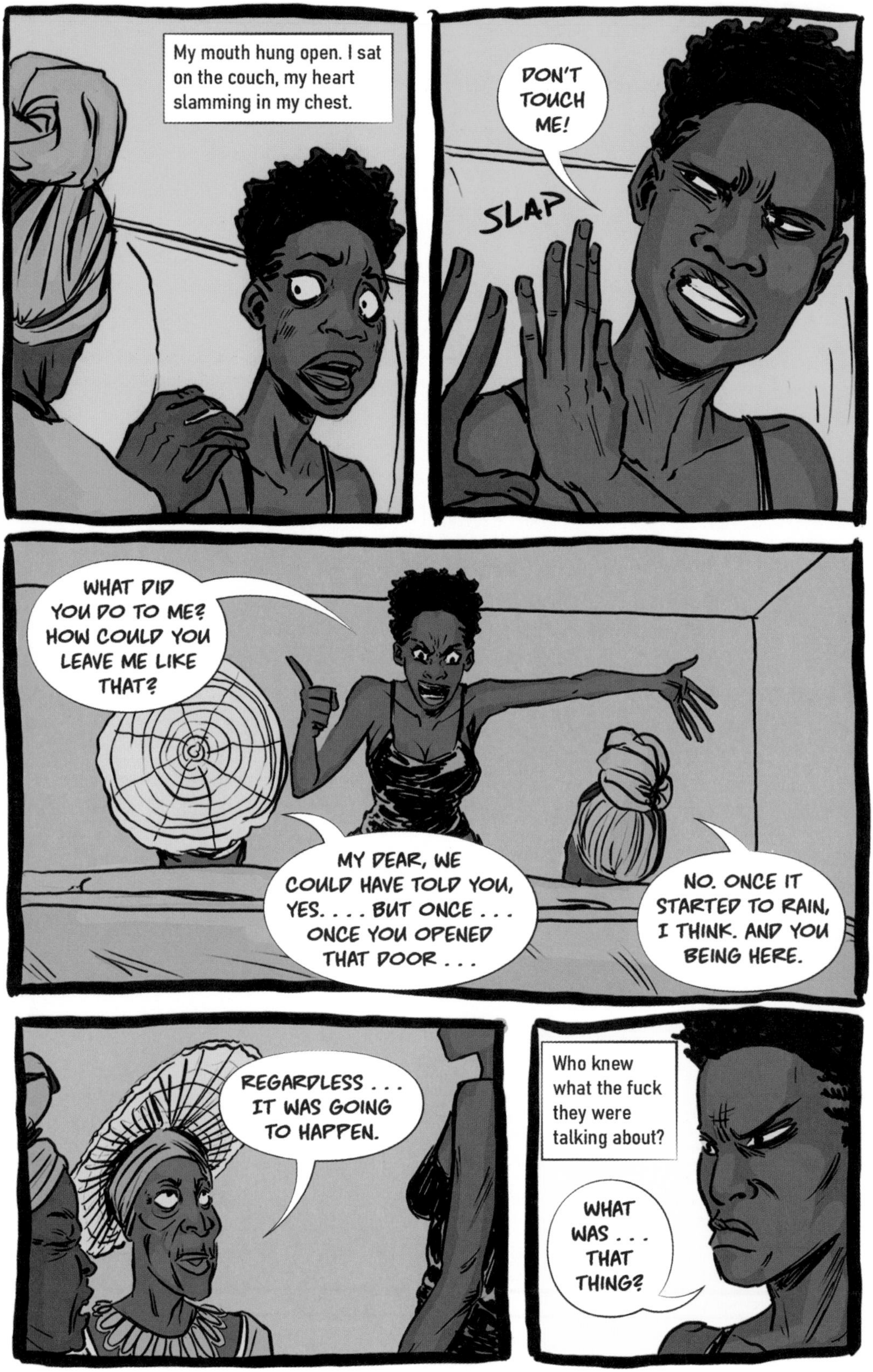
My mouth hung open. I sat on the couch, my heart slamming in my chest.
DON'T TOUCH ME!
SLAP
WHAT DID YOU DO TO ME? HOW COULD YOU LEAVE ME LIKE THAT?
MY DEAR, WE COULD HAVE TOLD YOU, YES. . . . BUT ONCE . . . ONCE YOU OPENED THAT DOOR . . .
NO. ONCE IT STARTED TO RAIN, I THINK. AND YOU BEING HERE.
REGARDLESS . . . IT WAS GOING TO HAPPEN.
Who knew what the fuck they were talking about?
WHAT WAS . . . THAT THING?

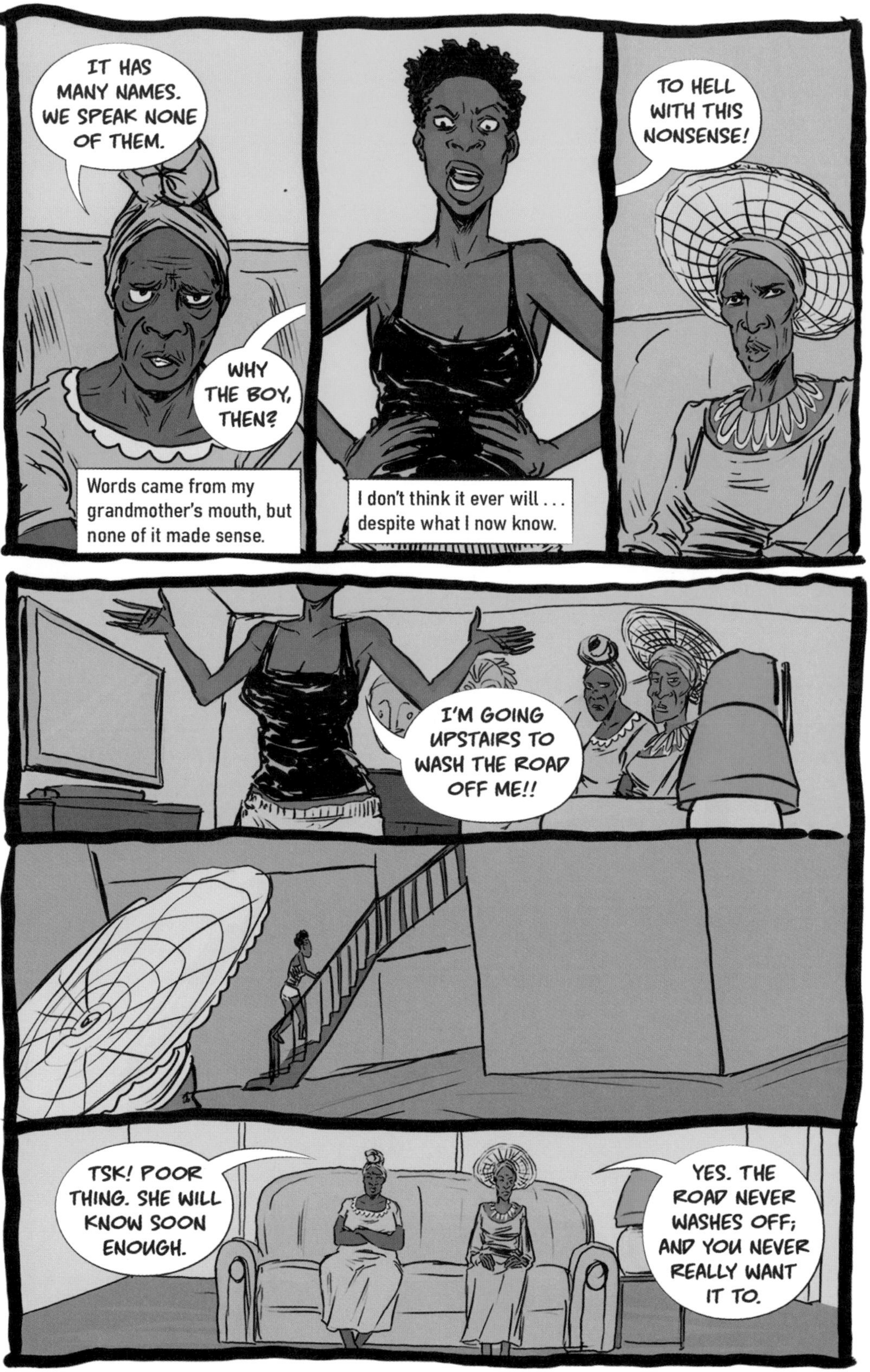
IT HAS MANY NAMES. WE SPEAK NONE OF THEM.
WHY THE BOY, THEN?
Words came from my grandmother's mouth, but none of it made sense.
I don't think it ever will . . . despite what I now know.
TO HELL WITH THIS NONSENSE!
I'M GOING UPSTAIRS TO WASH THE ROAD OFF ME!!
TSK! POOR THING. SHE WILL KNOW SOON ENOUGH.
YES. THE ROAD NEVER WASHES OFF; AND YOU NEVER REALLY WANT IT TO.

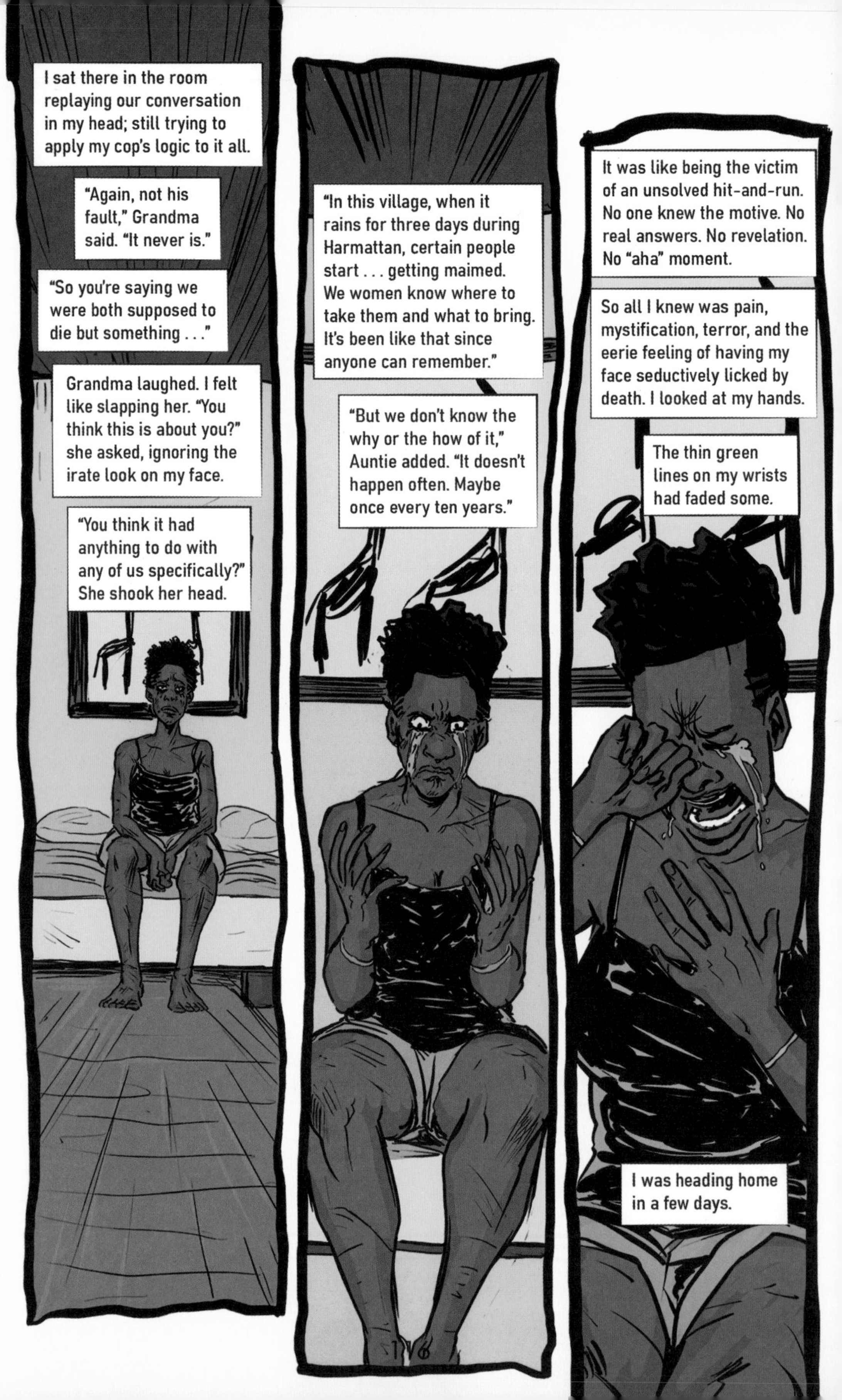
I sat there in the room replaying our conversation in my head; still trying to apply my cop's logic to it all.
"Again, not his fault," Grandma said. "It never is."
"So you're saying we were both supposed to die but something . . ."
Grandma laughed. I felt like slapping her. "You think this is about you?" she asked, ignoring the irate look on my face.
"You think it had anything to do with any of us specifically?" She shook her head.
"In this village, when it rains for three days during Harmattan, certain people start . . . getting maimed. We women know where to take them and what to bring. It's been like that since anyone can remember."
"But we don't know the why or the how of it," Auntie added. "It doesn't happen often. Maybe once every ten years."
It was like being the victim of an unsolved hit-and-run. No one knew the motive. No real answers. No revelation. No "aha" moment.
So all I knew was pain, mystification, terror, and the eerie feeling of having my face seductively licked by death. I looked at my hands.
The thin green lines on my wrists had faded some.
I was heading home in a few days.

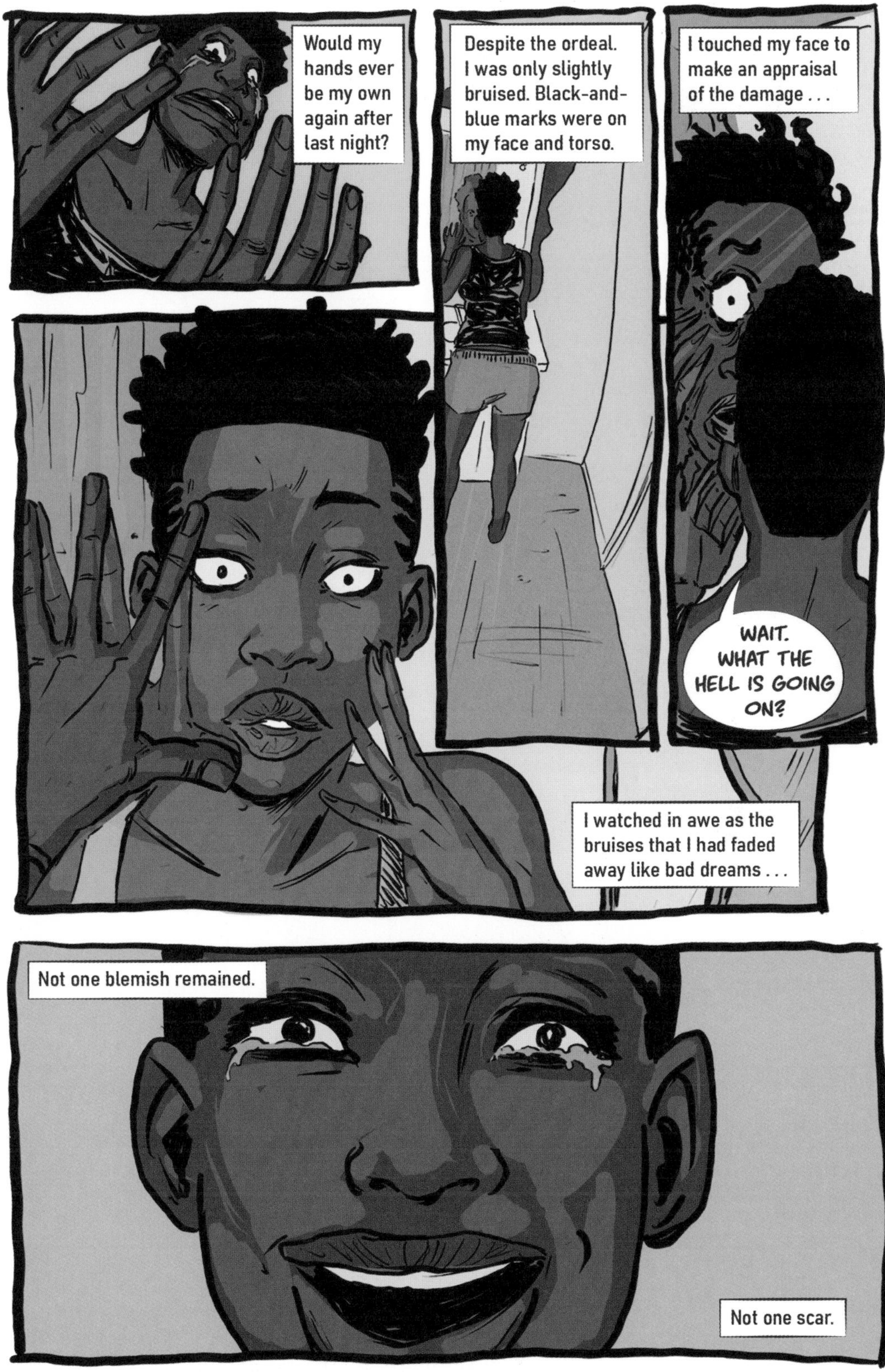
Would my hands ever be my own again after last night?
Despite the ordeal. I was only slightly bruised. Black-and-blue marks were on my face and torso.
I touched my face to make an appraisal of the damage . . .
WAIT. WHAT THE HELL IS GOING ON?
I watched in awe as the bruises that I had faded away like bad dreams . . .
Not one blemish remained.
Not one scar.

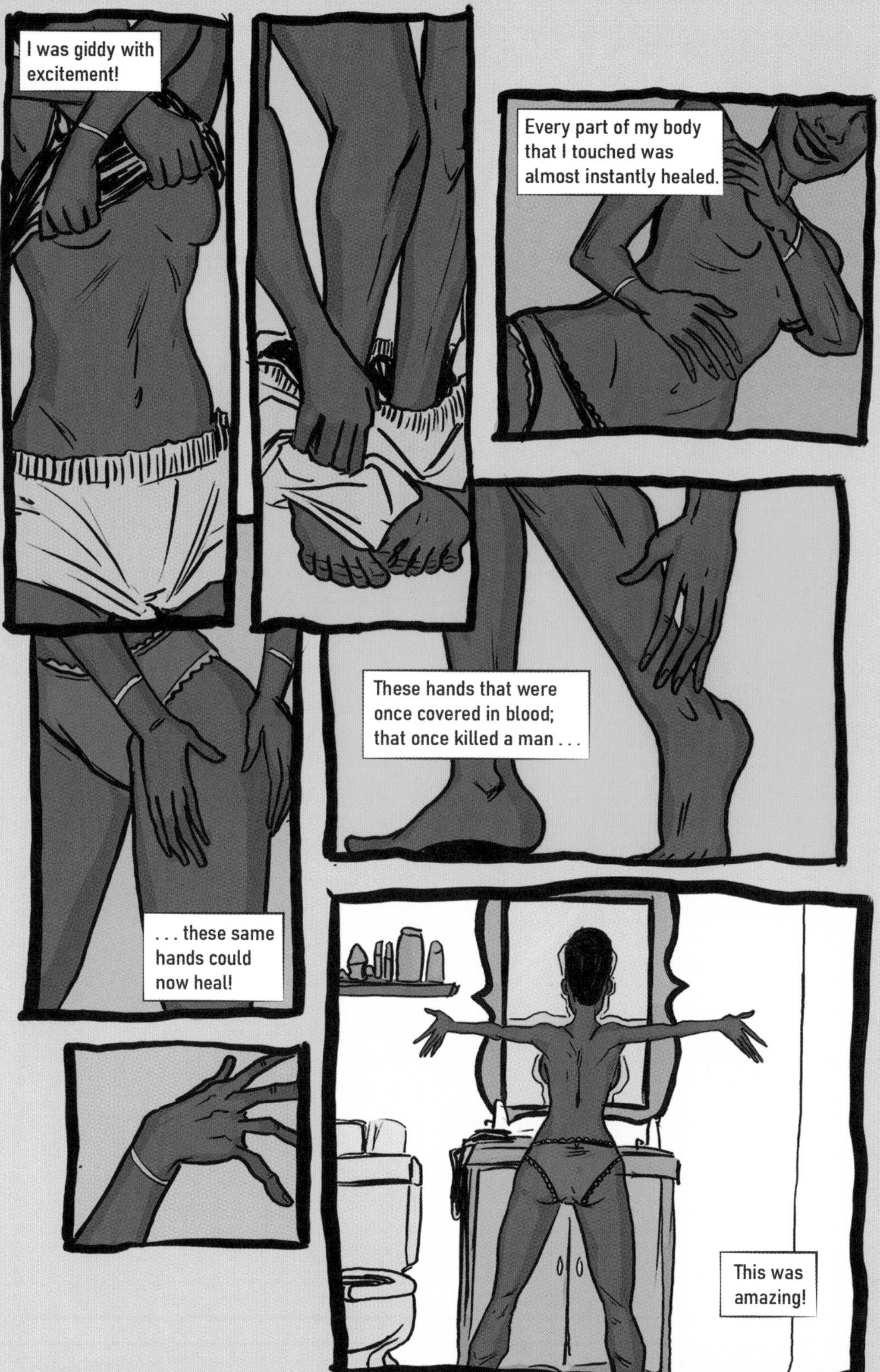
I was giddy with excitement!
Every part of my body that I touched was almost instantly healed.
These hands that were once covered in blood; that once killed a man . . .
. . . these same hands could now heal!
This was amazing!

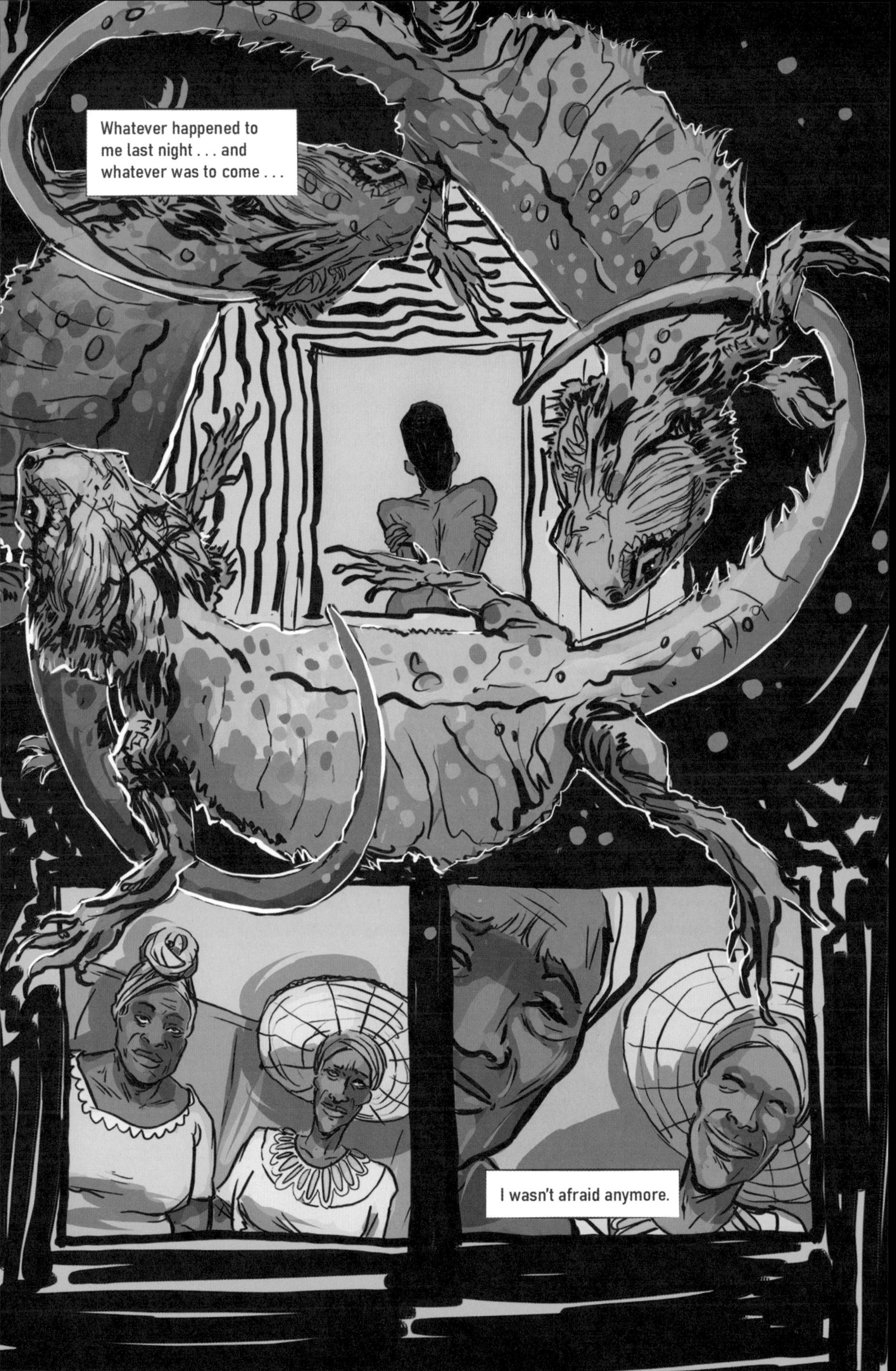
Whatever happened to me last night . . . and whatever was to come . . .
I wasn't afraid anymore.

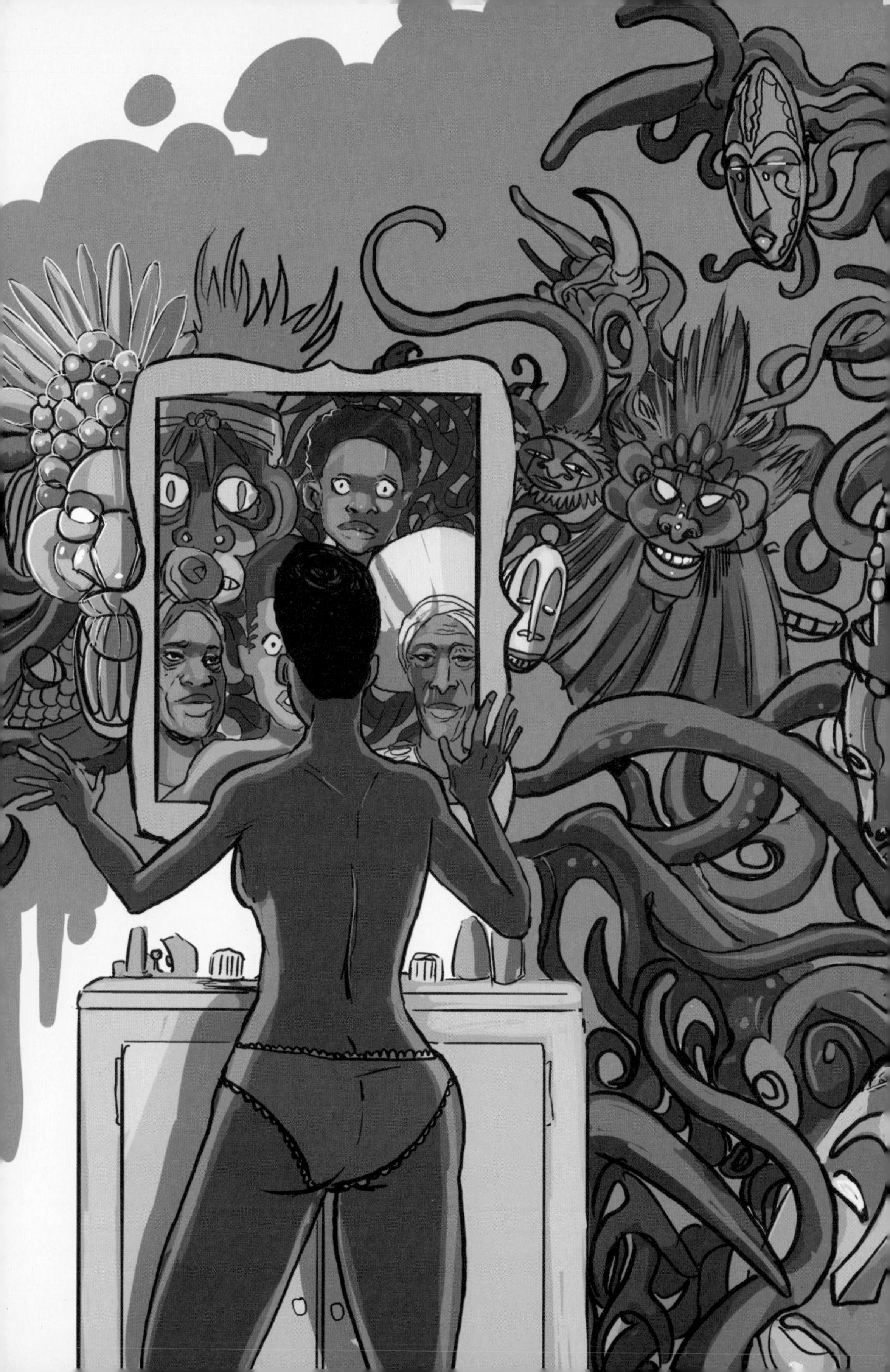

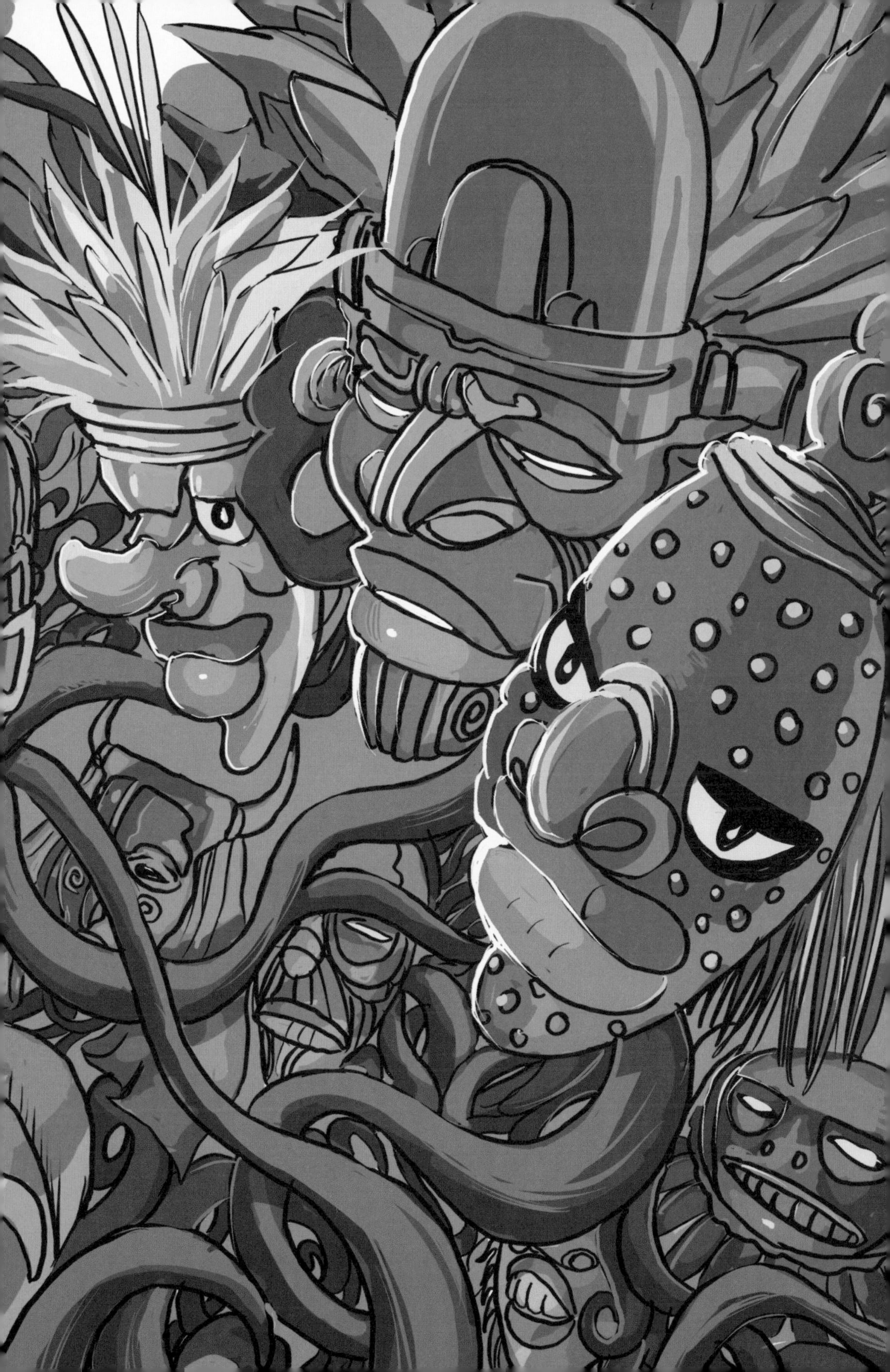

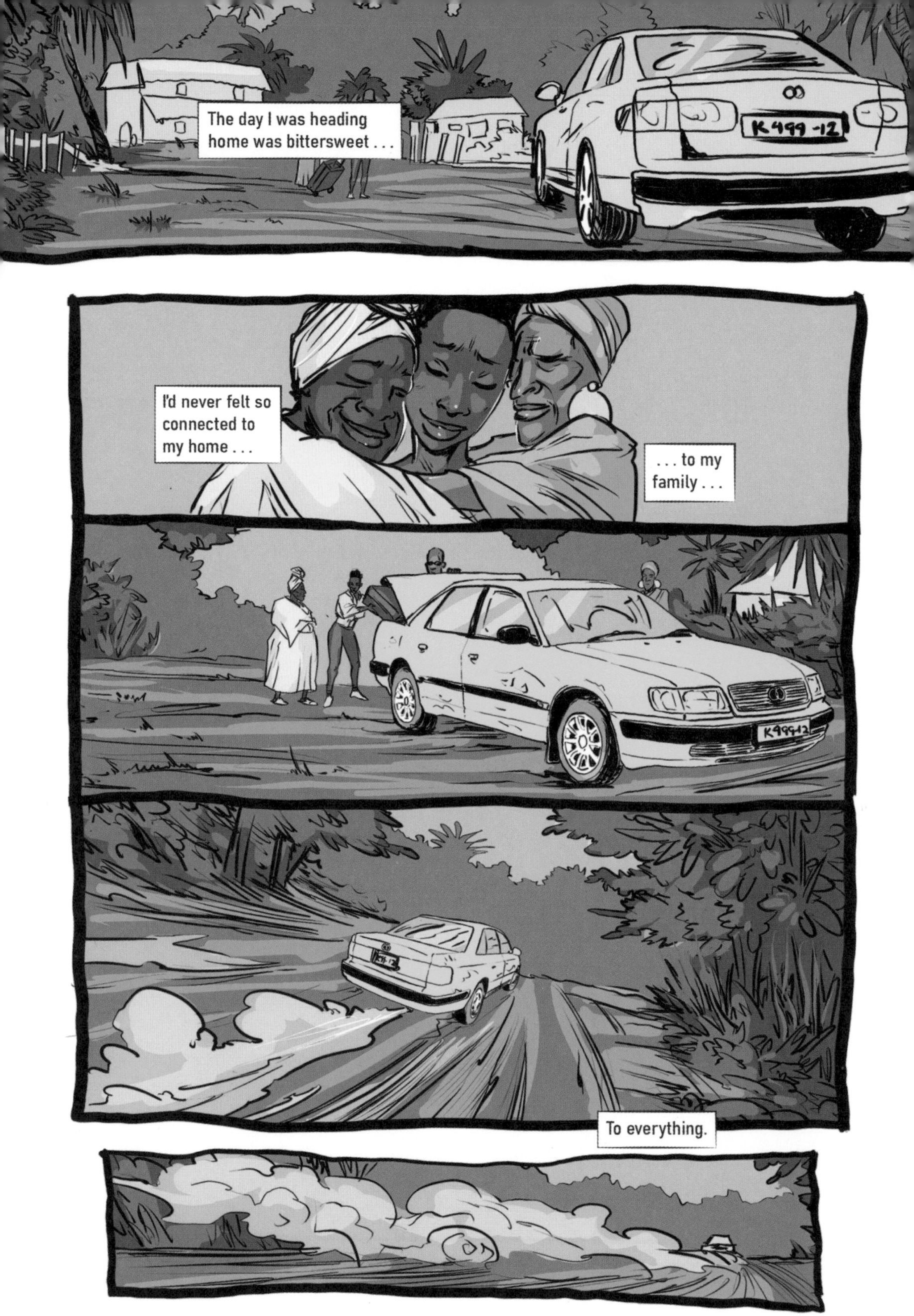
The day I was heading home was bittersweet . . .
K499-12
I'd never felt so connected to my home . . .
. . . to my family . . .
To everything.

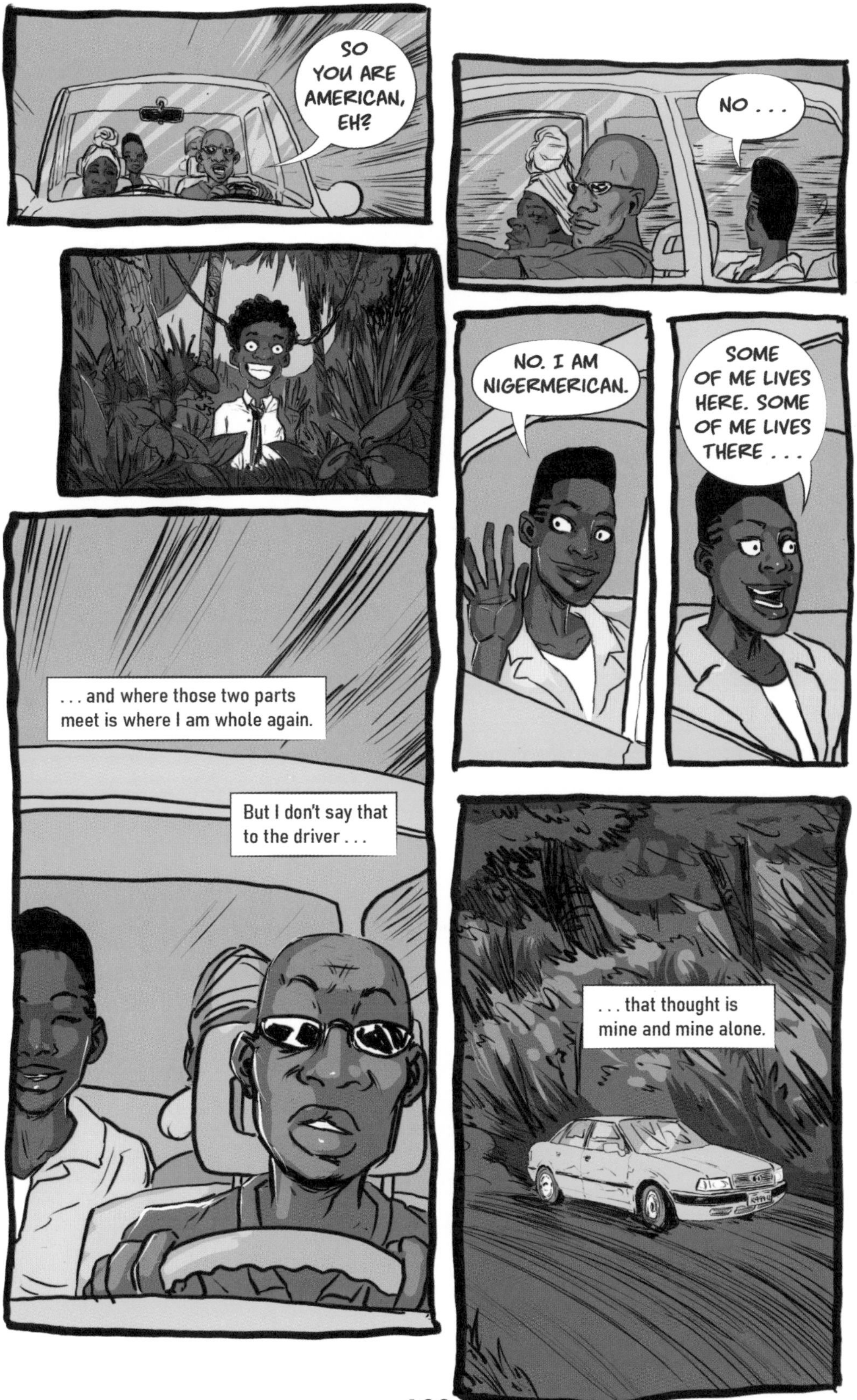
SO YOU ARE AMERICAN, EH?
NO . . .
NO. I AM NIGERMERICAN.
SOME OF ME LIVES HERE. SOME OF ME LIVES THERE . . .
. . . and where those two parts meet is where I am whole again.
But I don't say that to the driver . . .
. . . that thought is mine and mine alone.

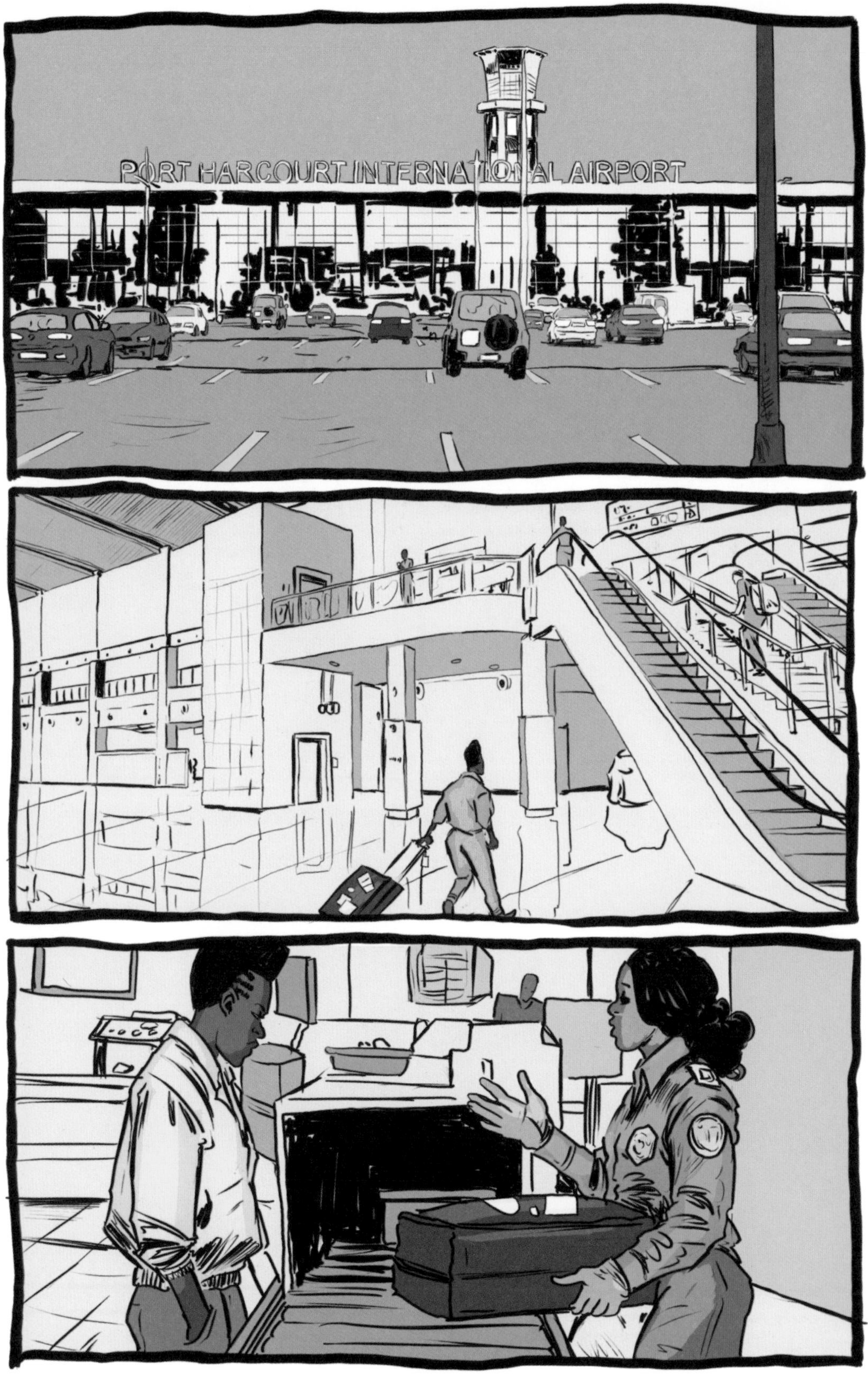
PORT HARCOURT INTERNATIONAL AIRPORT

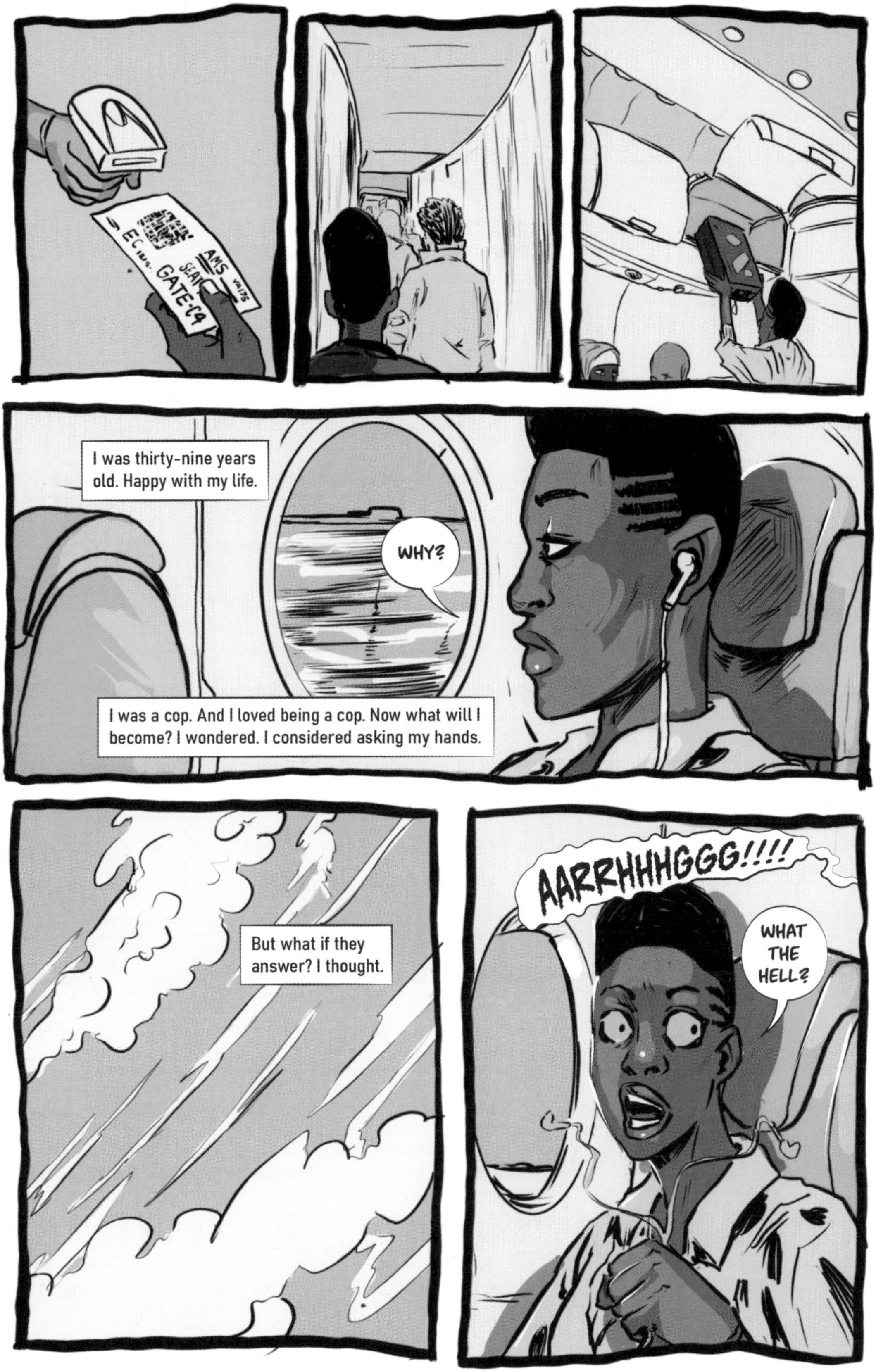
AMS
VA175
EC
GATE-C4
I was thirty-nine years old. Happy with my life.
WHY?
I was a cop. And I loved being a cop. Now what will I become? I wondered. I considered asking my hands.
But what if they answer? I thought.
AARRHHHGGG!!!!
WHAT THE HELL?

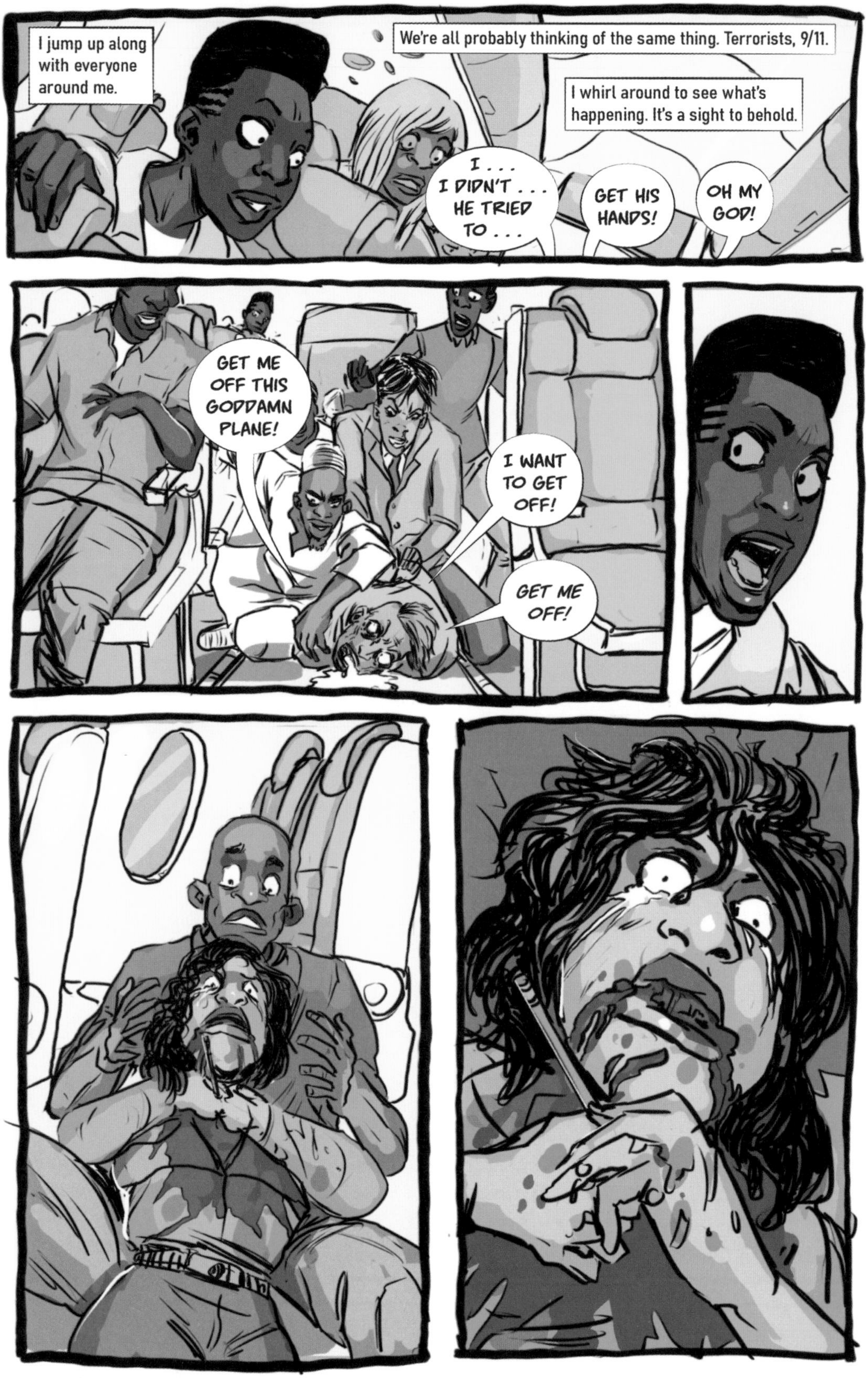
I jump up along with everyone around me.
We're all probably thinking of the same thing. Terrorists, 9/11.
I whirl around to see what's happening. It's a sight to behold.
I . . . I DIDN'T . . . HE TRIED TO . . .
GET HIS HANDS!
OH MY GOD!
GET ME OFF THIS GODDAMN PLANE!
I WANT TO GET OFF!
GET ME OFF!

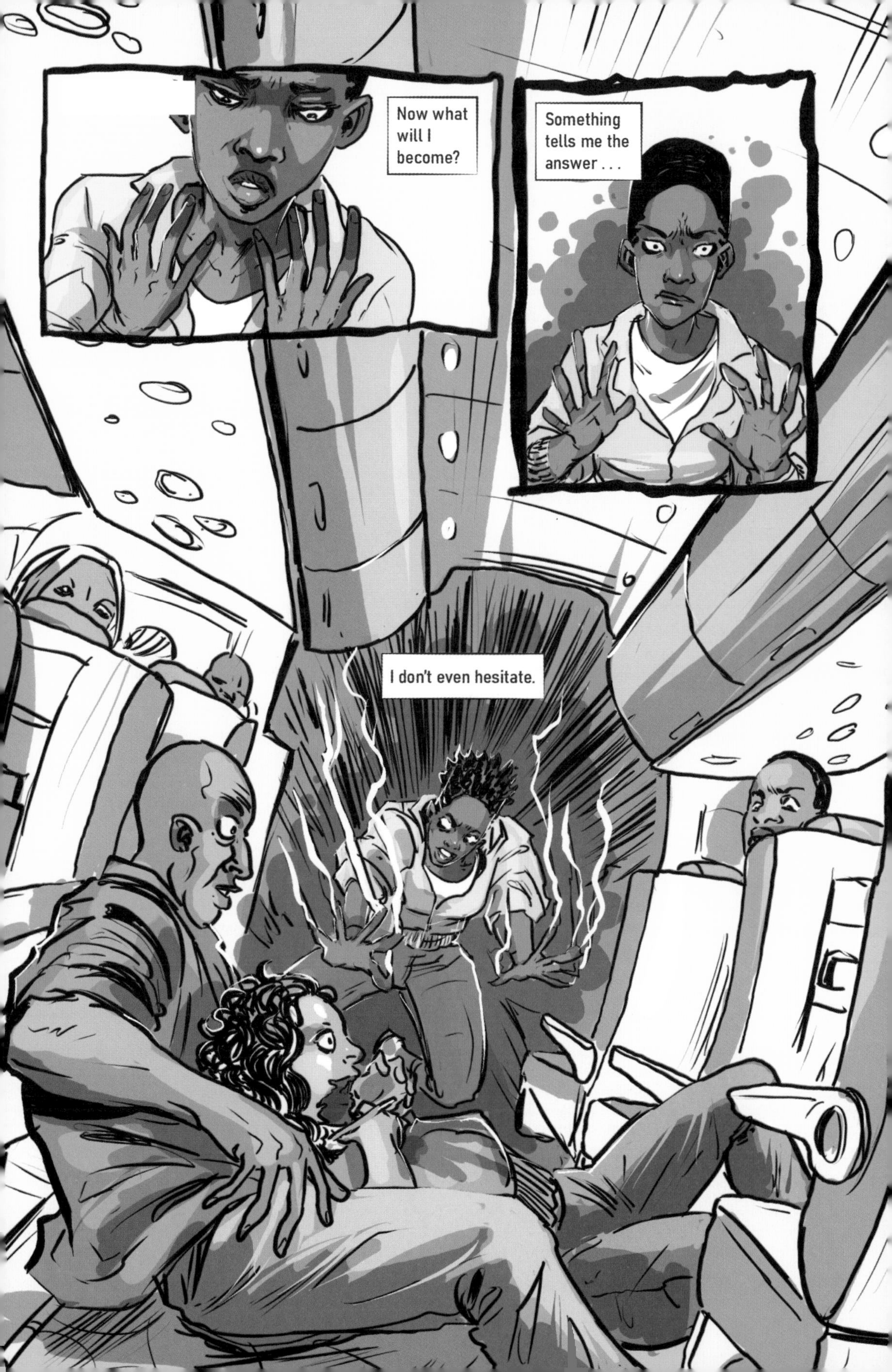
Now what will I become?
Something tells me the answer . . .
I don't even hesitate.

ACKNOWLEDGMENTS

I want to acknowledge my wife, Tawana, and my son, Jaxon, for not only helping to weather every storm but also for giving me the precious time to bring this book to life. I also want to thank my friend Nnedi Okorafor for trusting us with the translation of her words into sequential images. Thanks to the amazing David Brame for giving the adaptation such incredible lines for me to color. I also want to thank Damian Duffy for his hard work on the lovely lettering of every sound effect and voice. Thank you also to Michael, Charlie, Andrew, Charlotte, Maya, Kristen, Pamela, and the entire ABRAMS family for believing in MEGASCOPE. Finally, I want to thank our assistant editor, Jazmine Joyner, and our color production team: Cinique Lenoir, Stacey Robinson, Alex Batchelor, Anthony Moncada, and "Superior" Solomon Robinson. You make what we do so much better. **—John Jennings**

I am extremely proud of the work I have put into this book, but it couldn't have been completed without the amazing team we have been working with. They are the backbone and lifeblood of this machine. To my family, thank you for letting me disappear into the drawing dungeon for half of every day. And lastly, to my four lovely, mischievous dogs: You can't read, and get off the table! **—David Brame**